THE WORKS OF SHAKESPEARE

EDITED FOR THE SYNDICS OF THE
CAMBRIDGE UNIVERSITY PRESS

BY

JOHN DOVER WILSON

THE POEMS

EDITED BY

J. C. MAXWELL

J. D. Morrison
Sep 70

THE POEMS

CAMBRIDGE
AT THE UNIVERSITY PRESS
1969

PUBLISHED BY
THE SYNDICS OF THE CAMBRIDGE UNIVERSITY PRESS
Bentley House, 200 Euston Road, London, N.W. 1
American Branch: 32 East 57th Street, New York, N.Y. 10022

Standard Book Number:
521 07551 3 *clothbound*
521 09493 3 *paperback*

LIBRARY OF CONGRESS CATALOGUE
CARD NUMBER: 65–14345

First edition 1966
First paperback edition 1969

First printed in Great Britain at the University Press, Cambridge
Reprinted in Great Britain by Hazell Watson & Viney Ltd,
Aylesbury, Bucks

CONTENTS

CONTENTS

PREFATORY NOTE

In this admirable edition of Shakespeare's Poems, which seems likely to appear at much the same time as my own edition of the Sonnets, my friend Professor James Maxwell adds the last volume to the series of texts which he has been good enough to undertake during the past decade, and so enables me to reach the end of the long road entered upon in 1919. I am also heavily indebted to him for help, especially during my period of blindness, for corrections in earlier volumes as they came up for reprint; but my gratitude to him is boundless.

J.D.W.

November 1965

INTRODUCTION

Both the narrative poems belong to the period when, with only brief intervals, the London theatres were closed because of plague—August 1592 to April 1594—and there is no reason to doubt that it was this emergency which led Shakespeare to turn to the composition of these poems: a more dignified and, he may well have hoped, a more remunerative form of writing. If we could accept the story told by Rowe on the alleged authority of Davenant that Southampton 'at one time, gave him a thousand Pounds, to enable him to go through with a Purchase which he heard he had a mind to',[1] his most sanguine hopes must have been more than realized, but the story has little claim to belief.[2] At any rate, the greater prestige of the non-dramatic poem is quite enough to explain the unnecessarily puzzled-over description of *Venus and Adonis* in the Dedication as 'the first heir of my invention'. (It did, in fact, precede in publication the first plays to appear: *Titus Andronicus* and the Bad Quarto of *2 Henry VI* in 1594.)

After being extremely popular in their own day—by 1617 there had been ten (surviving) editions of *Venus and Adonis* and six of *The Rape of Lucrece*—these poems, though regularly reprinted in collected editions since 1778, sank into relative obscurity. With a very few exceptions, notably the brilliant comments by Coleridge in ch. xv of *Biographia Literaria*, all the substantial criticism of them belongs to the present century, so that the excellent sketch by J. W. Lever in

---

[1] E. K. Chambers, *William Shakespeare* (1930), II, 266–7.
[2] J. Dover Wilson, *The Essential Shakespeare* (1932), p. 66, treats it as possible, though with the sum probably exaggerated.

Shakespeare Survey, 15 (1962), of criticism since
George Wyndham's edition of 1898 comes close to
covering the whole field, and makes it unnecessary to
attempt a new survey.[1] *The Phoenix and the Turtle* is
also largely a twentieth-century discovery. *The Pas-
sionate Pilgrim* contains no certain example of Shake-
speare's work not found elsewhere and calls for no
comment.

I. VENUS AND ADONIS

The main source is, of course, the version of the story
in Ovid, *Metamorphoses*, x. 510–62, 705–39. Other
episodes in the *Metamorphoses* which contribute some-
thing are Salmacis and Hermaphroditus (IV. 285–388)
and Narcissus and Echo (III. 341–510).[2] Another
mythological figure that has been regarded as of im-
portance is that of Hippolytus.[3] As elsewhere, Shake-
speare would seem to have used both the original (see
notes on ll. 47, 1116) and Golding's translation. The
reluctance of Adonis is probably drawn from the
behaviour of Salmacis (and possibly Hippolytus)—
Ovid's Adonis, though the passive partner, is wholly
acquiescent.[4]

[1] There is also much relevant material cited by H. E.
Rollins in the New Variorum edition (1938).

[2] All three passages are reproduced in Golding's trans-
lation by G. Bullough, *Narrative and Dramatic Sources of
Shakespeare*, 1 (1957).

[3] D. C. Allen, 'On *Venus and Adonis*', *Elizabethan and
Jacobean Studies Presented to Frank Percy Wilson* (1959),
pp. 106–7.

[4] See Rollins, New Variorum edition (1938), pp. 392–3,
for a disdainful Adonis in *Hero and Leander* (I. 11–14) and
in Greene. F. T. Prince, Arden edition (1960), p. xxxii,
n. 3, adds Spenser, *Faerie Queene*, III. i; but this is not quite
correct. Venus there takes the initiative, but eventually 'So
did she steale his heedelesse hart away' (37. 1).

As far as derivation goes, then, this is a wholly Ovidian poem, and it is a poem for whose understanding the question of poetic kind is particularly important. The Ovidian mythological narrative is one of the most popular genres of the 1590's, and Shakespeare, though not its initiator, is among its first distinguished exponents. Except for actual translations, the narratives of the *Metamorphoses* had not been used as models for imitation until Lodge's *Scilla's Metamorphosis* (1589), whose influence on later examples of the genre is not easy to trace, though *Venus and Adonis* is in the same metre. It is in 1593 that it comes fully into its own with the only two poems of high distinction which it was to produce: *Hero and Leander*, Ovidian in spirit though not in source, and *Venus and Adonis*. It is, unfortunately, impossible to be sure of the chronological relationship between them. Shakespeare's poem was registered on 18 April. Marlowe is usually believed to have been occupied on *Hero and Leander* during the last months of his life, which ended on 30 May, and the poem was registered on 28 September, though it was not published, as far as we know, until 1598. It is clear, then, that if either poet knew the work of the other— as a few parallel phrases suggest—it must have been in manuscript. One would, of course, like to believe that the two poets showed each other their work in progress, and discussed it, but the only safe course is to treat the two as substantially independent and probably simultaneous compositions.

It is of the essence of an Ovidian narrative to be witty and pointed, but also to tell a story that has a bearing on the world as a whole. The two aspects must be held in focus. Indeed, much of the unbalanced criticism of *Venus and Adonis* has come from those who have held either that such a light and witty poem cannot have any serious meaning at all, or that a poem with the deeper implications that they rightly detect in it cannot really (or successfully) be light and witty at the same time. The word 'witty', rather than 'comic' or 'humorous', which have been popular in recent criticism, seems to be the one to keep hold of—it was the 'wittie soul of Ovid'[1] that Meres saw re-incarnated in Shakespeare—though the element of undisguised comedy is not to be underrated, either in Marlowe or in Shakespeare. We must certainly avoid the misreading of both poems of which C. S. Lewis is guilty. He rightly singles out the 'hardness'[2] of *Hero and Leander*, but wants us at the same time to banish 'our sense of humour',[3] and when he reaches *Venus and Adonis*, he finds its recurring words and images—'satiety', 'sweating', 'glutton', etc. —disgusting.[4] Such a response grossly exaggerates the prominence in the poem of the elements referred to, but I cite it here more especially for its rejection of even the possibility that Shakespeare was deliberately exploiting, among other things, the sheer comedy of sexuality. Whether wholly successfully or not is another matter, but surely it is a very stuffy reader who does not respond, say, to the erotic topography of ll. 229–40.[5]

Few descriptions of *Venus and Adonis* are as apt as what Hallett Smith writes of Ovid's own story of Salmacis and Hermaphroditus: 'The tone of the narrative is, as always with Ovid, a mixture of sensuous delight, humor, preciousness, and airy sophistication.

[1] E. K. Chambers, *William Shakespeare* (1930), II, 194.

[2] *English Literature in the Sixteenth Century* (1954), p. 487.

[3] *Ibid*. M. C. Bradbrook, *Shakespeare and Elizabethan Poetry* (1951), p. 59, rightly talks of the 'joyful and mocking comedy'.

[4] *Ibid*. pp. 498–9.

[5] For brief appreciative comments, see J. Middleton Murry, *Shakespeare* (1936), pp. 88–9.

The details and imagery are pictorial, not dramatic....
There is rhetorical heightening...but the rhetoric is
controlled and kept in place by the speed and verve of
the narrative.'[1] In this sense, Shakespeare is the most
Ovidian of all the Ovidians.[2] But, notoriously, Ovid
could be *moralisé*: how important is this for Shake-
speare? *Venus and Adonis* is certainly not a moral story
in any crude sense[3]—it is not a dissuasive from lust (or,
for that matter, from chastity)—but it is not just an
amusing narrative in which one of the principal figures
happens to be a goddess. For this reason one must be
disquieted, even apart from the question of how broadly
comic Shakespeare's effects are, by such an account as
that of Rufus Putney, who hails Venus as 'Shakespeare's
first great comic character' and invokes such parallels as
Falstaff and Juliet's nurse.[4] J. W. Lever's insistence is
very much to the point, that 'the poem is, in fact, not a

[1] *Elizabethan Poetry* (1952), pp. 65–6. Smith's chapter
on 'Ovidian Poetry' is the best treatment of the context
both of *Venus and Adonis* and of *The Rape of Lucrece*.

[2] Smith himself would not endorse the full laudatory
implications of this: see his pp. 86–9, where he finds that
Shakespeare 'betrays something of his own provincial
background' (p. 86).

[3] That, for instance, of Golding's prefatory address:
'By Venus [are meant] such as of the fleshe to filthie lust
are bent'.

[4] 'Venus Agonistes' in *University of Colorado Studies in
Language and Literature*, IV (1953), 53, 50. His earlier
essay, 'Venus and Adonis: Amour with Humor', *Philo-
logical Quarterly*, XX (1941), 533–48, gives a useful account
of the genre as a whole. A recent essay in the same vein is
Eugene B. Cantelupe's 'An Iconographical Interpretation
of *Venus and Adonis*, Shakespeare's Ovidian Comedy',
Shakespeare Quarterly, XIV (1963), 141–51, which is not in
fact very technically iconographical and which treats the
poem as 'satiris[ing] Neoplatonic love' (p. 150).

comedy or a tragedy. It is not a drama. It is occupied
with narrating a myth, and characteristically the aim is
to maintain a certain detachment or "distancing" of
sympathetic response.'[1] Venus is not just an amorous
female of ripe years—she is Love; Adonis is not just a
beautiful boy—he is Beauty;[2] the Boar is not just a Boar
—he is, well, let us not be too precise, but he is something
that can slay Beauty and frustrate Love. This is not a
matter of 'reading things into' the poem. It is the
paradox of Venus's situation that

> She's Love, she loves, and yet she is not loved. (l. 610)

In so far as this is true, the death of Adonis is not
hyperbolically but accurately summed up by her:

> For he being dead, with him is Beauty slain,
> And, Beauty dead, black Chaos comes again.
>
> (ll. 1019–20)

It is not just a piece of embroidery but part of what
makes this story what it is that the death of Adonis
should explain why love is what it now is in this
flawed world (ll. 1135–64). As Lever puts it, the figures
of myth 'interpret life through a fictional paradigm,
telling how nature became as we know it, how death or
winter came into the world, how paradise happened to
be lost'.[3] It is, of course, part of the charm of Ovidian
myth that we have a double vision: Venus is very much
the frustrated lover *within* the myth which purports to
explain how it first came about that love can be
frustrated. And when we think of the controversy there
has been in Milton criticism about how Adam and Eve

---

[1] *Shakespeare Survey*, 15 (1962), 81.
[2] This is a departure from tradition: see A. C. Hamilton
quoted below, p. xvii.
[3] *Shakespeare Survey*, 15 (1962), 81.

can fall without already seeming fallen beings, we may
well find it a considerable advantage for a poet to be
able to present such a myth in a setting basically comic
rather than tragic (and avowedly fictitious rather than
supposedly veridical). But does this save the coherence
of *Venus and Adonis*? Is it not, at least in its climax, a
tragedy, as some critics have claimed? When we are
reminded at l. 1020, as we must be, of Othello's 'Chaos
is come again', are we comparing the wholly incom-
parable? This is where the broadly comic interpreta-
tions, notably that of Rufus Putney, begin to break
down. Granted that Venus indulges in gross hyperbole
(e.g. ll. 1093–1104), which in one sense we cannot
take 'seriously', does this make it burlesque or mock-
heroic? Here we are driven back to the first really
penetrating piece of criticism of this poem, ch. xv of
Biographia Literaria.[1] Coleridge was more interested
in 'the specific symptoms of poetic power' than in
Venus and Adonis as a poem, but what he says is highly
relevant to the poem as a mythical narrative. He writes
of 'the alienation, and, if I may hazard the expression,
the utter *aloofness* of the poet's own feelings, from those
of which he is at once the painter and the analyst', and,
though perhaps unduly concerned about the indelicacy
of the subject, adds that 'Shakespeare has here repre-
sented the animal impulse itself, so as to preclude all
sympathy with it, by dissipating the reader's notice
among the thousand outward images, and now beauti-
ful, now fanciful circumstances, which form its dresses
and its scenery; or by diverting our attention from the
main subject by those frequent witty or profound
reflections, which the poet's ever active mind has
deduced from, or connected with, the imagery and the

[1] See also other versions in T. M. Raysor's edition of
Coleridge's *Shakespearian Criticism* (1930; Everyman
edition 1960).

incidents'.[1] And elsewhere, restricting himself less to
the specific question of 'the animal impulse': 'he works
exactly as if of another planet, as describing the move-
ments of two butterflies'.[2] This is Lever's 'distancing'.
We do not take the characters 'seriously', in the sense
in which dramatic characters can be taken seriously,
but the alternative is not to take them comically:
seeing them as mythical beings is something generically
different from either. Thus in the *Hippolytus* we do not
regard Aphrodite as a character on the same level as
Hippolytus and Phaedra; but this does not make her a
mere abstraction or piece of supernatural machinery:
she is 'not a member of the Pantheon of whom Euri-
pides disapproves, but a potentially disastrous element
in our nature'.[3] So in *Venus and Adonis*, not to take
Venus 'seriously' in one sense—to treat the story as
mere comic fable—would be to turn one's back on a
whole dimension of human experience which the poem
is about. There is a 'Shakespeare the Irrationalist' in the
sense in which E. R. Dodds wrote of 'Euripides the
Irrationalist',[4] who 'explored those dark tracts of the
spirit that lie outside the narrow illuminated field of
rational thought'.

Having said so much, I must stop short of some of the
interpretations heavily fraught with cosmic significance
that recent critics have offered. Ovid, no doubt, was a
'philosopher' in his way, and the Pythagoreanism of the
final book of the *Metamorphoses* is not mere eyewash.

[1] *Biographia Literaria*, ed. J. Shawcross (1907), II, 15–16.
[2] *Shakespearian Criticism*, ed. T. M. Raysor, Everyman
edition (1960), I, 193. H. N. Coleridge gave a padded-out
version of this in *Literary Remains* (1836): see *Lectures and
Notes on Shakespeare and Other Dramatists* (World's
Classics edition, 1931), p. 47.
[3] H. D. F. Kitto, *Greek Tragedy* (1939), p. 204.
[4] *Classical Review*, XLIII (1929), 97–104; p. 100 quoted.

Still, Ovid was not Euripides; neither was the Shakespeare of this poem the 'sage and serious Spenser' of the Mutability Cantos. Of the most stimulating of the 'deeper' interpretations of the poem, that by H. T. Price,[1] Lever reasonably raises the question 'whether these depths might be compatible with its surface brilliance'.[2] But there is one recent discussion of the poem which does justice to the mythical element while judiciously avoiding over-reading. This is A. C. Hamilton's 'Venus and Adonis' in *Studies in English Literature 1500–1900*, 1 (1961). Hamilton rejects the view that the poem was 'written against lust': if it was, then 'all [Shakespeare's] contemporaries were deceived'. Departing from the traditional identification of Venus with Beauty, and equating Venus with Love and Adonis with Beauty, Shakespeare makes use of 'the Platonic doctrine that love is the desire for beauty' (p. 9). 'Adonis sees Venus as lust....But Shakespeare does not, and neither may readers of the poem' (p. 10). 'The Boar expresses all these forces which seek to pluck the flower of Beauty. Accordingly, it functions as a poetic symbol through which Shakespeare explores the mystery of evil' (p. 13).

This still leaves indeterminate exactly what

[1] 'The Function of Imagery in *Venus and Adonis*', *Papers of the Michigan Academy of Science, Arts and Letters*, XXXI (1945), 275–97.

[2] *Shakespeare Survey*, 15 (1962), 21. This is the place to mention, but not discuss, the ingenious account of the numerology of the poem by Christopher Butler and Alastair Fowler, 'Time-Beguiling Sport: Number Symbolism in Shakespeare's *Venus and Adonis*', *Shakespeare 1564–1964: A Collection of Modern Essays by Various Hands*, ed. E. A. Bloom (1964), pp. 124–33. On the seasonal significance of the myth, this usefully quotes Sandys's commentary on *Metamorphoses*, X (p. 125).

Shakespeare has to *say* about the 'mystery of evil' through this symbol. It is at this point that one must ask how the slaying of Adonis is related to his rejection of Venus. Perhaps this should not be pressed—after all, this is how Adonis was traditionally slain—still, the opposition of love and hunting has been put in the forefront from line 4:

> Hunting he loved, but love he laughed to scorn.

And it is because of his rejection of Venus that Adonis perishes. It is here that it would be specially helpful to decide whether, as D. C. Allen thinks,[1] the Hippolytus story has made an important contribution to the story as Shakespeare sees it, for there the fate of Hippolytus is a punishment (not a just one but a divinely inflicted one) for his rejection of love. Certainly the one myth cannot be simply applied to the other—Venus is far removed from a vindictive Aphrodite, and the symbolic reading of H. T. Price must be firmly rejected: that Venus as 'the irrepressible desire to possess and to destroy is represented in three figures; she is the eagle (ll. 55–60), the horse (ll. 259–318), the boar (ll. 614–42, 1105–18)', and the boar becomes in Racinian vein 'Venus in her most horrible symbol'.[2] We cannot possibly depart from the surface meaning of the story in such a way as to make Venus and the boar anything but enemies; and if Venus toys with the conceit of the boar as lover (ll. 1109–20), this can be paralleled by 'Death the bridegroom' in *Romeo and Juliet*—Death is none the less Death. I suspect that the traditional story is treated as sufficient to make us accept the vulnerability of

[1] *Elizabethan and Jacobean Studies Presented to Frank Percy Wilson* (1959), pp. 106–7.

[2] *Papers of the Michigan Academy of Science, Arts and Letters*, XXXI (1945), 292.

beauty without linking it too closely with Shakespeare's (primarily comic) innovation of the unconquerable coldness of Adonis. In fact they fit in quite well with each other; even if we are not to think of Adonis's death as in any way a retribution, it certainly drives home the need for Beauty to propagate itself, which has bulked large in Venus's urgings; to this extent the customary linking of the poem with Sonnets 1–17 is fair enough.

I have stressed the role of the central myth in the poem because it is by keeping hold of this that it is easiest to avoid one-sided interpretations of various sorts. But such an account is of course far from exhausting the richness of the poem. The vividly realized rural setting, which led some earlier critics to imagine Shakespeare writing the poem in the Stratford of his early years, is essential to the effect, and the episode of the horse shows the dramatist's sense of the telling power of concrete *exemplum*.[1] It is these local felicities that have seemed to many critics to bulk too large in the poem, and to distract attention from its main narrative line. I do not myself feel that this happens, but clearly Shakespeare has gone at least as far as he safely can in naturalizing Ovid in an English setting. Even the sceptical critic must surely admit that any incongruity between the worlds of comedy and of myth is in some degree mitigated by such things as the easy, lightly touched unsentimental pathos—for which perhaps Burns affords the only parallel—of the description of the hare, and the unforced naturalism of the stallion and the mare. And if the final lament over the death of Adonis is in danger of striking the unattuned reader as over-strained and operatic, it can still be seen as falling

[1] Not only the dramatist's, of course: it is what Sidney in the *Apology* praises as the special virtue of the poet as such.

within the boundaries of Shakespeare's conception of comedy—a conception that, perhaps about the same time, was exemplified in the shadow that falls across the riotous farce of the Show of the Nine Worthies in *Love's Labour's Lost* with the news of the King's death. Such a comparison must not be allowed to blur the distinction between myth and comic drama—yet in Shakespeare's treatment of both there is the same generalizing power. In *Love's Labour's Lost*, just because the King is not even a character in the play, his death is all the more apt to stand for Death as such, and its impact on the business of everyday life. So, in *Venus and Adonis*, the distance from reality intrinsic to the mythological figures enables us to contemplate the vulnerability of Beauty without having to think away the comic reality presented by the whole structure of the poem.

II. THE RAPE OF LUCRECE

The question of sources is a little more difficult for *The Rape of Lucrece* than for *Venus and Adonis*, because here we have a single story told by two Latin authors, Ovid (*Fasti*, II. 721–852) and Livy (I. 57–60), as well as by several writers in English.[1] There can be no doubt that Shakespeare read Ovid, and that he also had access to certain material available in Livy but not in Ovid. Whether his knowledge of Livy was first-hand is harder to prove. As has been shown by T. W. Baldwin in particular, the relevant passages in Livy were freely quoted by Renaissance commentators on Ovid, and there are other derivatives (see note on ll. 1850–1). Of

---

[1] Geoffrey Bullough, *Narrative and Dramatic Sources of Shakespeare*, I (1957), prints Ovid, in the original and in a translation of 1640, Chaucer, and Painter's *Palace of Pleasure* (fairly closely translating Livy).

the two Middle English versions, Shakespeare had pretty certainly read Chaucer's (see notes on ll. 197–210, 365, 515, 596–630), and quite possibly Gower's (see notes on ll. 106–13, 170).

But what is most important about Shakespeare's re-handling of the story is not his use of earlier versions in detail, but the radically different impression that his poem as a whole makes. Not only is it greatly expanded, but it displays a type of interest in the figure of Tarquin that is quite new.[1] It is here, rather than in the story of Lucrece, that the poem points significantly forward to later Shakespearian tragedy. But before considering this aspect of it, we must look at it in the context of the 1590's.

The question of genre arises with *Lucrece* as with *Venus and Adonis*, but with differences that can be linked with the lesser degree of success of the later poem. *Lucrece* can be placed in the tradition of the complaint poem, which had leapt into prominence with Samuel Daniel's *Complaint of Rosamond* (1592). This was certainly known to Shakespeare, and Daniel in his turn seems to have drawn on *Lucrece* in revising and expanding his poem in 1594.[2]

The complaint poem, like the mythological-erotic poem, can be broadly classified as Ovidian, as it is by Hallett Smith in the title of ch. II of his *Elizabethan*

[1] The Argument, among its other divergences from the poem, completely lacks any such interest. For its sources, and for the view that it is not by Shakespeare, see J. M. Tolbert, *Studies in English* [University of Texas], XXVIII (1950), 77–90. For the view that it 'may transmit an early outline for the narrative superseded in some details by the actual poem', see E. A. J. Honigmann, *The Stability of Shakespeare's Text* (1965), p. 45.

[2] See D. Bush, *Mythology and the Renaissance Tradition in English Poetry* (1932), p. 152, n. 31.

Poetry.[1] But it is a much more mixed genre. The subject-matter of its first exemplar, Daniel's *Complaint of Rosamond*, admits Ovidian influence. In Hallett Smith's words: 'Because of the special nature of the new complaint poems, their concern with love and chastity, the Ovidian tradition had an opportunity to influence and color the complaint' (p. 103). But, though Shakespeare's contribution to it has a specific Ovidian source, the tone of the genre remains remote from Ovid. The grim shadow of the *Mirror for Magistrates* tradition hangs over it, and in its short career—the last example Hallett Smith discusses is Middleton's juvenile *The Ghost of Lucrece* (1600)—it produces no such assured masterpiece as *Hero and Leander* or *Venus and Adonis*. It is significant that the most accomplished poems that can be linked with it are Drayton's 'Heroical Epistles', in which complaint material is held within a firm framework supplied by Ovid—the *Heroides* instead of the *Metamorphoses*—so that the result is markedly superior to Drayton's earlier and much more diffuse *Piers Gaveston* (1594), which is strongly under the influence of Daniel and Shakespeare.

It would have been surprising, then, if Shakespeare had managed to achieve the same degree of unity and coherence as he has in *Venus and Adonis*, and he certainly did not.[2] But if *The Rape of Lucrece* is a less satisfactory poem, it is more interestingly related to Shakespeare's dramatic work. Its intrinsic qualities and defects are admirably assessed in F. T. Prince's Arden

---

[1] But he sometimes, as on p. 104, contrasts the 'Ovidian poem' with the complaint.

[2] The interesting essay by Horst Oppel, 'Das Bild der brennenden Troja in Shakespeares *Rape of Lucrece*', *Shakespeare Jahrbuch*, LXXVII–VIII (1951–2), revised in *Shakespeare, Studien zum Werk und zur Welt des Dichters* (1963), seems to me to make excessive claims for the poem.

Introduction (pp. xxxiii–viii): 'while the digressions in *Venus and Adonis* strengthen the whole, those in *Lucrece* consistently weaken it'; 'the greatest weakness in Shakespeare's Lucrece is... her remorseless eloquence'; and, most important of all, 'the poem offers, in turn, two centres of interest': Tarquin and Lucrece. It is, in fact, the tragic potentialities of Tarquin's role that make the second, and longer, half of the poem so unsatisfying. As Fr. Christopher Devlin puts it, Shakespeare 'is more concerned with Tarquin's soul than Lucrece's body',[1] and indeed the probing concern with Tarquin's soul brings out more clearly than would otherwise have been necessary the degree to which Lucrece *is* simply Lucrece's body, or, at best, the guardian of a valuable physical possession,[2] regarded in something like the fashion Coleridge credited to Beaumont and Fletcher, who 'always write as if virtue or goodness were a sort of talisman or strange something that might be lost without the least fault on the part of the owner. In short their chaste ladies value their chastity as a material thing, not as an act or state of being.'[3] Shakespeare, of course, is not satisfied to make Lucrece's chastity just a possession for her, and the better passages of this second half of the poem effectively convey her sense of intrinsic pollution. But the effect is blurred. It is possible to tell the story, as do Ovid and Chaucer, without raising any embarrassing questions; and of course the combination of subjective innocence and objective pollution can be the stuff of great tragedy, as in the story of Oedipus. But Shakespeare, by treating the situation of Tarquin in such an Augustinian fashion,

[1] *Life of Robert Southwell* (1956), p. 272.
[2] See especially the presentation of the body-soul relation in ll. 1163–76.
[3] *Coleridge's Miscellaneous Criticism*, ed. T. M. Raysor (1936), p. 81.

has made inescapable the Augustinian question about Lucrece: 'si adulterata, cur laudata? si pudica, cur occisa?' (see note on ll. 1723–4). The inconsistency reveals itself in the stanza in which Shakespeare makes the transition from Tarquin to Lucrece:

> He thence departs a heavy convertite;
> She there remains a hopeless castaway;
> He in his speed looks for the morning light;
> She prays she never may behold the day.
>
> (ll. 743–6)

The term 'castaway', with its strong theological connotations, is quite inappropriate to this tale of pagan honour, which can only be acceptable if its basic assumptions go unchallenged. It might still have been possible to present Lucrece's suicide as not, indeed, exemplary, but still as the only choice left open to her,[1] and there are passages in which the pathos of her predicament does emerge. As F. T. Prince says (*Arden* Introduction, p. xxxvi), 'the most moving passages are those in which she is silent, or nearly so: the interviews with the maid and with the groom. Here we are shown her grief momentarily from without, or indirectly, checked by social circumstance.' But the force of these passages is destroyed by the 'remorseless eloquence' elsewhere. The highly wrought set pieces, on Opportunity and Time, and on the Fall of Troy, have their own impressiveness, and it is easy to see how Shakespeare came to feel that they represented the only way the subject could be treated, but they emphasize rather than mitigate the failure of the poem as a whole.

Yet this failure sharpens our attention to those elements in the poem which seem to belong to the nature

---

[1] As good a case as can be made out for a reading of this sort is presented by Harold R. Walley, *PMLA* LXXVI (1961), 486–7.

of Shakespearian tragedy as it is later to develop, more
markedly than anything in *Titus Andronicus* or even in
Romeo and Juliet. It may be broadly true that 'if
Lucrece is a tragedy, it is of course a tragedy by the
author of *Titus Andronicus*, and not by the author of
Lear or *Othello*',[1] but it is still what casts our minds
forward to more mature Shakespeare that is of the
greatest interest. The subject has recently been dis-
cussed by Harold R. Walley,[2] who traces Shakespeare's
account of 'precisely what is involved in the commission
of an act like that of Tarquin', and 'how it comes
about that such an act is ever committed'.[3] Walley also
deals with the later part of the poem, which concen-
trates on 'the central interest of tragedy, the plight of the
victim',[4] but he is not notably more successful than
other critics in showing that this *is* the 'central interest'
of this particular poem. Indeed, taking 'victim' in its
natural sense, this would seem to be something that
distinguishes the poem from later tragedy, rather than
something that links them. Where, in Shakespearian
tragedy, does the central interest lie in the fate of a
victim who is other than the principal agent? But if
we are prepared to be satisfied with the more limited
local successes of the first part, there is much to reward
us. The epic plunge *in medias res*, in the opening
stanza, is extremely effective, with its immediate intro-
duction of the image of 'lightless fire' (l. 4), to be taken
up later in symbolic incidents (with no parallel in Ovid
or Livy) at ll. 309 ff., where

> The wind wars with his torch to make him stay,
> And blows the smoke of it into his face,
> Extinguishing his conduct in this case;

---

[1] *Arden* Introduction, pp. xxiv–v.
[2] *PMLA* LXXVI (1961), 480–7.
[3] *Ibid.* 482.   [4] *Ibid.* 484.

and ll. 673–4:

> This said, he sets his foot upon the light,
> For light and lust are deadly enemies.

Even more interesting is the emphasis on the compulsive and irrational nature of the crime, which all critics have linked with *Macbeth* (especially the soliloquy of Act 1, scene 7): the two stanzas, ll. 225–38, culminating in:

> But as he is my kinsman, my dear friend,
> The shame and fault finds no excuse nor end.

Even here the unevenness of the poem is manifest, since these fine stanzas are immediately followed by the *Spanish Tragedy* formulae:

> Shameful it is—ay, if the fact be known;
> Hateful it is—there is no hate in loving;....

Apart from the parallels that force themselves on the reader's notice, there is some warrant for thinking of *Lucrece* in terms of later Shakespearian tragedy in the fact that Shakespeare himself recalls both the story and his own handling of it up to the end of his career. Macbeth speaks of 'Tarquin's ravishing strides' (2. 1. 55), and Jachimo of 'our Tarquin' (*Cymbeline*, 2. 2. 12). It is, perhaps, not really surprising that, of the two early poems, it should have been the unsatisfactory, uneven and inchoate work that continued to solicit its creator's attention, whereas he could move forward leaving *Venus and Adonis* behind him as a limited, mannered but self-sufficient artistic achievement.

III. THE PHOENIX AND THE TURTLE

We shall probably never know why Shakespeare contributed to the 'Poeticall Essaies' appended to Robert Chester's *Love's Martyr* (1601). Unlike his fellow-

contributors Jonson and Marston, he does not appear
to have had any personal knowledge of Sir John
Salusbury, Chester's patron, and his poem contradicts
the personal allegory of Chester's poem. This deplor-
able and obscure piece of verse has a generally 'Platonic'
flavour, but it is pretty clear that, as Carleton Brown
demonstrated,[1] there is also a reference to the marriage
of Sir John Salusbury and Ursula Stanley in December
1586, and the birth of their daughter Jane in October
1587. In so far as the poem uses the Phoenix myth, a
final act of immolation is required, and Chester's inept
attempt to superimpose upon this the mystical union of
a (male) Turtle with a (female) Phoenix inevitably
gives rise to obscurity as to whether the lovers did or
did not perish (whatever that might symbolically stand
for) in the process of creating a new Phoenix. Those
who knew the actual facts (like Marston, who refers to
the new Phoenix as 'now...growne vnto maturitie'[2] by
1601) could cope with the situation. Shakespeare
would seem to have contented himself with a glance at
the subtitle, 'Allegorically shadowing the truth of Loue,
in the constant Fate of the Phoenix and Turtle', and

---

[1] *Poems by Sir John Salusbury and Robert Chester*, Early
English Text Society, E.S. CXIII (1914 for 1913). For the
gist of Brown's argument see H. E. Rollins's New Variorum
edition of the *Poems* (1938), pp. 575–7. Less plausible is the
view of T. P. Harrison, *Studies in English* [University of
Texas], XXX (1951), 82, that 'the new Phoenix is a symbol
of reconciliation between the Queen and Salisbury [Salus-
bury]'. The old view (that of Grosart) that the Phoenix is
Elizabeth is accepted, but not argued, on p. 124 of
Elizabeth Watson's 'Natural History in *Love's Martyr*'
(*Renaissance and Modern Studies*, VIII, Nottingham, 1964).

[2] *The Poems of John Marston*, ed. A. Davenport (1961),
p. 179. Carleton Brown, *op. cit.* pp. lxxi–ii, noted the
importance of this reference.

possibly at the stanzas which, on a casual reading, would suggest that both birds perish in the flame. (I argue below that Shakespeare makes something wholly new of this.) At any rate, it is futile to look for personal allusions in Shakespeare's poem, which must be interpreted from within itself, with such help as can be gained from literary or philosophical tradition.

Literary sources are hard to find. In what remains one of the most useful discussions, A. H. R. Fairchild[1] claimed as the clue to the poem the tradition of the Court of Love, and Chaucer in *The Parlement of Foules* in particular, on the one hand, and the emblematic tradition on the other. There is enough to suggest—in conjunction with evidence from other works that he knew the poem[2]—that Shakespeare took a few hints from *The Parlement of Foules*, but there is nothing in Chaucer that really throws much light on what is distinctive in *The Phoenix and the Turtle*; and while emblematic equivalences are certainly used, they are of a familiar kind. Perhaps a more promising specific source is the collection *The Phoenix Nest* (1593),[3] which contains an elegy on Sidney by M. Roydon, introducing the Phoenix, the Eagle, the Turtle and the Swan as mourners, and also a 'Dialogue between Constancie and Inconstancie', but the resemblances are not very striking. The whole phoenix tradition has been examined by various scholars, notably T. W. Baldwin, who also claims a special

[1] *Englische Studien*, XXXIII (1904).

[2] Nevill Coghill in *Elizabethan and Jacobean Studies Presented to Frank Percy Wilson* (1959), pp. 86–99; also *Notes and Queries*, CCV (1960), 16, 17–18.

[3] Noted in passing by Sidney Lee, *Life of Shakespeare* (1898), p. 184; elaborated by K. Muir and S. O'Loughlin, *The Voyage to Illyria* (1937), pp. 130–1, and R. Ellrodt, *Shakespeare Survey*, 15 (1962), 100–1.

connexion with Ovid, *Amores*, II. 6 (on the death of the parrot),[1] and Robert Ellrodt.[2]

Basically, our interpretation must be from within the poem itself. It did not greatly impress most critics until relatively recent times, and it is significant that it should have grown in repute with the growth of interest in 'metaphysical poetry' on the one hand and 'pure poetry' on the other. These two affinities suggest rather different, though not necessarily incompatible, ways of looking at the poem. Helen Gardner, though she includes it in *The Metaphysical Poets* (1957), places it among 'poems which in some ways anticipate the metaphysical manner', along with poems by Ralegh, Fulke Greville and Southwell, and writes that, compared with Donne, Shakespeare is 'too remote, and too symbolic, creating a static world where Love and Constancy are deified' (p. 23). Certainly *The Phoenix and the Turtle* is not characterized by 'the dialectical expression of personal drama', to borrow a phrase which J. B. Leishman regards as more aptly descriptive of Donne than 'metaphysical'.[3] Yet Miss Gardner has also written that it is 'the most "strong-lined" of all poems, if "strong lines" are riddles' and the central paradox of 'two and one' is eminently reminiscent of Donne.[4] What Shakespeare gives us is, in some measure, scholastic terminology,[5] but without the scholastic

[1] *Literary Genetics of Shakspere's Poems and Sonnets* (Urbana, 1950).

[2] *Shakespeare Survey*, 15 (1962), 99–110.

[3] *The Monarch of Wit* (1951), p. 18.

[4] For the importance of Shakespeare's substitution of '*neither* two nor one' for the Neoplatonic 'two *and* one', see Ellrodt, *op. cit.* p. 109, n. 28.

[5] See J. V. Cunningham, *ELH: A Journal of English Literary History*, XIX (1952), 265–76; reprinted in *Tradition and Poetic Structure* (Denver, 1960).

argumentation of Donne: instead, we have charged, incantatory statement.

The inclination to describe *The Phoenix and the Turtle* as 'pure poetry' may in part arise from a sense of the ways in which it is not 'metaphysical'. Yet the first critic to use this actual phrase, J. Middleton Murry, would perhaps not have sharply opposed the two. For he writes of the poem as 'pure poetry in the loftiest and most abstract meaning of the words: that is to say, it gives us the highest experience which it is possible for poetry to give, and it gives it without inter-mission'.[1] It is with a somewhat different emphasis that F. T. Prince writes of it as 'pure' poetry in the sense of Poe and Mallarmé.[2] The element of mystery and deliberate obscurity and compression of syntax certainly prompts such comparison, though Prince is equally right in pointing out the 'element of irony, hyperbole, and high fantasy which is generally missing in the Romantic and Victorian poets'.[3] The solemn, startling pronouncements are placed within a framework of bird-ritual which militates against over-solemnity: to quote Prince again, 'a homeliness like that of the burial of Cock-Robin is fused with apprehensions of the mystery of death and the migration of the soul'.[4] Yet, is it 'migration'? One of the striking things about the poem is that it is *not*, in any obvious way, about im-mortality or re-incarnation. The miracle of love is hymned, the lovers 'are fled | In a mutual flame from hence', but though 'fled' may hint at another world, the stress of the poem remains entirely elegiac: 'Love

---

[1] *Discoveries* (1924), 1930 ed., p. 25. Later (p. 42) it becomes 'absolute' poetry: 'the direct embodiment, through symbols which are necessarily dark, of a pure, comprehensive and self-satisfying experience'.

[2] Arden Introduction (1960), p. xliv.

[3] *Ibid.*   [4] *Ibid.* p. xliii.

and constancy is dead', 'their tragic scene', 'Truth and beauty buried be', and

> Death is now the phoenix' nest;
> And the turtle's loyal breast
> To eternity doth rest.

The very word that might be used to invoke a Time/Eternity opposition is used with startling plainness as a simple 'for ever', all the more striking because of the legendary nature of the Phoenix. To say that Shakespeare denies or rejects the notion of life after death would be absurd. But the fact that, in spite of the Phoenix symbol, it just does not arise in this poem, is one of the things that distinguish it from poems like, say, Donne's *Anniversaries*, which also seems to assert that 'Truth and Beauty buried be', but which superimpose ideas of a traditional heaven. There is, one might say, no longer any need for the death followed by resurrection of the traditional Phoenix. Shakespeare has in the fullest sense, as Helen Gardner says, 'created out of the myth a myth of his own'.[1] The love-union of the Phoenix and the Turtle simply *is* their death—'the exchanged death, and life, of a fully mutual love'[2]—not something on which the death tragically supervenes, though within the conventions of the poem it has to be emblematized as a real death. (From this point of view, what Shakespeare may have known or imagined about the family history of Sir John Salusbury is simply irrelevant.) And it *is* a real death in so far as the experience shadowed forth is unique and inaccessible to all others: 'But in them it were a wonder.'

Here we can see also the qualifications necessary in accepting another label we may be tempted to apply to

[1] *The Metaphysical Poets* (1957), p. 39, n. 1.
[2] C. S. Lewis, *English Literature in the Sixteenth Century* (1954), p. 509.

the poem: 'Platonic'. It is certainly Platonism with a difference. As Ellrodt writes, 'It invites no ascent along the well-known ladder leading up to the contemplation of the Heavenly Beauty, though a ray of it may flash through the flaming eyes of the Phoenix, her earthly reflexion. The poet is concerned only with the perfect union achieved by the lovers' souls, an idea perhaps more closely related to Christian mysticism than genuine Platonism.'[1] A selection from the language of Platonism (or Neoplatonism) is, in fact, just one of the modes of expression that Shakespeare finds ready to hand. As in *Antony and Cleopatra* the use of apocalyptic imagery, analysed by Miss Ethel Seaton,[2] does not make the play a religious allegory, but is rather a borrowing for Shakespeare's own purposes of a type of evocative language specially well adapted for conveying the relationship of the lovers and the significance of their fate, so in *The Phoenix and the Turtle*, in spite of Platonic echoes, and of a formulation reminiscent of the doctrine of the Trinity,[3] Shakespeare 'nowhere suggests an allegory of religious mysteries or even of divine love'.[4] It is just that such formulations give the nearest analogue to what can be said, or hinted, about this exemplary love. And in the upshot, the description 'metaphysical' is not, after all, so inapplicable, so long as we do not just take that epithet to mean 'like Donne'. To quote Ellrodt again, 'Intellectually, Shakespeare is less inventive, less witty than Donne: he rings the

---

[1] *Shakespeare Survey*, 15 (1962), 104. For the view that this 'Ladder' is also absent in the most overtly 'Platonic' of major Elizabethan poems, see C. S. Lewis on Spenser's *Hymns*: *English Literature in the Sixteenth Century* (1954), pp. 374–7.

[2] *Review of English Studies*, XXII (1946), 219–24.

[3] See note on l. 27.

[4] Ellrodt, *op. cit.* p. 105.

changes on one idea instead of striking out fresh con-
ceits from the traditional "two-in-one" paradox'.[1] But
at the same time, 'the Plotinian intuition of the One
and the paradoxes of negative theology make a kindred
appeal to the imaginative mind. In each case the sense
of transcendence arises from an utter denial of common
sense, an utter rejection of common experience.'[2] It is
because just once in his life Shakespeare took, or made,
the opportunity of fixing this 'utter rejection of com-
mon experience' in a way that is excluded by the
dramatic medium that this poem is both so utterly un-
like anything else he ever wrote[3] and yet, now that we
have it, such a rare and irreplaceable possession.

IV. A LOVER'S COMPLAINT

For a poem published along with the 1609 *Sonnets*, *A
Lover's Complaint* has been very little discussed.
Nothing of any real importance[4] was written about it
before the essay by J. W. Mackail in 1912,[5] a study so
important that H. E. Rollins, in his New Variorum
edition of the *Poems* (1938), subdivides criticism into
that 'before 1912' and that 'after 1912'. Even after
Mackail, the poem had to wait more than fifty years
for another full discussion, which it has now received
from Kenneth Muir in *Shakespeare 1594–1964: A*

[1] *Ibid.* p. 107.   [2] *Ibid.*

[3] 'We could not have guessed, I think, from internal
evidence that this poem was by Shakespeare' (C. S. Lewis,
English Literature in the Sixteenth Century, 1954, p. 509).

[4] E. K. Chambers, *William Shakespeare* (1930), I, 550,
in a very short bibliography, cited N. Delius's essay in
Jahrbuch, XX (1885). This is little more than a précis,
and not worth consulting. Almost all Delius's general
comments are quoted by Rollins, New Variorum, p. 589.

[5] *Essays and Studies of the English Association*, III (1912),
51–70.

Collection of Modern Essays by Various Hands, edited
by Edward A. Bloom (1964).[1]

These two essays present, respectively, the case
against and the case for Shakespeare's authorship.
Neither of them enters into the question of what
relationship, if any, the poem has to the *Sonnets*; and,
as one innocent of any theories about the *Sonnets*
(beyond a belief that they are all, or almost all, by
Shakespeare), I propose to follow their example,
though the young man who 'sexes both enchanted'
(l. 128) might prompt speculation.

The case against Shakespearian authorship is,
basically, the general impression that the poem is
neither good enough nor characteristic enough. The
number of words which do not occur elsewhere in
Shakespeare (or, occasionally, anywhere else at all), is
not in itself particularly striking (see Muir, pp. 155–6),
and some of them are Latinisms reminiscent of *Troilus
and Cressida*, but there is a general lack of ease and
fluency. Mackail (pp. 64–5) notes in particular the
way in which the fumbling opening contrasts with those
of *Venus* and *Lucrece*. Another suspicious feature is the
poverty of proverbial material. Tilley's index cites only
two passages (ll. 198, 290) and both are of the most
commonplace description. It is hard to dissent from
Mackail's verdict: 'A certain laboriousness, a certain
cramped, gritty, discontinuous quality, affects it subtly
but vitally throughout' (p. 63).

But if it is not by Shakespeare, who is it by? J. M.
Robertson[2] favoured Chapman, but Muir (pp. 157–8)
shows that the evidence is no better, if no worse, than
that which led Robertson to assign large portions of the
plays also to Chapman. Mackail accounted for its
presence in the *Sonnets* volume on the hypothesis that it
was by the 'Rival Poet' (which, on one view, would

[1] Pp. 154–66.   [2] *Shakespeare and Chapman* (1917).

coincide with Robertson's verdict). But this is a desperate speculation.

I feel myself driven, rather reluctantly, to the conclusion that the 1609 attribution is correct. Muir has analysed some striking similarities to passages in the plays (see notes on ll. 18, 173), and a few more may be added (see notes on ll. 298, 315). There are also some details of verbal forms and spelling that, without proving a Shakespearian origin, fit in well with it (see notes on ll. 20, 112, 118). None of this would be enough to warrant the attribution of an anonymous poem to Shakespeare, but it would be surprising if they were all, by chance, present in one falsely attributed to him in a volume which also contains a collection of genuine work.

On one point, Mackail and Muir agree: that if the poem is by Shakespeare, its defects are not to be explained by its being of very early date. I am sure they are right. The vocabulary belongs to the Shakespeare of the 1600's, not the early 1590's, and the play to which it seems closest is *Troilus and Cressida*. A certain awkwardness, a lack of sureness of touch, may also make us think of *All's Well*. If I had to choose a year, it would be 1601 or 1602.

Rollins (p. 586) wrote that 'what a writer thinks of the authorship largely determines his judgement of the literary value and the date of composition'. I feel myself an exception to this generalization, since I believe it to be a poem of Shakespeare's maturity, but a poem of very little merit.

Yet rather than labour my lack of admiration of the poem, I had better confess to a possible blind spot, though it is one shared by many other critics, and record that both the critics who have made the most notable contributions to the study of the poem have found something to admire, though neither thinks it a success as a

whole. For Mackail, 'there are more than a few passages
in the poem which are like Shakespeare at his best, and
of which one would say at first sight that no one but
Shakespeare could have written them, so wonderfully
do they combine his effortless power and his incom-
parable sweetness' (p. 62). And Muir concludes his
essay: 'The poem is inferior in most ways to Shake-
speare's other narrative poems, and it is inferior to the
best of the sonnets; but it is not without its own special
flavour, and it adds something to the total impression
we have of Shakespeare as a poet' (p. 166).

J. C. M.

May 1965

POSTSCRIPT

Since completing this Introduction, I have received a
copy of *Shakespeare's A Lover's Complaint: Its Date
and Authenticity*, by MacD. P. Jackson (University of
Auckland, 1965), which, after a fuller discussion, comes
to much the same conclusions as Muir's essay (of which
it is independent). I have been able to insert Jackson's
name in connexion with one parallel (note on l. 81).

A recent essay on *The Phoenix and the Turtle*, 'The
Dead Phoenix' by Murray Copland (*Essays in Criticism*,
xv (1965), 279–87), objects to this traditional title as
a 'howler' (p. 279), and insists on *The Phoenix and
Turtle*: 'the subject is *one* thing, not two'. I think this
is much ado about very little, but probably ought to
have noted that the usual title is modern (1807, accord-
ing to Rollins, New Variorum, p. 560). The poem is
untitled in *Love's Martyr*, but the main title-page has
'the Phoenix and Turtle' (see p. xxvii above) and the
separate title page for the additional poems refers to
'Diverse Poeticall Essaies on the former Subiect; viz:
the *Turtle* and *Phoenix*'.

September 1965

THE POEMS

THE POEMS

VENUS AND ADONIS

Vilia miretur vulgus; mihi flavus Apollo
Pocula Castalia plena ministret aqua

TO THE

TO THE

RIGHT HONOURABLE
HENRY WRIOTHESLEY,

EARL OF SOUTHAMPTON, AND BARON
OF TITCHFIELD

RIGHT HONOURABLE,

I know not how I shall offend in dedicating my un-polished lines to your lordship, nor how the world will censure me for choosing so strong a prop to support so weak a burden: only, if your honour seem but pleased, I account my self highly praised, and vow to take advantage of all idle hours, till I have honoured you with some graver labour. But if the first heir of my invention prove deformed, I shall be sorry it had so noble a godfather, and never after ear so barren a land, for fear it yield me still so bad a harvest. I leave it to your honourable survey, and your honour to your heart's content; which I wish may always answer your own wish, and the world's hopeful expectation.

Your honour's in all duty,

William Shakespeare

VENUS AND ADONIS

Even as the sun with purple-coloured face
Had ta'en his last leave of the weeping morn,
Rose-cheeked Adonis hied him to the chase;
Hunting he loved, but love he laughed to scorn.
    Sick-thoughted Venus makes amain unto him,   5
    And like a bold-faced suitor 'gins to woo him.

'Thrice fairer than myself,' thus she began,
'The field's chief flower, sweet above compare,
Stain to all nymphs, more lovely than a man,
More white and red than doves or roses are;   10
    Nature that made thee with herself at strife
    Saith that the world hath ending with thy life.

'Vouchsafe, thou wonder, to alight thy steed,
And rein his proud head to the saddle-bow;
If thou wilt deign this favour, for thy meed   15
A thousand honey secrets shalt thou know.
    Here come and sit, where never serpent hisses,
    And being set, I'll smother thee with kisses;

'And yet not cloy thy lips with loathed satiety,
But rather famish them amid their plenty,   20
Making them red and pale with fresh variety;
Ten kisses short as one, one long as twenty.
    A summer's day will seem an hour but short,
    Being wasted in such time-beguiling sport.'

With this she seizeth on his sweating palm,   25
The precedent of pith and livelihood,
And, trembling in her passion, calls it balm,
Earth's sovereign salve to do a goddess good.
    Being so enraged, desire doth lend her force
    Courageously to pluck him from his horse.   30

Over one arm the lusty courser's rein,
Under her other was the tender boy,
Who blushed and pouted in a dull disdain,
With leaden appetite, unapt to toy;
35   She red and hot as coals of glowing fire,
He red for shame, but frosty in desire.

The studded bridle on a ragged bough
Nimbly she fastens—O, how quick is love!
The steed is stallèd up, and even now
40 To tie the rider she begins to prove.   *try*
        Backward she pushed him, as she would be thrust,
        And governed him in strength, though not in lust.

So soon was she along as he was down,
Each leaning on their elbows and their hips;
45 Now doth she stroke his cheek, now doth he frown,
And 'gins to chide, but soon she stops his lips,
        And kissing speaks, with lustful language broken,
        'If thou wilt chide, thy lips shall never open.'

He burns with bashful shame; she with her tears
50 Doth quench the maiden burning of his cheeks;
Then with her windy sighs and golden hairs
To fan and blow them dry again she seeks.
        He saith she is immodest, blames her miss;   *fault*
        What follows more she murders with a kiss.

55 Even as an empty eagle, sharp by fast,
Tires with her beak on feathers, flesh and bone,
Shaking her wings, devouring all in haste,
Till either gorge be stuffed or prey be gone;
        Even so she kissed his brow, his cheek, his chin,
60   And where she ends she doth anew begin.

Forced to content, but never to obey,
Panting he lies and breatheth in her face;
She feedeth on the steam as on a prey,
And calls it heavenly moisture, air of grace,
   Wishing her cheeks were gardens full of flowers, 65
   So they were dewed with such distilling showers.

Look how a bird lies tangled in a net,
So fast'ned in her arms Adonis lies;
Pure shame and awed resistance made him fret,
Which bred more beauty in his angry eyes. 70
   Rain added to a river that is rank
   Perforce will force it overflow the bank.

Still she entreats, and prettily entreats,
For to a pretty ear she tunes her tale;
Still is he sullen, still he lours and frets, 75
'Twixt crimson shame and anger ashy-pale;
   Being red, she loves him best, and being white,
   Her best is bettered with a more delight.

Look how he can, she cannot choose but love;
And by her fair immortal hand she swears 80
From his soft bosom never to remove
Till he take truce with her contending tears,
   Which long have rained, making her cheeks all wet;
   And one sweet kiss shall pay this countless debt.

Upon this promise did he raise his chin, 85
Like a dive-dapper peering through a wave, _dabchick_
Who, being looked on, ducks as quickly in;
So offers he to give what she did crave;
   But when her lips were ready for his pay,
   He winks, and turns his lips another way. 90

Never did passenger in summer's heat
More thirst for drink than she for this good turn.
Her help she sees, but help she cannot get;
She bathes in water, yet her fire must burn.
95   'O, pity,' 'gan she cry, 'flint-hearted boy!
      'Tis but a kiss I beg; why art thou coy?

'I have been wooed, as I entreat thee now,
Even by the stern and direful god of war,
Whose sinewy neck in battle ne'er did bow,
100 Who conquers where he comes in every jar;
      Yet hath he been my captive and my slave,
      And begged for that which thou unasked shalt have.

'Over my altars hath he hung his lance,
His batt'red shield, his uncontrollèd crest,
105 And for my sake hath learned to sport and dance,
To toy, to wanton, dally, smile and jest,
      Scorning his churlish drum and ensign red,
      Making my arms his field, his tent my bed.

'Thus he that overruled I overswayèd,
110 Leading him prisoner in a red-rose chain;
Strong-tempered steel his stronger strength obeyèd,
Yet was he servile to my coy disdain.
      O, be not proud, nor brag not of thy might,
      For mast'ring her that foiled the god of fight!

115 'Touch but my lips with those fair lips of thine—
Though mine be not so fair, yet are they red—
The kiss shall be thine own as well as mine.
What see'st thou in the ground? hold up thy head;
      Look in mine eyeballs, there thy beauty lies;
120   Then why not lips on lips, since eyes in eyes?

'Art thou ashamed to kiss? then wink again,
And I will wink; so shall the day seem night.
Love keeps his revels where there are but twain;
Be bold to play, our sport is not in sight.
    These blue-veined violets whereon we lean   125
    Never can blab, nor know not what we mean.

'The tender spring upon thy tempting lip
Shews thee unripe; yet mayst thou well be tasted;
Make use of time, let not advantage slip;
Beauty within itself should not be wasted.   130
    Fair flowers that are not gath'red in their prime
    Rot and consume themselves in little time.

'Were I hard-favoured, foul, or wrinkled-old,
Ill-nurtured, crooked, churlish, harsh in voice,
O'erworn, despiséd, rheumatic and cold,   135
Thick-sighted, barren, lean, and lacking juice,
    Then mightst thou pause, for then I were not for thee;
    But having no defects, why dost abhor me?

'Thou canst not see one wrinkle in my brow;
Mine eyes are grey and bright and quick in turning; 140
My beauty as the spring doth yearly grow,
My flesh is soft and plump, my marrow burning;
    My smooth moist hand, were it with thy hand felt,
    Would in thy palm dissolve, or seem to melt.

'Bid me discourse, I will enchant thine ear,   145
Or, like a fairy, trip upon the green,
Or, like a nymph, with long dishevelléd hair,
Dance on the sands, and yet no footing seen.
    Love is a spirit all compact of fire,
    Not gross to sink, but light, and will aspire.   150

'Witness this primrose bank whereon I lie;
These forceless flowers like sturdy trees support me;
Two strengthless doves will draw me through the sky
From morn till night, even where I list to sport me..
155   Is love so light, sweet boy, and may it be
       That thou should think it heavy unto thee?

'Is thine own heart to thine own face affected?
Can thy right hand seize love upon thy left?
Then woo thyself, be of thyself rejected,
160 Steal thine own freedom, and complain on theft.
       Narcissus so himself himself forsook,
       And died to kiss his shadow in the brook.

'Torches are made to light, jewels to wear,
Dainties to taste, fresh beauty for the use,
165 Herbs for their smell, and sappy plants to bear;
Things growing to themselves are growth's abuse.
       Seeds spring from seeds and beauty breedeth beauty;
       Thou wast begot; to get it is thy duty.

'Upon the earth's increase why shouldst thou feed,
170 Unless the earth with thy increase be fed?
By law of nature thou art bound to breed,
That thine may live when thou thyself art dead;
       And so in spite of death thou dost survive,
       In that thy likeness still is left alive.'

175 By this, the love-sick queen began to sweat,
For where they lay the shadow had forsook them,
And Titan, tiréd in the mid-day heat,
With burning eye did hotly overlook them,
       Wishing Adonis had his team to guide,
180   So he were like him, and by Venus' side.

And now Adonis, with a lazy sprite,
And with a heavy, dark, disliking eye,
His louring brows o'erwhelming his fair sight,
Like misty vapours when they blot the sky, 185
 Souring his cheeks, cries 'Fie, no more of love!
 The sun doth burn my face; I must remove.'

'Ay me,' quoth Venus, 'young, and so unkind!
What bare excuses mak'st thou to be gone!
I'll sigh celestial breath, whose gentle wind 190
Shall cool the heat of this descending sun;
 I'll make a shadow for thee of my hairs;
 If they burn too, I'll quench them with my tears.

'The sun that shines from heaven shines but warm,
And lo, I lie between that sun and thee; 195
The heat I have from thence doth little harm;
Thine eye darts forth the fire that burneth me;
 And were I not immortal, life were done
 Between this heavenly and earthly sun.

'Art thou obdurate, flinty, hard as steel? 200
Nay, more than flint, for stone at rain relenteth.
Art thou a woman's son, and canst not feel
What 'tis to love, how want of love tormenteth?
 O, had thy mother borne so hard a mind,
 She had not brought forth thee, but died unkind.

'What am I that thou shouldst contemn me this? 205
Or what great danger dwells upon my suit?
What were thy lips the worse for one poor kiss?
Speak, fair; but speak fair words, or else be mute.
 Give me one kiss, I'll give it thee again,
 And one for int'rest, if thou wilt have twain. 210

'Fie, lifeless picture, cold and senseless stone,
Well painted idol, image dull and dead,
Statue contenting but the eye alone,
Thing like a man, but of no woman bred!
215   Thou art no man, though of a man's complexion,
For men will kiss even by their own direction.'

This said, impatience chokes her pleading tongue,
And swelling passion doth provoke a pause;
Red cheeks and fiery eyes blaze forth her wrong;
220 Being judge in love, she cannot right her cause;
And now she weeps, and now she fain would speak,
And now her sobs do her intendments break.

Sometime she shakes her head, and then his hand,
Now gazeth she on him, now on the ground;
225 Sometime her arms infold him like a band;
She would, he will not in her arms be bound;
And when from thence he struggles to be gone,
She locks her lily fingers one in one.

'Fondling,' she saith, 'since I have hemmed thee here
230 Within the circuit of this ivory pale,
I'll be a park, and thou shalt be my deer;
Feed where thou wilt, on mountain or in dale;
Graze on my lips, and if those hills be dry,
Stray lower, where the pleasant fountains lie.

235 'Within this limit is relief enough,
Sweet bottom-grass and high delightful plain,
Round rising hillocks, brakes obscure and rough,
To shelter thee from tempest and from rain:
Then be my deer, since I am such a park;
240   No dog shall rouse thee, though a thousand bark.'

At this Adonis smiles as in disdain,
That in each cheek appears a pretty dimple.
Love made those hollows, if himself were slain,
He might be buried in a tomb so simple;
   Foreknowing well, if there he came to lie,   245
   Why, there Love lived, and there he could not die.

These lovely caves, these round enchanting pits,
Opened their mouths to swallow Venus' liking.
Being mad before, how doth she now for wits?
Struck dead at first, what needs a second striking?   250
   Poor queen of love, in thine own law forlorn,
   To love a cheek that smiles at thee in scorn!

Now which way shall she turn? what shall she say?
Her words are done, her woes the more increasing;
The time is spent, her object will away,   255
And from her twining arms doth urge releasing.
   'Pity,' she cries, 'some favour, some remorse!'
   Away he springs, and hasteth to his horse.

But lo, from forth a copse that neighbours by,
A breeding jennet, lusty, young and proud,   260
Adonis' trampling courser doth espy,
And forth she rushes, snorts and neighs aloud.
   The strong-necked steed, being tied unto a tree,
   Breaketh his rein and to her straight goes he.

Imperiously he leaps, he neighs, he bounds,   265
And now his woven girths he breaks asunder;
The bearing earth with his hard hoof he wounds,
Whose hollow womb resounds like heaven's thunder;
   The iron bit he crusheth 'tween his teeth,
   Controlling what he was controlléd with.   270

His ears up-pricked; his braided hanging mane
Upon his compassed crest now stand on end;
His nostrils drink the air, and forth again,
As from a furnace, vapours doth he send;
275   His eye, which scornfully glisters like fire,
    Shows his hot courage and his high desire.

Sometime he trots, as if he told the steps,
With gentle majesty and modest pride;
Anon he rears upright, curvets and leaps,
280 As who should say 'Lo, thus my strength is tried,
    And this I do to captivate the eye
    Of the fair breeder that is standing by.'

What recketh he his rider's angry stir,
His flattering 'Holla' or his 'Stand, I say'?
285 What cares he now for curb or pricking spur?
   For rich caparisons or trappings gay?
    He sees his love, and nothing else he sees,
    For nothing else with his proud sight agrees.

Look when a painter would surpass the life
290 In limning out a well-proportionéd steed,
His art with nature's workmanship at strife,
As if the dead the living should exceed;
    So did this horse excel a common one
    In shape, in courage, colour, pace and bone.

295 Round-hoofed, short-jointed, fetlocks shag and long,
Broad breast, full eye, small head and nostril wide,
High crest, short ears, straight legs and passing strong,
Thin mane, thick tail, broad buttock, tender hide;
    Look what a horse should have he did not lack,
300   Save a proud rider on so proud a back.

Sometime he scuds far off, and there he stares;
Anon he starts at stirring of a feather;
To bid the wind a base he now prepares,
And whe'er he run or fly they know not whether;
   For through his mane and tail the high wind sings, 305
   Fanning the hairs, who wave like feath'red wings.

He looks upon his love and neighs unto her;
She answers him as if she knew his mind;
Being proud, as females are, to see him woo her,
She puts on outward strangeness, seems unkind,   310
   Spurns at his love and scorns the heat he feels,
   Beating his kind embracements with her heels.

Then, like a melancholy malcontent,
He vails his tail, that, like a falling plume,
Cool shadow to his melting buttock lent;   315
He stamps, and bites the poor flies in his fume.
   His love, perceiving how he was enraged,
   Grew kinder, and his fury was assuaged.

His testy master goeth about to take him,
When, lo, the unbacked breeder, full of fear,   320
Jealous of catching, swiftly doth forsake him,
With her the horse, and left Adonis there.
   As they were mad, unto the wood they hie them,
   Out-stripping crows that strive to over-fly them.

All swoln with chafing, down Adonis sits,   325
Banning his boist'rous and unruly beast;
And now the happy season once more fits
That love-sick Love by pleading may be blest;
   For lovers say the heart hath treble wrong
   When it is barred the aidance of the tongue.   330

An oven that is stopped, or river stayed,
Burneth more hotly, swelleth with more rage;
So of concealéd sorrow may be said,
Free vent of words love's fire doth assuage;
335　　But when the heart's attorney once is mute,
　　　The client breaks, as desperate in his suit.

He sees her coming, and begins to glow,
Even as a dying coal revives with wind,
And with his bonnet hides his angry brow,
340 Looks on the dull earth with disturbéd mind,
　　　Taking no notice that she is so nigh,
　　　For all askance he holds her in his eye.

O, what a sight it was, wistly to view
How she came stealing to the wayward boy!
345 To note the fighting conflict of her hue,
How white and red each other did destroy!
　　　But now her cheek was pale, and by and by
　　　It flashed forth fire, as lightning from the sky.

Now was she just before him as he sat,
350 And like a lowly lover down she kneels;
With one fair hand she heaveth up his hat,
Her other tender hand his fair cheek feels;
　　　His tend'rer cheek receives her soft hand's print
　　　As apt as new-fall'n snow takes any dint.

355 O, what a war of looks was then between them,
Her eyes petitioners to his eyes suing!
His eyes saw her eyes as they had not seen them;
Her eyes wooed still, his eyes disdained the wooing;
　　　And all this dumb play had his acts made plain
360　　With tears which chorus-like her eyes did rain.

Full gently now she takes him by the hand,
A lily prisoned in a gaol of snow,
Or ivory in an alabaster band;
So white a friend engirts so white a foe:
 This beauteous combat, wilful and unwilling, 365
 Showed like two silver doves that sit a-billing.

Once more the engine of her thoughts began:
'O fairest mover on this mortal round,
Would thou wert as I am, and I a man,
My heart all whole as thine, thy heart my wound; 370
 For one sweet look thy help I would assure thee,
 Though nothing but my body's bane would cure
  thee.'

'Give me my hand,' saith he; 'why dost thou feel it?'
'Give me my heart,' saith she, 'and thou shalt have it;
O, give it me, lest thy hard heart do steel it, 375
And being steeled, soft sighs can never grave it;
 Then love's deep groans I never shall regard,
 Because Adonis' heart hath made mine hard.'

'For shame,' he cries, 'let go, and let me go;
My day's delight is past, my horse is gone, 380
And 'tis your fault I am bereft him so.
I pray you hence, and leave me here alone;
 For all my mind, my thought, my busy care,
 Is how to get my palfrey from the mare.'

Thus she replies: 'Thy palfrey, as he should, 385
Welcomes the warm approach of sweet desire.
Affection is a coal that must be cooled;
Else, suffered, it will set the heart on fire.
 The sea hath bounds, but deep desire hath none,
 Therefore no marvel though thy horse be gone. 390

'How like a jade he stood tied to the tree,
Servilely mastered with a leathern rein!
But when he saw his love, his youth's fair fee,
He held such petty bondage in disdain,
395   Throwing the base thong from his bending crest,
      Enfranchising his mouth, his back, his breast.

'Who sees his true-love in her naked bed,
Teaching the sheets a whiter hue than white,
But, when his glutton eye so full hath fed,
400 His other agents aim at like delight?
      Who is so faint that dares not be so bold
      To touch the fire, the weather being cold?

'Let me excuse thy courser, gentle boy;
And learn of him, I heartily beseech thee,
405 To take advantage on presented joy;
      Though I were dumb, yet his proceedings teach thee.
        O, learn to love; the lesson is but plain,
        And once made perfect, never lost again.'

'I know not love,' quoth he, 'nor will not know it,
410 Unless it be a boar, and then I chase it.
'Tis much to borrow, and I will not owe it.
My love to love is love but to disgrace it;
      For I have heard it is a life in death,
      That laughs, and weeps, and all but with a breath.

415 'Who wears a garment shapeless and unfinished?
Who plucks the bud before one leaf put forth?
If springing things be any jot diminished,
They wither in their prime, prove nothing worth.
      The colt that's backed and burdened being young
420   Loseth his pride, and never waxeth strong.

'You hurt my hand with wringing; let us part,
And leave this idle theme, this bootless chat;
Remove your siege from my unyielding heart;
To love's alarms it will not ope the gate.
 Dismiss your vows, your feignéd tears, your flatt'ry; 425
 For where a heart is hard they make no batt'ry.'

'What, canst thou talk?' quoth she, 'hast thou a tongue?
O, would thou hadst not, or I had no hearing!
Thy mermaid's voice hath done me double wrong;
I had my load before, now pressed with bearing: 430
 Melodious discord, heavenly tune harsh sounding,
 Ears' deep-sweet music, and heart's deep-sore
  wounding.

'Had I no eyes but ears, my ears would love
That inward beauty and invisible;
Or were I deaf, thy outward parts would move 435
Each part in me that were but sensible.
 Though neither eyes nor ears, to hear nor see,
 Yet should I be in love by touching thee.

'Say that the sense of feeling were bereft me,
And that I could not see, nor hear, nor touch, 440
And nothing but the very smell were left me,
Yet would my love to thee be still as much;
 For from the stillitory of thy face excelling
 Comes breath perfumed, that breedeth love by
  smelling.

'But O, what banquet wert thou to the taste, 445
Being nurse and feeder of the other four!
Would they not wish the feast might ever last,
And bid Suspicion double-lock the door,
 Lest Jealousy, that sour unwelcome guest,
 Should by his stealing in disturb the feast?' 450

Once more the ruby-coloured portal opened,
Which to his speech did honey passage yield;
Like a red morn, that ever yet betokened
Wrack to the seaman, tempest to the field,
455　　Sorrow to shepherds, woe unto the birds,
　　　　Gusts and foul flaws to herdmen and to herds.

This ill presage advisedly she marketh.
Even as the wind is hushed before it raineth,
Or as the wolf doth grin before he barketh,
460 Or as the berry breaks before it staineth,
　　　　Or like the deadly bullet of a gun,
　　　　His meaning struck her ere his words begun.

And at his look she flatly falleth down,
For looks kill love, and love by looks reviveth;
465 A smile recures the wounding of a frown.
　　　　But blessèd bankrupt that by loss so thriveth!
　　　　The silly boy, believing she is dead,
　　　　Claps her pale cheek, till clapping makes it red;

And all amazed brake off his late intent,
470 For sharply he did think to reprehend her,
Which cunning love did wittily prevent.
Fair fall the wit that can so well defend her!
　　　　For on the grass she lies as she were slain,
　　　　Till his breath breatheth life in her again.

475 He wrings her nose, he strikes her on the cheeks,
He bends her fingers, holds her pulses hard,
He chafes her lips, a thousand ways he seeks
To mend the hurt that his unkindness marred;
　　　　He kisses her; and she, by her good will,
480　　Will never rise, so he will kiss her still.

The night of sorrow now is turned to day:
Her two blue windows faintly she upheaveth,
Like the fair sun, when in his fresh array
He cheers the morn, and all the earth relieveth;
   And as the bright sun glorifies the sky,   485
   So is her face illumined with her eye;

Whose beams upon his hairless face are fixed,
As if from thence they borrowéd all their shine.
Were never four such lamps together mixed,
Had not his clouded with his brow's repine;   490
   But hers, which through the crystal tears gave light,
   Shone like the moon in water seen by night.

'O, where am I?' quoth she; 'in earth or heaven,
Or in the ocean drenched, or in the fire?
What hour is this? or morn or weary even?   495
Do I delight to die, or life desire?
   But now I lived, and life was death's annoy;
   But now I died, and death was lively joy.

'O, thou didst kill me: kill me once again.
Thy eyes' shrewd tutor, that hard heart of thine,   500
Hath taught them scornful tricks, and such disdain
That they have murd'red this poor heart of mine;
   And these mine eyes, true leaders to their queen,
   But for thy piteous lips no more had seen.

'Long may they kiss each other, for this cure!   505
O, never let their crimson liveries wear!
And as they last, their verdure still endure
To drive infection from the dangerous year!
   That the star-gazers, having writ on death,
   May say, the plague is banished by thy breath.   510

'Pure lips, sweet seals in my soft lips imprinted,
What bargains may I make, still to be sealing?
To sell myself I can be well contented,
So thou wilt buy, and pay, and use good dealing;
515   Which purchase if thou make, for fear of slips
      Set thy seal manual on my wax-red lips.

'A thousand kisses buys my heart from me;
And pay them at thy leisure, one by one.
What is ten hundred touches unto thee?
520 Are they not quickly told and quickly gone?
      Say for non-payment that the debt should double,
      Is twenty hundred kisses such a trouble?'

'Fair queen,' quoth he, 'if any love you owe me,
Measure my strangeness with my unripe years;
525 Before I know myself, seek not to know me;
No fisher but the ungrown fry forbears.
      The mellow plum doth fall, the green sticks fast,
      Or being early plucked is sour to taste.

'Look, the world's comforter, with weary gait,
530 His day's hot task hath ended in the west;
The owl, night's herald, shrieks 'tis very late;
The sheep are gone to fold, birds to their nest;
      And coal-black clouds that shadow heaven's light
      Do summon us to part, and bid good night.

535 'Now let me say "Good night", and so say you;
If you will say so, you shall have a kiss.'
'Good night', quoth she; and, ere he says 'Adieu',
The honey fee of parting tend'red is:
      Her arms do lend his neck a sweet embrace;
540   Incorporate then they seem; face grows to face.

Till breathless he disjoined, and backward drew
The heavenly moisture, that sweet coral mouth,
Whose precious taste her thirsty lips well knew,
Whereon they surfeit, yet complain on drouth.
    He with her plenty pressed, she faint with dearth,   545
    Their lips together glued, fall to the earth.

Now quick desire hath caught the yielding prey,
And glutton-like she feeds, yet never filleth;
Her lips are conquerors, his lips obey,
Paying what ransom the insulter willeth;   550
    Whose vulture thought doth pitch the price so high
    That she will draw his lips' rich treasure dry.

And having felt the sweetness of the spoil,
With blindfold fury she begins to forage;
Her face doth reek and smoke, her blood doth boil,   555
And careless lust stirs up a desperate courage,
    Planting oblivion, beating reason back,
    Forgetting shame's pure blush and honour's wrack.

Hot, faint and weary, with her hard embracing,
Like a wild bird being tamed with too much handling, 560
Or as the fleet-foot roe that's tired with chasing,
Or like the froward infant stilled with dandling,
    He now obeys and now no more resisteth,
    While she takes all she can, not all she listeth.

What wax so frozen but dissolves with temp'ring,   565
And yields at last to every light impression?
Things out of hope are compass'd oft with vent'ring,
Chiefly in love, whose leave exceeds commission:
    Affection faints not like a pale-faced coward,
    But then woos best when most his choice is froward. 570

When he did frown, O, had she then gave over,
Such nectar from his lips she had not sucked.
Foul words and frowns must not repel a lover;
What though the rose have prickles, yet 'tis plucked.
575   Were beauty under twenty locks kept fast,
      Yet love breaks through, and picks them all at last.

For pity now she can no more detain him;
The poor fool prays her that he may depart.
She is resolved no longer to restrain him;
580 Bids him farewell, and look well to her heart,
      The which by Cupid's bow she doth protest
      He carries thence incagéd in his breast.

'Sweet boy,' she says, 'this night I'll waste in sorrow,
For my sick heart commands mine eyes to watch.
585 Tell me, love's master, shall we meet to-morrow?
Say, shall we? shall we? wilt thou make the match?'
      He tells her, no; to-morrow he intends
      To hunt the boar with certain of his friends.

'The boar!' quoth she; whereat a sudden pale,
590 Like lawn being spread upon the blushing rose,
Usurps her cheek; she trembles at his tale,
And on his neck her yoking arms she throws.
      She sinketh down, still hanging by his neck,
      He on her belly falls, she on her back.

595 Now is she in the very lists of love,
Her champion mounted for the hot encounter.
All is imaginary she doth prove;
He will not manage her, although he mount her;
      That worse than Tantalus' is her annoy,
600   To clip Elysium and to lack her joy.

Even so poor birds, deceived with painted grapes,
Do surfeit by the eye and pine the maw;
Even so she languisheth in her mishaps
As those poor birds that helpless berries saw.
　　The warm effects which she in him finds missing　　605
　　She seeks to kindle with continual kissing.

But all in vain, good queen, it will not be.
She hath assayed as much as may be proved;
Her pleading hath deserved a greater fee;
She's Love, she loves, and yet she is not loved.　　610
　　'Fie, fie,' he says, 'you crush me; let me go;
　　You have no reason to withhold me so.'

'Thou hadst been gone,' quoth she, 'sweet boy, ere this,
But that thou told'st me thou wouldst hunt the boar.
O, be advised: thou know'st not what it is　　615
With javelin's point a churlish swine to gore,
　　Whose tushes never sheathed he whetteth still,
　　Like to a mortal butcher bent to kill.

'On his bow-back he hath a battle set
Of bristly pikes that ever threat his foes;　　620
His eyes like glow-worms shine when he doth fret;
His snout digs sepulchres where'er he goes;
　　Being moved, he strikes whate'er is in his way,
　　And whom he strikes his crookéd tushes slay.

'His brawny sides, with hairy bristles arméd,　　625
Are better proof than thy spear's point can enter;
His short thick neck cannot be easily harméd;
Being ireful, on the lion he will venter:
　　The thorny brambles and embracing bushes,
　　As fearful of him, part; through whom he rushes.　　630 ·

'Alas, he nought esteems that face of thine,
To which Love's eyes pays tributary gazes;
Nor thy soft hands, sweet lips and crystal eyne,
Whose full perfection all the world amazes;
635   But having thee at vantage—wondrous dread!—
Would root these beauties as he roots the mead.

'O, let him keep his loathsome cabin still;
Beauty hath nought to do with such foul fiends.
Come not within his danger by thy will;
640 They that thrive well take counsel of their friends.
When thou didst name the boar, not to dissemble,
I feared thy fortune, and my joints did tremble.

'Didst thou not mark my face? was it not white?
Saw'st thou not signs of fear lurk in mine eye?
645 Grew I not faint? and fell I not downright?
Within my bosom, whereon thou dost lie,
My boding heart pants, beats, and takes no rest,
But, like an earthquake, shakes thee on my breast.

'For where Love reigns, disturbing Jealousy
650 Doth call himself Affection's sentinel;
Gives false alarms, suggesteth mutiny,
And in a peaceful hour doth cry "Kill, kill!"
Distemp'ring gentle Love in his desire,
As air and water do abate the fire.

655 'This sour informer, this bate-breeding spy,
This canker that eats up Love's tender spring,
This carry-tale, dissentious Jealousy,
That sometime true news, sometime false doth bring,
Knocks at my heart, and whispers in mine ear
660   That if I love thee I thy death should fear;

'And more than so, presenteth to mine eye
The picture of an angry chafing boar
Under whose sharp fangs on his back doth lie
An image like thyself, all stained with gore;
   Whose blood upon the fresh flowers being shed   665
   Doth make them droop with grief and hang the head.

'What should I do, seeing thee so indeed,
That tremble at th'imagination?
The thought of it doth make my faint heart bleed,
And fear doth teach it divination: 670
   I prophesy thy death, my living sorrow,
   If thou encounter with the boar to-morrow.

'But if thou needs wilt hunt, be ruled by me;
Uncouple at the timorous flying hare,
Or at the fox which lives by subtlety,   675
Or at the roe which no encounter dare.
   Pursue these fearful creatures o'er the downs,
   And on thy well-breathed horse keep with thy hounds.

'And when thou hast on foot the purblind hare,
Mark the poor wretch, to overshoot his troubles,   680
How he outruns the wind, and with what care
He cranks and crosses with a thousand doubles.
   The many musits through the which he goes
   Are like a labyrinth to amaze his foes.

'Sometime he runs among a flock of sheep,   685
To make the cunning hounds mistake their smell,
And sometime where earth-delving conies keep,
To stop the loud pursuers in their yell;
   And sometime sorteth with a herd of deer.
   Danger deviseth shifts; wit waits on fear.   690

'For there his smell with others being mingled,
The hot scent-snuffing hounds are driven to doubt,
Ceasing their clamorous cry till they have singled
With much ado the cold fault cleanly out.
695   Then do they spend their mouths; Echo replies,
As if another chase were in the skies.

'By this, poor Wat, far off upon a hill,
Stands on his hinder legs with list'ning ear,
To hearken if his foes pursue him still;
700 Anon their loud alarums he doth hear;
And now his grief may be compared well
To one sore sick that hears the passing-bell.

'Then shalt thou see the dew-bedabbled wretch
Turn, and return, indenting with the way;
705 Each envious brier his weary legs do scratch,
Each shadow makes him stop, each murmur stay;
For misery is trodden on by many,
And being low never relieved by any.

'Lie quietly and hear a little more;
710 Nay, do not struggle, for thou shalt not rise.
To make thee hate the hunting of the boar,
Unlike myself thou hear'st me moralize,
Applying this to that, and so to so;
For love can comment upon every woe.

715 'Where did I leave?' 'No matter where,' quoth he;
'Leave me, and then the story aptly ends.
The night is spent.' 'Why, what of that?' quoth she.
'I am', quoth he, 'expected of my friends;
And now 'tis dark, and going I shall fall.'
720   'In night', quoth she, 'desire sees best of all.

'But if thou fall, O, then imagine this,
The earth, in love with thee, thy footing trips,
And all is but to rob thee of a kiss.
Rich preys make true men thieves; so do thy lips
    Make modest Dian cloudy and forlorn,   725
    Lest she should steal a kiss, and die forsworn.

'Now of this dark night I perceive the reason:
Cynthia for shame obscures her silver shine,
Till forging Nature be condemned of treason,
For stealing moulds from heaven that were divine,   730
    Wherein she framed thee, in high heaven's despite,
    To shame the sun by day and her by night.

'And therefore hath she bribed the Destinies
To cross the curious workmanship of Nature,
To mingle beauty with infirmities   735
And pure perfection with impure defeature,
    Making it subject to the tyranny
    Of mad mischances and much misery;

'As burning fevers, agues pale and faint,
Life-poisoning pestilence and frenzies wood,   740
The marrow-eating sickness whose attaint
Disorder breeds by heating of the blood,
    Surfeits, imposthumes, grief and damned despair,
    Swear Nature's death for framing thee so fair.

'And not the least of all these maladies   745
But in one minute's fight brings beauty under.
Both favour, savour, hue and qualities,
Whereat th'impartial gazer late did wonder,
    Are on the sudden wasted, thawed and done,
    As mountain snow melts with the midday sun.   750

'Therefore, despite of fruitless chastity,
Love-lacking vestals and self-loving nuns,
That on the earth would breed a scarcity
And barren dearth of daughters and of sons,
755　Be prodigal: the lamp that burns by night
　　　Dries up his oil to lend the world his light.

'What is thy body but a swallowing grave,
Seeming to bury that posterity
Which by the rights of time thou needs must have,
760 If thou destroy them not in dark obscurity?
　　　If so, the world will hold thee in disdain,
　　　Sith in thy pride so fair a hope is slain.

'So in thyself thyself art made away;
A mischief worse than civil home-bred strife,
765 Or theirs whose desperate hands themselves do slay,
Or butcher sire that reaves his son of life.
　　　Foul cank'ring rust the hidden treasure frets,
　　　But gold that's put to use more gold begets.'

'Nay, then,' quoth Adon, 'you will fall again
770 Into your idle over-handled theme;
The kiss I gave you is bestowed in vain,
And all in vain you strive against the stream;
　　　For, by this black-faced night, desire's foul nurse,
　　　Your treatise makes me like you worse and worse.

775 'If love have lent you twenty thousand tongues,
And every tongue more moving than your own,
Bewitching like the wanton mermaid's songs,
Yet from mine ear the tempting tune is blown;
　　　For know, my heart stands arméd in mine ear,
780　And will not let a false sound enter there,

'Lest the deceiving harmony should run
Into the quiet closure of my breast;
And then my little heart were quite undone,
In his bedchamber to be barred of rest.
    No, lady, no; my heart longs not to groan,   785
    But soundly sleeps, while now it sleeps alone.

'What have you urged that I cannot reprove?
The path is smooth that leadeth on to danger;
I hate not love, but your device in love
That lends embracements unto every stranger.   790
    You do it for increase: O strange excuse,
    When reason is the bawd to lust's abuse!

'Call it not love, for Love to heaven is fled
Since sweating Lust on earth usurped his name;
Under whose simple semblance he hath fed   795
Upon fresh beauty, blotting it with blame;
    Which the hot tyrant stains and soon bereaves,
    As caterpillars do the tender leaves.

'Love comforteth like sunshine after rain,
But Lust's effect is tempest after sun;   800
Love's gentle spring doth always fresh remain,
Lust's winter comes ere summer half be done;
    Love surfeits not, Lust like a glutton dies;
    Love is all truth, Lust full of forgéd lies.

'More I could tell, but more I dare not say;   805
The text is old, the orator too green.
Therefore, in sadness, now I will away;
My face is full of shame, my heart of teen:
    Mine ears that to your wanton talk attended
    Do burn themselves for having so offended.'   810

With this, he breaketh from the sweet embrace
Of those fair arms which bound him to her breast,
And homeward through the dark lawnd runs apace;
Leaves Love upon her back deeply distressed.
815   Look how a bright star shooteth from the sky,
    So glides he in the night from Venus' eye;

Which after him she darts, as onc on shore
Gazing upon a late-embarkéd friend,
Till the wild waves will have him seen no more,
820 Whose ridges with the meeting clouds contend;
    So did the merciless and pitchy night
    Fold in the object that did feed her sight.

Whereat amazed as one that unaware
Hath dropped a precious jewel in the flood,
825 Or 'stonished as night-wand'rers often are,
    Their light blown out in some mistrustful wood;
    Even so confounded in the dark she lay,
    Having lost the fair discovery of her way.

And now she beats her heart, whereat it groans,
830 That all the neighbour caves, as seeming troubled,
Make verbal repetition of her moans;
Passion on passion deeply is redoubled:
    'Ay me!' she cries, and twenty times, 'Woe, woe!'
    And twenty echoes twenty times cry so.

835 She, marking them, begins a wailing note,
And sings extemporally a woeful ditty;
How love makes young men thrall, and old men dote;
How love is wise in folly, foolish witty:
    Her heavy anthem still concludes in woe,
840   And still the choir of echoes answer so.

Her song was tedious, and outwore the night,
For lovers' hours are long, though seeming short;
If pleased themselves, others, they think, delight
In such-like circumstance, with such-like sport.
    Their copious stories, oftentimes begun,   845
    End without audience, and are never done.

For who hath she to spend the night withal
But idle sounds resembling parasites,
Like shrill-tongued tapsters answering every call,
Soothing the humour of fantastic wits?   850
    She says ''Tis so'; they answer all ''Tis so';
    And would say after her, if she said 'No'.

Lo, here the gentle lark, weary of rest,
From his moist cabinet mounts up on high,
And wakes the morning, from whose silver breast   855
The sun ariseth in his majesty;
    Who doth the world so gloriously behold
    That cedar-tops and hills seem burnished gold.

Venus salutes him with this fair good-morrow:
'O thou clear god, and patron of all light,   860
From whom each lamp and shining star doth borrow
The beauteous influence that makes him bright,
    There lives a son that sucked an earthly mother
    May lend thee light, as thou dost lend to other.'

This said, she hasteth to a myrtle grove,   865
Musing the morning is so much o'erworn,
And yet she hears no tidings of her love;
She hearkens for his hounds and for his horn.
    Anon she hears them chant it lustily,
    And all in haste she coasteth to the cry.   870

And as she runs, the bushes in the way
Some catch her by the neck, some kiss her face,
Some twind about her thigh to make her stay;
She wildly breaketh from their strict embrace,
875 Like a milch doe, whose swelling dugs do ache,
  Hasting to feed her fawn hid in some brake.

By this she hears the hounds are at a bay;
Whereat she starts, like one that spies an adder
Wreathed up in fatal folds just in his way,
880 The fear whereof doth make him shake and shudder;
  Even so the timorous yelping of the hounds
  Appals her senses and her spirit confounds.

For now she knows it is no gentle chase,
But the blunt boar, rough bear, or lion proud,
885 Because the cry remaineth in one place,
Where fearfully the dogs exclaim aloud.
  Finding their enemy to be so curst,
  They all strain court'sy who shall cope him first.

This dismal cry rings sadly in her ear,
890 Through which it enters to surprise her heart;
Who, overcome by doubt and bloodless fear,
With cold-pale weakness numbs each feeling part;
  Like soldiers, when their captain once doth yield,
  They basely fly and dare not stay the field.

895 Thus stands she in a trembling ecstasy;
Till, cheering up her senses all dismayed,
She tells them 'tis a causeless fantasy,
And childish error, that they are afraid;
  Bids them leave quaking, bids them fear no more;
900 And with that word she spied the hunted boar,

Whose frothy mouth, bepainted all with red,
Like milk and blood being mingled both together,
A second fear through all her sinews spread,
Which madly hurries her she knows not whither:
    This way she runs, and now she will no further, 905
    But back retires to rate the boar for murther.

A thousand spleens bear her a thousand ways;
She treads the path that she untreads again;
Her more than haste is mated with delays,
Like the proceedings of a drunken brain, 910
    Full of respects, yet nought at all respecting,
    In hand with all things, nought at all effecting.

Here kennelled in a brake she finds a hound,
And asks the weary caitiff for his master;
And there another licking of his wound, 915
'Gainst venomed sores the only sovereign plaster;
    And here she meets another sadly scowling,
    To whom she speaks, and he replies with howling.

When he hath ceased his ill-resounding noise,
Another flap-mouthed mourner, black and grim, 920
Against the welkin volleys out his voice;
Another and another answer him,
    Clapping their proud tails to the ground below,
    Shaking their scratched ears, bleeding as they go.

Look how the world's poor people are amazéd 925
At apparitions, signs and prodigies,
Whereon with fearful eyes they long have gazéd,
Infusing them with dreadful prophecies;
    So she at these sad signs draws up her breath,
    And, sighing it again, exclaims on Death. 930

'Hard-favoured tyrant, ugly, meagre, lean,
Hateful divorce of love'—thus chides she Death—
'Grim-grinning ghost, earth's worm, what dost
  thou mean
To stifle beauty and to steal his breath
935 Who when he lived, his breath and beauty set
  Gloss on the rose, smell to the violet?

'If he be dead—O no, it cannot be,
Seeing his beauty, thou shouldst strike at it—
O yes, it may; thou hast no eyes to see,
940 But hatefully at random dost thou hit.
  Thy mark is feeble age; but thy false dart
  Mistakes that aim, and cleaves an infant's heart.

'Hadst thou but bid beware, then he had spoke,
And, hearing him, thy power had lost his power.
945 The Destinies will curse thee for this stroke;
  They bid thee crop a weed, thou pluck'st a flower.
  Love's golden arrow at him should have fled,
  And not Death's ebon dart, to strike him dead.

'Dost thou drink tears, that thou provokest
  such weeping?
950 What may a heavy groan advantage thee?
Why hast thou cast into eternal sleeping
Those eyes that taught all other eyes to see?
  Now Nature cares not for thy mortal vigour,
  Since her best work is ruined with thy rigour.'

955 Here overcome as one full of despair,
She vailed her eyelids, who, like sluices, stopped
The crystal tide that from her two cheeks fair
In the sweet channel of her bosom dropped;
  But through the flood-gates breaks the silver rain,
960 And with his strong course opens them again.

O, how her eyes and tears did lend and borrow!
Her eye seen in the tears, tears in her eye;
Both crystals, where they viewed each other's sorrow,
Sorrow that friendly sighs sought still to dry;
    But like a stormy day, now wind, now rain,   965
    Sighs dry her cheeks, tears make them wet again.

Variable passions throng her constant woe,
As striving who should best become her grief;
All entertained, each passion labours so
That every present sorrow seemeth chief,   970
    But none is best. Then join they all together,
    Like many clouds consulting for foul weather.

By this, far off she hears some huntsman holla;
A nurse's song ne'er pleased her babe so well.
The dire imagination she did follow   975
This sound of hope doth labour to expel;
    For now reviving joy bids her rejoice,
    And flatters her it is Adonis' voice.

Whereat her tears began to turn their tide,
Being prisoned in her eye like pearls in glass;   980
Yet sometimes falls an orient drop beside,
Which her cheek melts, as scorning it should pass
    To wash the foul face of the sluttish ground,
    Who is but drunken when she seemeth drowned.

O hard-believing love, how strange it seems   985
Not to believe, and yet too credulous!
Thy weal and woe are both of them extremes;
Despair, and hope, makes thee ridiculous:
    The one doth flatter thee in thoughts unlikely,
    In likely thoughts the other kills thee quickly.   990

Now she unweaves the web that she hath wrought;
Adonis lives, and Death is not to blame;
It was not she that called him all to nought.
Now she adds honours to his hateful name;
995   She clepes him king of graves, and grave for kings,
    Imperious supreme of all mortal things.

'No, no,' quoth she, 'sweet Death, I did but jest;
Yet pardon me, I felt a kind of fear
When as I met the boar, that bloody beast,
1000 Which knows no pity, but is still severe.
    Then, gentle shadow—truth I must confess—
    I railed on thee, fearing my love's decease.

''Tis not my fault: the boar provoked my tongue;
Be wreaked on him, invisible commander;
1005 'Tis he, foul creature, that hath done thee wrong;
I did but act, he's author of thy slander.
    Grief hath two tongues, and never woman yet
    Could rule them both without ten women's wit.'

Thus, hoping that Adonis is alive,
1010 Her rash suspect she doth extenuate;
And that his beauty may the better thrive,
With Death she humbly doth insinuate;
    Tells him of trophies, statues, tombs, and stories
    His victories, his triumphs and his glories.

1015 'O Jove,' quoth she, 'how much a fool was I
To be of such a weak and silly mind
To wail his death who lives and must not die
Till mutual overthrow of mortal kind!
    For he being dead, with him is Beauty slain,
1020   And, Beauty dead, black Chaos comes again.

'Fie, fie, fond love, thou art as full of fear
As one with treasure laden, hemmed with thieves;
Trifles unwitnesséd with eye or ear
Thy coward heart with false bethinking grieves.'
   Even at this word she hears a merry horn, 1025
   Whereat she leaps that was but late forlorn.

As falcons to the lure, away she flies;
The grass stoops not, she treads on it so light;
And in her haste unfortunately spies
The foul boar's conquest on her fair delight; 1030
   Which seen, her eyes, as murd'red with the view,
   Like stars ashamed of day, themselves withdrew;

Or as the snail, whose tender horns being hit,
Shrinks backward in his shelly cave with pain,
And there all smoth'red up in shade doth sit, 1035
Long after fearing to creep forth again;
   So at his bloody view her eyes are fled
   Into the deep-dark cabins of her head;

Where they resign their office and their light
To the disposing of her troubled brain; 1040
Who bids them still consort with ugly night,
And never wound the heart with looks again;
   Who, like a king perplexéd in his throne,
   By their suggestion gives a deadly groan,

Whereat each tributary subject quakes; 1045
As when the wind, imprisoned in the ground,
Struggling for passage, earth's foundation shakes,
Which with cold terror doth men's minds confound.
   This mutiny each part doth so surprise,
   That from their dark beds once more leap her eyes; 1050

And being opened, threw unwilling light
Upon the wide wound that the boar had trenched
In his soft flank; whose wonted lily white
With purple tears that his wound wept was drenched:
1055   No flower was nigh, no grass, herb, leaf or weed,
    But stole his blood and seemed with him to bleed.

This solemn sympathy poor Venus noteth;
Over one shoulder doth she hang her head;
Dumbly she passions, franticly she doteth;
1060 She thinks he could not die, he is not dead.
    Her voice is stopped, her joints forget to bow;
    Her eyes are mad that they have wept till now.

Upon his hurt she looks so steadfastly
That her sight dazzling makes the wound seem three;
1065 And then she reprehends her mangling eye
That makes more gashes where no breach should be:
    His face seems twain, each several limb is doubled;
    For oft the eye mistakes, the brain being troubled.

'My tongue cannot express my grief for one,
1070 And yet,' quoth she, 'behold two Adons dead!
My sighs are blown away, my salt tears gone,
Mine eyes are turned to fire, my heart to lead;
    Heavy heart's lead, melt at mine eyes' red fire!
    So shall I die by drops of hot desire.

1075 'Alas, poor world, what treasure hast thou lost!
What face remains alive that's worth the viewing?
Whose tongue is music now? what canst thou boast
Of things long since, or any thing ensuing?
    The flowers are sweet, their colours fresh and trim;
1080   But true sweet beauty lived and died with him.

'Bonnet nor veil henceforth no creature wear;
Nor sun nor wind will ever strive to kiss you.
Having no fair to lose, you need not fear;
The sun doth scorn you, and the wind doth hiss you.
    But when Adonis lived, sun and sharp air   1085
    Lurked like two thieves to rob him of his fair;

'And therefore would he put his bonnet on,
Under whose brim the gaudy sun would peep;
The wind would blow it off, and, being gone,
Play with his locks. Then would Adonis weep;   1090
    And straight, in pity of his tender years,
    They both would strive who first should dry his tears.

'To see his face the lion walked along
Behind some hedge, because he would not fear him;
To recreate himself when he hath sung,   1095
The tiger would be tame and gently hear him;
    If he had spoke, the wolf would leave his prey,
    And never fright the silly lamb that day.

'When he beheld his shadow in the brook,
The fishes spread on it their golden gills;   1100
When he was by, the birds such pleasure took
That some would sing, some other in their bills
    Would bring him mulberries and ripe-red cherries;
    He fed them with his sight, they him with berries.

'But this foul, grim, and urchin-snouted boar,   1105
Whose downward eye still looketh for a grave,
Ne'er saw the beauteous livery that he wore;
Witness the entertainment that he gave.
    If he did see his face, why then I know
    He thought to kiss him, and hath killed him so.   1110

"'Tis true, 'tis true; thus was Adonis slain:
He ran upon the boar with his sharp spear,
Who did not whet his teeth at him again,
But by a kiss thought to persuade him there;
1115   And nuzzling in his flank, the loving swine
Sheathed unaware the tusk in his soft groin.

'Had I been toothed like him, I must confess,
With kissing him I should have killed him first;
But he is dead, and never did he bless
1120 My youth with his; the more am I accurst.'
With this, she falleth in the place she stood,
And stains her face with his congealéd blood.

She looks upon his lips, and they are pale;
She takes him by the hand, and that is cold;
1125 She whispers in his ears a heavy tale,
As if they heard the woeful words she told;
She lifts the coffer-lids that close his eyes,
Where, lo, two lamps, burnt out, in darkness lies;

Two glasses, where herself herself beheld
1130 A thousand times, and now no more, reflect;
Their virtue lost wherein they late excelled,
And every beauty robbed of his effect.
'Wonder of time,' quoth she, 'this is my spite,
That, thou being dead, the day should yet be light.

1135 'Since thou art dead, lo, here I prophesy
Sorrow on love hereafter shall attend;
It shall be waited on with jealousy,
Find sweet beginning but unsavoury end;
Ne'er settled equally, but high or low,
1140   That all love's pleasure shall not match his woe.

'It shall be fickle, false and full of fraud;
Bud, and be blasted, in a breathing while;
The bottom poison, and the top o'erstrawed
With sweets that shall the truest sight beguile;
    The strongest body shall it make most weak,   1145
      Strike the wise dumb, and teach the fool to speak.

'It shall be sparing, and too full of riot,
Teaching decrepit age to tread the measures;
The staring ruffian shall it keep in quiet,
Pluck down the rich, enrich the poor with treasures; 1150
    It shall be raging-mad, and silly-mild,
      Make the young old, the old become a child.

'It shall suspect where is no cause of fear;
It shall not fear where it should most mistrust;
It shall be merciful and too severe,   1155
And most deceiving when it seems most just;
    Perverse it shall be where it shows most toward,
      Put fear to valour, courage to the coward.

'It shall be cause of war and dire events,
And set dissension 'twixt the son and sire;   1160
Subject and servile to all discontents,
As dry combustious matter is to fire.
    Sith in his prime death doth my love destroy,
      They that love best their loves shall not enjoy.'

By this the boy that by her side lay killed   1165
Was melted like a vapour from her sight,
And in his blood that on the ground lay spilled
A purple flower sprung up, chequ'red with white,
    Resembling well his pale cheeks, and the blood
      Which in round drops upon their whiteness stood. 1170

She bows her head the new-sprung flower to smell,
Comparing it to her Adonis' breath;
And says within her bosom it shall dwell,
Since he himself is reft from her by death;
1175 She crops the stalk, and in the breach appears
Green-dropping sap, which she compares to tears.

'Poor flower,' quoth she, 'this was thy father's guise—
Sweet issue of a more sweet-smelling sire—
For every little grief to wet his eyes.
1180 To grow unto himself was his desire,
And so 'tis thine; but know, it is as good
To wither in my breast as in his blood.

'Here was thy father's bed, here in my breast;
Thou art the next of blood, and 'tis thy right.
1185 Lo, in this hollow cradle take thy rest;
My throbbing heart shall rock thee day and night;
There shall not be one minute in an hour
Wherein I will not kiss my sweet love's flower.'

Thus weary of the world, away she hies,
1190 And yokes her silver doves, by whose swift aid
Their mistress, mounted, through the empty skies
In her light chariot quickly is conveyed,
Holding their course to Paphos, where their queen
Means to immure herself and not be seen.

THE RAPE OF LUCRECE

THE RAPE OF LUCRECE

TO THE

RIGHT HONOURABLE,
HENRY WRIOTHESLEY,
EARL OF SOUTHHAMPTON, AND BARON
OF TITCHFIELD

The love I dedicate to your lordship is without end: whereof this pamphlet without beginning is but a superfluous moiety. The warrant I have of your honourable disposition, not the worth of my untutored lines, makes it assured of acceptance. What I have done is yours; what I have to do is yours; being part in all I have, devoted yours. Were my worth greater, my duty would show greater; meantime, as it is, it is bound to your lordship, to whom I wish long life still lengthened with all happiness.

Your lordship's in all duty,

William Shakespeare

THE ARGUMENT

LUCIUS TARQUINIUS, for his excessive pride surnamed
Superbus, after he had caused his own father-in-law
Servius Tullius to be cruelly murdered, and, contrary
to the Roman laws and customs, not requiring or staying
for the people's suffrages, had possessed himself of the
kingdom, went, accompanied with his sons and other
noblemen of Rome, to besiege Ardea. During which
siege the principal men of the army meeting one evening
at the tent of Sextus Tarquinius, the king's son, in their
discourses after supper every one commended the
virtues of his own wife; among whom Collatinus ex-
tolled the incomparable chastity of his wife Lucretia.
In that pleasant humour they all posted to Rome; and
intending, by their secret and sudden arrival, to make
trial of that which every one had before avouched, only
Collatinus finds his wife, though it were late in the night,
spinning amongst her maids: the other ladies were all
found dancing and revelling, or in several disports.
Whereupon the noblemen yielded Collatinus the vic-
tory, and his wife the fame. At that time Sextus
Tarquinius being inflamed with Lucrece' beauty, yet
smothering his passions for the present, departed with
the rest back to the camp; from whence he shortly after
privily withdrew himself, and was, according to his
estate, royally entertained and lodged by Lucrece at
Collatium. The same night he treacherously stealeth
into her chamber, violently ravished her, and early in
the morning speedeth away. Lucrece, in this lamentable
plight, hastily dispatcheth messengers, one to Rome for
her father, another to the camp for Collatine. They
came, the one accompanied with Junius Brutus, the
other with Publius Valerius; and finding Lucrece
attired in mourning habit, demanded the cause of her

sorrow. She, first taking an oath of them for her revenge, revealed the actor and whole manner of his dealing, and withal suddenly stabbed herself. Which done, with one consent they all vowed to root out the whole hated family of the Tarquins; and bearing the dead body to Rome, Brutus acquainted the people with the doer and manner of the vile deed, with a bitter invective against the tyranny of the king: wherewith the people were so moved, that with one consent and a general acclamation the Tarquins were all exiled, and the state government changed from kings to consuls.

THE RAPE OF LUCRECE

Fʀᴏᴍ the besiegéd Ardea all in post,
Borne by the trustless wings of false desire,
Lust-breathéd Tarquin leaves the Roman host,
And to Collatium bears the lightless fire
Which, in pale embers hid, lurks to aspire   5
    And girdle with embracing flames the waist
    Of Collatine's fair love, Lucrece the chaste.

Haply that name of chaste unhapp'ly set
This bateless edge on his keen appetite;
When Collatine unwisely did not let   10
To praise the clear unmatchéd red and white
Which triumphed in that sky of his delight,
    Where mortal stars, as bright as heaven's beauties,
    With pure aspects did him peculiar duties.

For he the night before, in Tarquin's tent,   15
Unlocked the treasure of his happy state;
What priceless wealth the heavens had him lent
In the possession of his beauteous mate;
Reck'ning his fortune at such high-proud rate
    That kings might be espouséd to more fame,   20
    But king nor peer to such a peerless dame.

O happiness enjoyed but of a few!
And, if possessed, as soon decayed and done
As is the morning silver-melting dew
Against the golden splendour of the sun!   25
An expired date, cancelled ere well begun:
    Honour and beauty, in the owner's arms,
    Are weakly fortressed from a world of harms.

Beauty itself doth of itself persuade
30 The eyes of men without an orator;
What needeth then apology be made,
To set forth that which is so singular?
Or why is Collatine the publisher
    Of that rich jewel he should keep unknown
35   From thievish ears, because it is his own?

Perchance his boast of Lucrece' sov'reignty
Suggested this proud issue of a king;
For by our ears our hearts oft tainted be.
Perchance that envy of so rich a thing,
40 Braving compare, disdainfully did sting
    His high-pitched thoughts, that meaner men
        should vaunt
    That golden hap which their superiors want.

But some untimely thought did instigate
His all too timeless speed, if none of those.
45 His honour, his affairs, his friends, his state,
Neglected all, with swift intent he goes
To quench the coal which in his liver glows.
    O rash-false heat, wrapped in repentant cold,
    Thy hasty spring still blasts, and ne'er grows old!

50 When at Collatium this false lord arrivéd,
Well was he welcomed by the Roman dame,
Within whose face beauty and virtue strivéd
Which of them both should underprop her fame:
When virtue bragged, beauty would blush for shame;
55   When beauty boasted blushes, in despite
        Virtue would stain that o'er with silver white.

But beauty, in that white entituléd,
From Venus' doves doth challenge that fair field;
Then virtue claims from beauty beauty's red,

c.p. 1.268

c.p. Nymph
complaining

Which virtue gave the golden age to gild   60
Their silver cheeks, and called it then their shield;
  Teaching them thus to use it in the fight,
  When shame assailed, the red should fence the white.

This heraldry in Lucrece' face was seen,
Argued by beauty's red and virtue's white;   65
Of either's colour was the other queen,
Proving from world's minority their right;
Yet their ambition makes them still to fight,
  The sovereignty of either being so great
  That oft they interchange each other's seat.   70

This silent war of lilies and of roses
Which Tarquin viewed in her fair face's field,   *MARVELL*
In their pure ranks his traitor eye encloses;   *"lilies without, roses within"*
Where, lest between them both it should be killed,
The coward captive vanquishéd doth yield   75
  To those two armies that would let him go
  Rather than triumph in so false a foe.

Now thinks he that her husband's shallow tongue,
The niggard prodigal that praised her so,
In that high task hath done her beauty wrong,   80
Which far exceeds his barren skill to show;
Therefore that praise which Collatine doth owe
  Enchanted Tarquin answers with surmise,
  In silent wonder of still-gazing eyes.

This earthly saint, adored by this devil,   85
Little suspecteth the false worshipper;
"For unstained thoughts do seldom dream on evil;
"Birds never limed no secret bushes fear.
So guiltless she securely gives good cheer
  And reverend welcome to her princely guest,   90
  Whose inward ill no outward harm expressed;

For that he coloured with his high estate,
Hiding base sin in pleats of majesty;
That nothing in him seemed inordinate,
95 Save sometime too much wonder of his eye,
Which, having all, all could not satisfy;
    But, poorly rich, so wanteth in his store
    That cloyed with much he pineth still for more.

cp. Macb.

But she, that never coped with stranger eyes,
100 Could pick no meaning from their parling looks,
Nor read the subtle-shining secrecies
Writ in the glassy margents of such books.
She touched no unknown baits, nor feared no hooks;
    Nor could she moralize his wanton sight,
105   More than his eyes were opened to the light.

He stories to her ears her husband's fame,
Won in the fields of fruitful Italy;
And decks with praises Collatine's high name,
Made glorious by his manly chivalry
110 With bruiséd arms and wreaths of victory.
    Her joy with heaved-up hand she doth express, 2 dramatic
    And wordless so greets heaven for his success.   visual

Far from the purpose of his coming thither,
He makes excuses for his being there.
115 No cloudy show of stormy blust'ring weather
Doth yet in his fair welkin once appear;
Till sable Night, mother of dread and fear,
    Upon the world dim darkness doth display,
    And in her vaulty prison stows the day.

120 For then is Tarquin brought unto his bed,
Intending weariness with heavy sprite;
For after supper long he questionéd

With modest Lucrece, and wore out the night.
Now leaden slumber with life's strength doth fight;
  And every one to rest himself betakes,   125
  Save thieves and cares and troubled minds that wakes.

As one of which doth Tarquin lie revolving
The sundry dangers of his will's obtaining;
Yet ever to obtain his will resolving,
Though weak-built hopes persuade him to abstaining; 130
Despair to gain doth traffic oft for gaining,
  And when great treasure is the meed proposéd,
  Though death be adjunct, there's no death supposéd.

Those that much covet are with gain so fond
That what they have not, that which they possess,   135
They scatter and unloose it from their bond,
And so, by hoping more, they have but less;
Or, gaining more, the profit of excess
  Is but to surfeit, and such griefs sustain
  That they prove bankrupt in this poor-rich gain.   140

The aim of all is but to nurse the life
With honour, wealth and ease, in waning age;
And in this aim there is such thwarting strife
That one for all or all for one we gage:
As life for honour in fell battle's rage;   145
  Honour for wealth; and oft that wealth doth cost
  The death of all, and all together lost.

So that in vent'ring ill we leave to be
The things we are for that which we expect;
And this ambitious foul infirmity,   150
In having much, torments us with defect
Of that we have; so then we do neglect
  The thing we have, and, all for want of wit,
  Make something nothing by augmenting it.

155 Such hazard now must doting Tarquin make,
Pawning his honour to obtain his lust;
And for himself himself he must forsake:
Then where is truth, if there be no self-trust?
When shall he think to find a stranger just
160   When he himself himself confounds, betrays
    To sland'rous tongues and wretched hateful days?

Now stole upon the time the dead of night,
When heavy sleep had closed up mortal eyes;
No comfortable star did lend his light,
165 No noise but owls' and wolves'. death-boding cries;
Now serves the season that they may surprise
    The silly lambs. Pure thoughts are dead and still,
    While lust and murder wakes to stain and kill.

And now this lustful lord, leaped from his bed,
170 Throwing his mantle rudely o'er his arm,
Is madly tossed between desire and dread;
Th'one sweetly flatters, th'other feareth harm;
But honest fear, bewitched with lust's foul charm,
    Doth too too oft betake him to retire,
175   Beaten away by brain-sick rude desire.

His falchion on a flint he softly smiteth,
That from the cold stone sparks of fire do fly,
Whereat a waxen torch forthwith he lighteth,
Which must be lode-star to his lustful eye;
180 And to the flame thus speaks advisedly:
    'As from this cold flint I enforced this fire,
    So Lucrece must I force to my desire.'

Here pale with fear he doth premeditate
The dangers of his loathsome enterprise,
185 And in his inward mind he doth debate

What following sorrow may on this arise;
Then, looking scornfully, he doth despise
  His naked armour of still-slaughteréd lust,
  And justly thus controls his thoughts unjust:

'Fair torch, burn out thy light, and lend it not   190
To darken her whose light excelleth thine;
And die, unhallowéd thoughts, before you blot
With your uncleanness that which is divine;
Offer pure incense to so pure a shrine;
  Let fair humanity abhor the deed   195
  That spots and stains love's modest snow-white weed.

'O shame to knighthood and to shining arms!
O foul dishonour to my household's grave!
O impious act, including all foul harms!
A martial man to be soft fancy's slave!   200
True valour still a true respect should have;
  Then my digression is so vile, so base,
  That it will live engraven in my face.

'Yea, though I die, the scandal will survive,
And be an eye-sore in my golden coat;   205
Some loathsome dash the herald will contrive,
To cipher me how fondly I did dote;
That my posterity, shamed with the note,
  Shall curse my bones, and hold it for no sin
  To wish that I their father had not been.   210

'What win I, if I gain the thing I seek?
A dream, a breath, a froth of fleeting joy.
Who buys a minute's mirth to wail a week?
Or sells eternity to get a toy?
For one sweet grape who will the vine destroy?   215
  Or what fond beggar, but to touch the crown,
  Would with the sceptre straight be strucken down?

'If Collatinus dream of my intent,
Will he not wake, and in a desp'rate rage
220 Post hither, this vile purpose to prevent?—
This siege that hath engirt his marriage,
This blur to youth, this sorrow to the sage,
    This dying virtue, this surviving shame,
    Whose crime will bear an ever-during blame.

225 'O what excuse can my invention make,
When thou shalt charge me with so black a deed?
Will not my tongue be mute, my frail joints shake,
Mine eyes forego their light, my false heart bleed?
The guilt being great, the fear doth still exceed;
230   And extreme fear can neither fight nor fly,
    But coward-like with trembling terror die.

'Had Collatinus killed my son or sire,
Or lain in ambush to betray my life,
Or were he not my dear friend, this desire
235 Might have excuse to work upon his wife,
As in revenge or quittal of such strife;
    But as he is my kinsman, my dear friend,
    The shame and fault finds no excuse nor end.

'Shameful it is—ay, if the fact be known;
240 Hateful it is—there is no hate in loving;
I'll beg her love—but she is not her own;
The worst is but denial and reproving.
My will is strong, past reason's weak removing.—
    Who fears a sentence or an old man's saw
245   Shall by a painted cloth be kept in awe.'

Thus graceless holds he disputation
'Tween frozen conscience and hot-burning will,
And with good thoughts makes dispensation,

Urging the worser sense for vantage still;
Which in a moment doth confound and kill 250
   All pure effects, and doth so far proceed
   That what is vile shows like a virtuous deed.

Quoth he, 'She took me kindly by the hand,
And gazed for tidings in my eager eyes,
Fearing some hard news from the warlike band 255
Where her belovéd Collatinus lies.
O how her fear did make her colour rise!
   First red as roses that on lawn we lay,
   Then white as lawn, the roses took away.

'And how her hand, in my hand being locked, 260
Forced it to tremble with her loyal fear!
Which struck her sad, and then it faster rocked
Until her husband's welfare she did hear;
Whereat she smiléd with so sweet a cheer
   That had Narcissus seen her as she stood 265
   Self-love had never drowned him in the flood.

'Why hunt I then for colour or excuses?
All orators are dumb when beauty pleadeth; *c.p. 1.29-30*
Poor wretches have remorse in poor abuses;
Love thrives not in the heart that shadows dreadeth; 270
Affection is my captain, and he leadeth;
   And when his gaudy banner is displayed,
   The coward fights and will not be dismayed.

'Then childish fear avaunt! debating die!
Respect and reason wait on wrinkled age! 275
My heart shall never countermand mine eye;
Sad pause and deep regard beseems the sage;
My part is youth, and beats these from the stage:
   Desire my pilot is, beauty my prize;
   Then who fears sinking where such treasure lies?' 280

As corn o'ergrown by weeds, so heedful fear
Is almost choked by unresisted lust.
Away he steals with open list'ning ear,
Full of foul hope and full of fond mistrust;
285 Both which, as servitors to the unjust,
 So cross him with their opposite persuasion
 That now he vows a league, and now invasion.

Within his thought her heavenly image sits,
And in the selfsame seat sits Collatine.
290 That eye which looks on her confounds his wits;
That eye which him beholds, as more divine,
Unto a view so false will not incline;
 But with a pure appeal seeks to the heart,
 Which once corrupted takes the worser part;

295 And therein heartens up his servile powers,
 Who, flatt'red by their leader's jocund show,
 Stuff up his lust, as minutes fill up hours;
 And as their captain, so their pride doth grow,
 Paying more slavish tribute than they owe.
300 By reprobate desire thus madly led,
 The Roman lord marcheth to Lucrece' bed.

The locks between her chamber and his will,
Each one by him enforced, retires his ward;
But, as they open, they all rate his ill,
305 Which drives the creeping thief to some regard.
 The threshold grates the door to have him heard;
 Night-wand'ring weasels shriek to see him there;
 They fright him, yet he still pursues his fear.

As each unwilling portal yields him way,
310 Through little vents and crannies of the place
The wind wars with his torch to make him stay,

And blows the smoke of it into his face,
Extinguishing his conduct in this case;
  But his hot heart, which fond desire doth scorch,
  Puffs forth another wind that fires the torch;   315

And being lighted, by the light he spies
Lucretia's glove, wherein her needle sticks;
He takes it from the rushes where it lies,
And griping it, the needle his finger pricks,
As who should say 'This glove to wanton tricks   320
  Is not inured. Return again in haste;
  Thou see'st our mistress' ornaments are chaste.'

But all these poor forbiddings could not stay him;
He in the worst sense consters their denial:
The doors, the wind, the glove, that did delay him,   325
He takes for accidental things of trial;
Or as those bars which stop the hourly dial,
  Who with a ling'ring stay his course doth let,
  Till every minute pays the hour his debt.

'So, so,' quoth he, 'these lets attend the time,   330
Like little frosts that sometime threat the spring,
To add a more rejoicing to the prime,
And give the sneapéd birds more cause to sing.
Pain pays the income of each precious thing;
  Huge rocks, high winds, strong pirates, shelves   335
    and sands
  The merchant fears, ere rich at home he lands.'

Now is he come unto the chamber door
That shuts him from the heaven of his thought,
Which with a yielding latch, and with no more,
Hath barred him from the blesséd thing he sought.   340
So from himself impiety hath wrought,

That for his prey to pray he doth begin,
As if the heavens should countenance his sin.

But in the midst of his unfruitful prayer,
345 Having solicited th'eternal power
That his foul thoughts might compass his fair fair,
And they would stand auspicious to the hour,
Even there he starts; quoth he 'I must deflower:
    The powers to whom I pray abhor this fact;
350   How can they then assist me in the act?

'Then Love and Fortune be my gods, my guide!
My will is backed with resolution.
Thoughts are but dreams till their effects be tried;
The blackest sin is cleared with absolution;
355 Against love's fire fear's frost hath dissolution.
    The eye of heaven is out, and misty night
    Covers the shame that follows sweet delight.'

This said, his guilty hand plucked up the latch,
And with his knee the door he opens wide.
360 The dove sleeps fast that this night-owl will catch.
Thus treason works ere traitors be espied.
Who sees the lurking serpent steps aside;
    But she, sound sleeping, fearing no such thing,
    Lies at the mercy of his mortal sting.

365 Into the chamber wickedly he stalks
And gazeth on her yet unstainéd bed.
The curtains being close, about he walks,
Rolling his greedy eyeballs in his head.
By their high treason is his heart misled,
370   Which gives the watch-word to his hand full soon
    To draw the cloud that hides the silver moon.

Look as the fair and fiery-pointed sun,
Rushing from forth a cloud, bereaves our sight;
Even so, the curtain drawn, his eyes begun
To wink, being blinded with a greater light;   375
Whether it is that she reflects so bright
    That dazzleth them, or else some shame supposéd,
    But blind they are, and keep themselves encloséd.

O, had they in that darksome prison died!
Then had they seen the period of their ill;   380
Then Collatine again, by Lucrece' side,
In his clear bed might have reposéd still;
But they must ope, this blesséd league to kill;
    And holy-thoughted Lucrece to their sight
    Must sell her joy, her life, her world's delight.   385

Her lily hand her rosy cheek lies under,
Coz'ning the pillow of a lawful kiss;
Who, therefore angry, seems to part in sunder,
Swelling on either side to want his bliss;
Between whose hills her head entombéd is;   390
    Where, like a virtuous monument, she lies,
    To be admired of lewd unhallowéd eyes.

Without the bed her other fair hand was,
On the green coverlet; whose perfect white
Showed like an April daisy on the grass,   395
With pearly sweat resembling dew of night.
Her eyes, like marigolds, had sheathed their light,
    And canopied in darkness sweetly lay,
    Till they might open to adorn the day.

Her hair, like golden threads, played with her breath— 400
O modest wantons! wanton modesty!—
Showing life's triumph in the map of death,

And death's dim look in life's mortality:
Each in her sleep themselves so beautify
405 As if between them twain there were no strife,
But that life lived in death and death in life.

Her breasts, like ivory globes circled with blue,
A pair of maiden worlds unconqueréd,
Save of their lord no bearing yoke they knew,
410 And him by oath they truly honouréd.
These worlds in Tarquin new ambition bred,
    Who like a foul usurper went about
    From this fair throne to heave the owner out.

What could he see but mightily he noted?
415 What did he note but strongly he desiréd?
What he beheld, on that he firmly doted,
And in his will his wilful eye he tiréd.
With more than admiration he admiréd
    Her azure veins, her alabaster skin,
420   Her coral lips, her snow-white dimpled chin.

As the grim lion fawneth o'er his prey,
Sharp hunger by the conquest satisfied,
So o'er this sleeping soul doth Tarquin stay,
His rage of lust by gazing qualified;
425 Slacked, not suppressed; for standing by her side,
    His eye, which late this mutiny restrains,
    Unto a greater uproar tempts his veins;

And they, like straggling slaves for pillage fighting,
Obdurate vassals fell exploits effecting,
430 In bloody death and ravishment delighting,
Nor children's tears nor mothers' groans respecting,
Swell in their pride, the onset still expecting.
    Anon his beating heart, alarum striking,
    Gives the hot charge, and bids them do their liking.

His drumming heart cheers up his burning eye,   435
His eye commends the leading to his hand;
His hand, as proud of such a dignity,
Smoking with pride, marched on to make his stand
On her bare breast, the heart of all her land;
    Whose ranks of blue veins as his hand did scale,   440
    Left their round turrets destitute and pale.

They, must'ring to the quiet cabinet
Where their dear governess and lady lies,
Do tell her she is dreadfully beset,
And fright her with confusion of their cries.   445
She, much amazed, breaks ope her locked-up eyes,
    Who, peeping forth this tumult to behold,
    Are by his flaming torch dimmed and controlled.

Imagine her as one in dead of night
From forth dull sleep by dreadful fancy waking,   450
That thinks she hath beheld some ghastly sprite,
Whose grim aspect sets every joint a-shaking;
What terror 'tis! but she, in worser taking,
    From sleep disturbéd, heedfully doth view
    The sight which makes supposéd terror true.   455

Wrapped and confounded in a thousand fears,
Like to a new-killed bird she trembling lies;
She dares not look; yet, winking, there appears
Quick-shifting antics, ugly in her eyes.
"Such shadows are the weak brain's forgeries,   460
    Who, angry that the eyes fly from their lights,
    In darkness daunts them with more dreadful sights.

His hand that yet remains upon her breast—
Rude ram, to batter such an ivory wall!—
May feel her heart, poor citizen, distressed,   465

Wounding itself to death, rise up and fall,
Beating her bulk, that his hand shakes withal.
   This moves in him more rage and lesser pity,
   To make the breach and enter this sweet city.

470 First like a trumpet doth his tongue begin
To sound a parley to his heartless foe,
Who o'er the white sheet peers her whiter chin,
The reason of this rash alarm to know,
Which he by dumb demeanour seeks to show;
475   But she with vehement prayers urgeth still
   Under what colour he commits this ill.

Thus he replies: 'The colour in thy face,
That even for anger makes the lily pale
And the red rose blush at her own disgrace,
480 Shall plead for me and tell my loving tale.
Under that colour am I come to scale
   Thy never-conqueréd fort. The fault is thine,
   For those thine eyes betray thee unto mine.

'Thus I forestall thee, if thou mean to chide:
485 Thy beauty hath ensnared thee to this night,
Where thou with patience must my will abide,
My will that marks thee for my earth's delight,
Which I to conquer sought with all my might;
   But as reproof and reason beat it dead,
490   By thy bright beauty was it newly bred.

'I see what crosses my attempt will bring;
I know what thorns the growing rose defends;
I think the honey guarded with a sting;
All this beforehand counsel comprehends.
495 But will is deaf and hears no heedful friends;
   Only he hath an eye to gaze on beauty,
   And dotes on what he looks, 'gainst law or duty.

'I have debated, even in my soul,
What wrong, what shame, what sorrow I shall breed;
But nothing can affection's course control,   500
Or stop the headlong fury of his speed.
I know repentant tears ensue the deed,
    Reproach, disdain and deadly enmity;
    Yet strive I to embrace mine infamy.'

This said, he shakes aloft his Roman blade,   505
Which, like a falcon tow'ring in the skies,
Coucheth the fowl below with his wings' shade,
Whose crooked beak threats if he mount he dies.
So under his insulting falchion lies
    Harmless Lucretia, marking what he tells   510
    With trembling fear, as fowl hear falcons' bells.

'Lucrece,' quoth he, 'this night I must enjoy thee.
If thou deny, then force must work my way,
For in thy bed I purpose to destroy thee;
That done, some worthless slave of thine I'll slay,   515
To kill thine honour with thy life's decay;
    And in thy dead arms do I mean to place him,
    Swearing I slew him, seeing thee embrace him.

'So thy surviving husband shall remain
The scornful mark of every open eye;   520
Thy kinsmen hang their heads at this disdain,
Thy issue blurred with nameless bastardy;
And thou, the author of their obloquy,
    Shalt have thy trespass cited up in rhymes
    And sung by children in succeeding times.   525

'But if thou yield, I rest thy secret friend:
The fault unknown is as a thought unacted;
"A little harm done to a great good end

For lawful policy remains enacted.
530 "The poisonous simple sometime is compacted
    In a pure compound; being so applied,
    His venom in effect is purified.

    'Then, for thy husband and thy children's sake,
    Tender my suit; bequeath not to their lot
535 The shame that from them no device can take,
    The blemish that will never be forgot;
    Worse than a slavish wipe or birth-hour's blot;
      For marks descried in men's nativity
      Are nature's faults, not their own infamy.'

540 Here with a cockatrice' dead-killing eye
    He rouseth up himself, and makes a pause;
    While she, the picture of pure piety,
    Like a white hind under the gripe's sharp claws,
    Pleads in a wilderness where are no laws
545   To the rough beast that knows no gentle right,
      Nor aught obeys but his foul appetite.

    But when a black-faced cloud the world doth threat,
    In his dim mist th'aspiring mountains hiding,
    From earth's dark womb some gentle gust doth get,
550 Which blows these pitchy vapours from their biding,
    Hind'ring their present fall by this dividing;
      So his unhallowéd haste her words delays,
      And moody Pluto winks while Orpheus plays.

    Yet, foul night-waking cat, he doth but dally,
555 While in his hold-fast foot the weak mouse panteth;
    Her sad behaviour feeds his vulture folly,
    A swallowing gulf that even in plenty wanteth;
    His ear her prayers admits, but his heart granteth
      No penetrable entrance to her plaining.
560   "Tears harden lust, though marble wear with raining.

Her pity-pleading eyes are sadly fixéd
In the remorseless wrinkles of his face;
Her modest eloquence with sighs is mixéd,
Which to her oratory adds more grace.
She puts the period often from his place,   565
   And midst the sentence so her accent breaks
   That twice she doth begin ere once she speaks.

She conjures him by high almighty Jove,
By knighthood, gentry, and sweet friendship's oath,
By her untimely tears, her husband's love,   570
By holy human law and common troth,
By heaven and earth, and all the power of both,
   That to his borrowéd bed he make retire,
   And stoop to honour, not to foul desire.

Quoth she: 'Reward not hospitality   575
With such black payment as thou hast pretended;
Mud not the fountain that gave drink to thee;
Mar not the thing that cannot be amended;
End thy ill aim before thy shoot be ended.
   He is no woodman that doth bend his bow   580
   To strike a poor unseasonable doe.   } cp. Nymph Comp.

'My husband is thy friend—for his sake spare me;
Thyself art mighty—for thine own sake leave me;
Myself a weakling—do not then ensnare me;
Thou look'st not like deceit—do not deceive me.   585
My sighs like whirlwinds labour hence to heave thee.
   If ever man were moved with woman's moans,
   Be movéd with my tears, my sighs, my groans;

'All which together, like a troubled ocean,
Beat at thy rocky and wrack-threat'ning heart,   590
To soften it with their continual motion;

For stones dissolved to water do convert.
O, if no harder than a stone thou art,
  Melt at my tears, and be compassionate!
595 Soft pity enters at an iron gate.

'In Tarquin's likeness I did entertain thee;
Hast thou put on his shape to do him shame?
To all the host of heaven I complain me
Thou wrong'st his honour, wound'st his princely name.
600 Thou art not what thou seem'st; and if the same,
  Thou seem'st not what thou art, a god, a king;
  For kings like gods should govern every thing.

'How will thy shame be seeded in thine age,
When thus thy vices bud before thy spring?
605 If in thy hope thou dar'st do such outrage,
What dar'st thou not when once thou art a king?
  O, be rememb'red, no outrageous thing
  From vassal actors can be wiped away;
  Then kings' misdeeds cannot be hid in clay.

610 'This deed will make thee only loved for fear,
But happy monarchs still are feared for love;
With foul offenders thou perforce must bear,
When they in thee the like offences prove.
If but for fear of this, thy will remove;
615 For princes are the glass, the school, the book,
  Where subjects' eyes do learn, do read, do look.

'And wilt thou be the school where Lust shall learn?
Must he in thee read lectures of such shame?
Wilt thou be glass wherein it shall discern
620 Authority for sin, warrant for blame,
  To privilege dishonour in thy name?
  Thou back'st reproach against long-living laud,
  And mak'st fair reputation but a bawd.

'Hast thou command? by him that gave it thee,
From a pure heart command thy rebel will; 625
Draw not thy sword to guard iniquity,
For it was lent thee all that brood to kill.
Thy princely office how canst thou fulfil,
    When patterned by thy fault foul sin may say
    He learned to sin, and thou didst teach the way? 630

'Think but how vile a spectacle it were
To view thy present trespass in another.
Men's faults do seldom to themselves appear;
Their own transgressions partially they smother;
This guilt would seem death-worthy in thy brother. 635
    O, how are they wrapped in with infamies
    That from their own misdeeds askance their eyes!

'To thee, to thee, my heaved-up hands appeal,
Not to seducing lust, thy rash relier;
I sue for exiled majesty's repeal; 640
Let him return, and flatt'ring thoughts retire.
His true respect will prison false desire,
    And wipe the dim mist from thy doting eyne,
    That thou shalt see thy state and pity mine.'

'Have done,' quoth he, 'my uncontrollèd tide 645
Turns not, but swells the higher by this let.
Small lights are soon blown out, huge fires abide,
And with the wind in greater fury fret.
The petty streams that pay a daily debt
    To their salt sovereign, with their fresh falls' haste 650
    Add to his flow, but alter not his taste.'

'Thou art', quoth she, 'a sea, a sovereign king;
And, lo, there falls into thy boundless flood
Black lust, dishonour, shame, misgoverning,

655 Who seek to stain the ocean of thy blood.
If all these petty ills shall change thy good;
    Thy sea within a puddle's womb is hearséd,
    And not the puddle in thy sea disperséd.

'So shall these slaves be king, and thou their slave;
660 Thou nobly base, they basely dignified;
Thou their fair life, and they thy fouler grave;
Thou loathéd in their shame, they in thy pride.
The lesser thing should not the greater hide;
    The cedar stoops not to the base shrub's foot,
665   But low shrubs wither at the cedar's root.

'So let thy thoughts, low vassals to thy state'—
'No more,' quoth he; 'by heaven, I will not hear thee.
Yield to my love; if not, enforcéd hate,
Instead of love's coy touch, shall rudely tear thee;
670 That done, despitefully I mean to bear thee
    Unto the base bed of some rascal groom,
    To be thy partner in this shameful doom.'

This said, he sets his foot upon the light,
For light and lust are deadly enemies;
675 Shame folded up in blind concealing night,
When most unseen, then most doth tyrannize.
The wolf hath seized his prey, the poor lamb cries,
    Till with her own white fleece her voice controlled
    Entombs her outcry in her lips' sweet fold;

680 For with the nightly linen that she wears
He pens her piteous clamours in her head,
Cooling his hot face in the chastest tears
That ever modest eyes with sorrow shed.
O, that prone lust should stain so pure a bed!
685   The spots whereof could weeping purify,
    Her tears should drop on them perpetually.

But she hath lost a dearer thing than life,
And he hath won what he would lose again.
This forcéd league doth force a further strife;
This momentary joy breeds months of pain;   690
This hot desire converts to cold disdain;
   Pure Chastity is rifled of her store,
    And Lust, the thief, far poorer than before.

Look as the full-fed hound or gorgéd hawk,
Unapt for tender smell or speedy flight,   695
Make slow pursuit, or altogether balk
The prey wherein by nature they delight,
So surfeit-taking Tarquin fares this night:
   His taste delicious, in digestion souring,
    Devours his will, that lived by foul devouring.   700

O, deeper sin than bottomless conceit
Can comprehend in still imagination!
Drunken Desire must vomit his receipt,
Ere he can see his own abomination.
While Lust is in his pride, no exclamation   705
   Can curb his heat or rein his rash desire,
    Till, like a jade, Self-will himself doth tire.

And then with lank and lean discoloured cheek,
With heavy eye, knit brow, and strengthless pace,
Feeble Desire, all recreant, poor and meek,   710
Like to a bankrupt beggar wails his case:
The flesh being proud, Desire doth fight with Grace,
   For there it revels, and when that decays
    The guilty rebel for remission prays.

So fares it with this faultful lord of Rome,   715
Who this accomplishment so hotly chaséd;
For now against himself he sounds this doom,

That through the length of times he stands disgracéd;
Besides, his soul's fair temple is defacéd,
720   To whose weak ruins muster troops of cares,
    To ask the spotted princess how she fares.

She says her subjects with foul insurrection
Have battered down her consecrated wall,
And by their mortal fault brought in subjection
725 Her immortality, and made her thrall
To living death and pain perpetual;
    Which in her prescience she controlléd still,
    But her foresight could not forestall their will.

Ev'n in this thought through the dark night he stealeth,
730 A captive victor that hath lost in gain;
Bearing away the wound that nothing healeth,
The scar that will, despite of cure, remain;
Leaving his spoil perplexed in greater pain.
    She bears the load of lust he left behind,
735   And he the burden of a guilty mind.

He like a thievish dog creeps sadly thence;
She like a wearied lamb lies panting there;
He scowls, and hates himself for his offence;
She, desperate, with her nails her flesh doth tear;
740 He faintly flies, sweating with guilty fear;
    She stays, exclaiming on the direful night;
    He runs, and chides his vanished, loathed delight.

He thence departs a heavy convertite;
She there remains a hopeless castaway;
745 He in his speed looks for the morning light;
She prays she never may behold the day.
    'For day', quoth she, 'night's scapes doth open lay,
    And my true eyes have never practised how
    To cloak offences with a cunning brow.

'They think not but that every eye can see   750
The same disgrace which they themselves behold;
And therefore would they still in darkness be,
To have their unseen sin remain untold;
For they their guilt with weeping will unfold,
    And grave, like water that doth eat in steel,   755
    Upon my cheeks what helpless shame I feel.'

Here she exclaims against repose and rest,
And bids her eyes hereafter still be blind.
She wakes her heart by beating on her breast,
And bids it leap from thence, where it may find   760
Some purer chest to close so pure a mind.
    Frantic with grief thus breathes she forth her spite
    Against the unseen secrecy of night:

'O comfort-killing Night, image of hell!
Dim register and notary of shame!   765
Black stage for tragedies and murders fell!
Vast sin-concealing chaos! nurse of blame!
Blind muffled bawd! dark harbour for defame!
    Grim cave of death! whisp'ring conspirator
    With close-tongued treason and the ravisher!   770

'O hateful, vaporous and foggy Night!
Since thou art guilty of my cureless crime,
Muster thy mists to meet the eastern light,
Make war against proportioned course of time;
Or if thou wilt permit the sun to climb   775
    His wonted height, yet ere he go to bed,
    Knit poisonous clouds about his golden head.

'With rotten damps ravish the morning air;
Let their exhaled unwholesome breaths make sick
The life of purity, the supreme fair,   780

Ere he arrive his weary noon-tide prick;
And let thy musty vapours march so thick
   That in their smoky ranks his smoth'red light
   May set at noon and make perpetual night.

785 'Were Tarquin Night, as he is but Night's child,
The silver-shining queen he would distain;
Her twinkling handmaids too, by him defiled,
Through Night's black bosom should not peep again;
So should I have co-partners in my pain;
790   And fellowship in woe doth woe assuage,
   As palmers' chat makes short their pilgrimage.

'Where now I have no one to blush with me,
To cross their arms and hang their heads with mine,
To mask their brows and hide their infamy;
795 But I alone alone must sit and pine,
   Seasoning the earth with show'rs of silver brine,
   Mingling my talk with tears, my grief with groans,
   Poor wasting monuments of lasting moans.

'O Night, thou furnace of foul-reeking smoke,
800 Let not the jealous Day behold that face
Which underneath thy black all-hiding cloak
Immodestly lies martyred with disgrace!
Keep still possession of thy gloomy place,
   That all the faults which in thy reign are made
805   May likewise be sepulchred in thy shade!

'Make me not object to the tell-tale Day.
The light will show, charactered in my brow,
The story of sweet chastity's decay,
The impious breach of holy wedlock vow;
810 Yea, the illiterate, that know not how
   To cipher what is writ in learnéd books,
   Will quote my loathsome trespass in my looks.

'The nurse, to still her child, will tell my story,
And fright her crying babe with Tarquin's name;
The orator, to deck his oratory,   815
Will couple my reproach to Tarquin's shame;
Feast-finding minstrels, tuning my defame,
    Will tie the hearers to attend each line,
    How Tarquin wrongéd me, I Collatine.

'Let my good name, that senseless reputation,   820
For Collatine's dear love be kept unspotted;
If that be made a theme for disputation,
The branches of another root are rotted,
And undeserved reproach to him allotted
    That is as clear from this attaint of mine   825
    As I ere this was pure to Collatine.

'O unseen shame! invisible disgrace!
O unfelt sore! crest-wounding, private scar!
Reproach is stamped in Collatinus' face,
And Tarquin's eye may read the mot afar,   830
"How he in peace is wounded, not in war.
    "Alas, how many bear such shameful blows,
    Which not themselves, but he that gives them knows!

'If, Collatine, thine honour lay in me,
From me by strong assault it is bereft.   835
My honey lost, and I, a drone-like bee,
Have no perfection of my summer left,
But robbed and ransacked by injurious theft.
    In thy weak hive a wand'ring wasp hath crept,
    And sucked the honey which thy chaste bee kept.   840

'Yet am I guilty of thy honour's wrack;
Yet for thy honour did I entertain him;
Coming from thee, I could not put him back,

For it had been dishonour to disdain him;
845 Besides, of weariness he did complain him,
  And talked of virtue: O unlooked-for evil,
  When virtue is profaned in such a devil!

'Why should the worm intrude the maiden bud?
Or hateful cuckoos hatch in sparrows' nests?
850 Or toads infect fair founts with venom mud?
Or tyrant folly lurk in gentle breasts?
Or kings be breakers of their own behests?
  "But no perfection is so absolute
  That some impurity doth not pollute.

855 'The agéd man that coffers up his gold
Is plagued with cramps and gouts and painful fits,
And scarce hath eyes his treasure to behold,
But like still-pining Tantalus he sits,
And useless barns the harvest of his wits,
860   Having no other pleasure of his gain
  But torment that it cannot cure his pain.

'So then he hath it when he cannot use it,
And leaves it to be mast'red by his young;
Who in their pride do presently abuse it.
865 Their father was too weak, and they too strong,
To hold their curséd-bléssed fortune long.
  "The sweets we wish for turn to loathéd sours
  "Even in the moment that we call them ours.

'Unruly blasts wait on the tender spring;
870 Unwholesome weeds take root with precious flowers:
The adder hisses where the sweet birds sing;
What virtue breeds iniquity devours.
We have no good that we can say is ours
  But ill-annexéd Opportunity
875   Or kills his life or else his quality.

'O Opportunity, thy guilt is great!
'Tis thou that execut'st the traitor's treason;
Thou sets the wolf where he the lamb may get;
Whoever plots the sin, thou point'st the season;
'Tis thou that spurn'st at right, at law, at reason;   880
   And in thy shady cell, where none may spy him,
   Sits Sin, to seize the souls that wander by him.

'Thou mak'st the vestal violate her oath;
Thou blow'st the fire when temperance is thawed;
Thou smother'st honesty, thou murd'rest troth;   885
Thou foul abettor! thou notorious bawd!
Thou plantest scandal and displacest laud.
   Thou ravisher, thou traitor, thou false thief,
   Thy honey turns to gall, thy joy to grief!

'Thy secret pleasure turns to open shame,   890
Thy private feasting to a public fast,
Thy smoothing titles to a ragged name,
Thy sugared tongue to bitter wormwood taste;
Thy violent vanities can never last.
   How comes it then, vile Opportunity,   895
   Being so bad, such numbers seek for thee?

'When wilt thou be the humble suppliant's friend,
And bring him where his suit may be obtainéd?
When wilt thou sort an hour great strifes to end?
Or free that soul which wretchedness hath chainéd?   900
Give physic to the sick, ease to the painéd?
   The poor, lame, blind, halt, creep, cry out for thee;
   But they ne'er meet with Opportunity.

'The patient dies while the physician sleeps;
The orphan pines while the oppressor feeds;   905
Justice is feasting while the widow weeps;

Advice is sporting while infection breeds;
Thou grant'st no time for charitable deeds;
  Wrath, envy, treason, rape, and murder's rages,
910 Thy heinous hours wait on them as their pages.

'When Truth and Virtue have to do with thee,
A thousand crosses keep them from thy aid;
They buy thy help, but Sin ne'er gives a fee;
He gratis comes, and thou art well appaid
915 As well to hear as grant what he hath said.
  My Collatine would else have come to me
  When Tarquin did, but he was stayed by thee.

'Guilty thou art of murder and of theft,
Guilty of perjury and subornation,
920 Guilty of treason, forgery and shift,
Guilty of incest, that abomination;
An accessary by thine inclination
  To all sins past and all that are to come,
  From the creation to the general doom.

925 'Misshapen Time, copesmate of ugly Night,
Swift subtle post, carrier of grisly care,
Eater of youth, false slave to false delight,
Base watch of woes, sin's pack-horse, virtue's snare;
Thou nursest all and murd'rest all that are.
930 O, hear me then, injurious, shifting Time!
  Be guilty of my death, since of my crime.

'Why hath thy servant Opportunity
Betrayed the hours thou gavest me to repose,
Cancelled my fortunes and enchainéd me
935 To endless date of never-ending woes?
  Time's office is to fine the hate of foes,
    To eat up errors by opinion bred,
    Not spend the dowry of a lawful bed.

'Time's glory is to calm contending kings,
To unmask falsehood and bring truth to light,   940
To stamp the seal of time in agéd things,
To wake the morn and sentinel the night,
To wrong the wronger till he render right,
　　To ruinate proud buildings with thy hours
　　And smear with dust their glitt'ring golden towers; 945

'To fill with worm-holes stately monuments,
To feed oblivion with decay of things,
To blot old books and alter their contents,
To pluck the quills from ancient ravens' wings,
To dry the old oak's sap and cherish springs,   950
　　To spoil antiquities of hammered steel
　　And turn the giddy round of Fortune's wheel;

'To show the beldam daughters of her daughter,
To make the child a man, the man a child,
To slay the tiger that doth live by slaughter,   955
To tame the unicorn and lion wild,
To mock the subtle in themselves beguiled,
　　To cheer the ploughman with increaseful crops,
　　And waste huge stones with little water-drops.

'Why work'st thou mischief in thy pilgrimage,   960
Unless thou couldst return to make amends?
One poor retiring minute in an age
Would purchase thee a thousand thousand friends,
Lending him wit that to bad debtors lends.
　　O, this dread night, wouldst thou one hour come back, 965
　　I could prevent this storm and shun thy wrack!

'Thou ceaseless lackey to eternity,
With some mischance cross Tarquin in his flight;
Devise extremes beyond extremity,

970 To make him curse this curséd crimeful night;
Let ghastly shadows his lewd eyes affright,
  And the dire thought of his committed evil
  Shape every bush a hideous shapeless devil.

'Disturb his hours of rest with restless trances,
975 Afflict him in his bed with bedrid groans;
Let there bechance him pitiful mischances,
To make him moan, but pity not his moans.
Stone him with hard'ned hearts, harder than stones;
  And let mild women to him lose their mildness,
980   Wilder to him than tigers in their wildness.

'Let him have time to tear his curléd hair,
Let him have time against himself to rave,
Let him have time of time's help to despair,
Let him have time to live a loathéd slave,
985 Let him have time a beggar's orts to crave,
  And time to see one that by alms doth live
  Disdain to him disdainéd scraps to give.

'Let him have time to see his friends his foes,
And merry fools to mock at him resort;
990 Let him have time to mark how slow time goes
In time of sorrow, and how swift and short
His time of folly and his time of sport;
  And ever let his unrecalling crime
  Have time to wail th'abusing of his time.

995 'O Time, thou tutor both to good and bad,
Teach me to curse him that thou taught'st this ill!
At his own shadow let the thief run mad,
Himself himself seek every hour to kill!
Such wretched hands such wretched blood should spill;
1000   For who so base would such an office have
  As sland'rous deathsman to so base a slave?

'The baser is he, coming from a king,
To shame his hope with deeds degenerate.
The mightier man, the mightier is the thing
That makes him honoured or begets him hate;   1005
For greatest scandal waits on greatest state.
    The moon being clouded presently is missed,
    But little stars may hide them when they list.

'The crow may bathe his coal-black wings in mire
And unperceived fly with the filth away;   1010
But if the like the snow-white swan desire,
The stain upon his silver down will stay.
Poor grooms are sightless night, kings glorious day.
    Gnats are unnoted wheresoe'er they fly,
    But eagles gazed upon with every eye.   1015

'Out, idle words, servants to shallow fools!
Unprofitable sounds, weak arbitrators!
Busy yourselves in skill-contending schools;
Debate where leisure serves with dull debaters;
To trembling clients be you mediators.   1020
    For me, I force not argument a straw,
    Since that my case is past the help of law.

'In vain I rail at Opportunity,
At Time, at Tarquin, and uncheerful Night;
In vain I cavil with mine infamy,   1025
In vain I spurn at my confirmed despite:
This helpless smoke of words doth me no right.
    The remedy indeed to do me good
    Is to let forth my foul-defiléd blood.

'Poor hand, why quiver'st thou at this decree?   1030
Honour thyself to rid me of this shame;
For if I die, my honour lives in thee,

But if I live, thou livest in my defame.
Since thou couldst not defend thy loyal dame
1035   And wast afeard to scratch her wicked foe,
Kill both thyself and her for yielding so.'

This said, from her betumbled couch she starteth,
To find some desp'rate instrument of death.
But this no slaughterhouse no tool imparteth
1040 To make more vent for passage of her breath,
Which, thronging through her lips, so vanisheth
As smoke from Etna that in air consumes,
Or that which from dischargéd cannon fumes.

'In vain,' quoth she, 'I live, and seek in vain
1045 Some happy mean to end a hapless life.
I feared by Tarquin's falchion to be slain,
Yet for the selfsame purpose seek a knife;
But when I feared I was a loyal wife;
So am I now—O no, that cannot be;
1050   Of that true type hath Tarquin rifled me.

'O, that is gone for which I sought to live,
And therefore now I need not fear to die.
To clear this spot by death, at least I give
A badge of fame to slander's livery,
1055 A dying life to living infamy.
Poor helpless help, the treasure stol'n away,
To burn the guiltless casket where it lay!

'Well, well, dear Collatine, thou shalt not know
The stainéd taste of violated troth;
1060 I will not wrong thy true affection so,
To flatter thee with an infringéd oath;
This bastard graff shall never come to growth;
He shall not boast who did thy stock pollute
That thou art doting father of his fruit.

'Nor shall he smile at thee in secret thought,   1065
Nor laugh with his companions at thy state;
But thou shalt know thy int'rest was not bought
Basely with gold, but stol'n from forth thy gate.
For me, I am the mistress of my fate,
    And with my trespass never will dispense,   1070
    Till life to death acquit my forced offence.

'I will not poison thee with my attaint,
Nor fold my fault in cleanly-coined excuses;
My sable ground of sin I will not paint
To hide the truth of this false night's abuses.   1075
My tongue shall utter all; mine eyes, like sluices,
    As from a mountain-spring that feeds a dale,
    Shall gush pure streams to purge my impure tale.'

By this, lamenting Philomel had ended
The well-tuned warble of her nightly sorrow,   1080
And solemn night with slow sad gait descended
To ugly hell; when lo, the blushing morrow
Lends light to all fair eyes that light will borrow;
    But cloudy Lucrece shames herself to see,
    And therefore still in night would cloist'red be.   1085

Revealing day through every cranny spies,
And seems to point her out where she sits weeping;
To whom she sobbing speaks: 'O eye of eyes,
Why pry'st thou through my window? leave
    thy peeping;
Mock with thy tickling beams eyes that are sleeping;   1090
    Brand not my forehead with thy piercing light,
    For day hath nought to do what's done by night.'

Thus cavils she with every thing she sees.
True grief is fond and testy as a child,
Who wayward once, his mood with nought agrees.   1095

Old woes, not infant sorrows, bear them mild;
Continuance tames the one; the other wild,
 Like an unpractised swimmer plunging still
 With too much labour drowns for want of skill.

1100 So she, deep-drenchéd in a sea of care,
Holds disputation with each thing she views,
And to herself all sorrow doth compare;
No object but her passion's strength renews,
And as one shifts, another straight ensues.
1105 Sometime her grief is dumb and hath no words;
 Sometime 'tis mad and too much talk affords.

The little birds that tune their morning's joy
Make her moans mad with their sweet melody;
"For mirth doth search the bottom of annoy;
1110 "Sad souls are slain in merry company;
"Grief best is pleased with grief's society.
 True sorrow then is feelingly sufficed
 When with like semblance it is sympathized.

"'Tis double death to drown in ken of shore;
1115 "He ten times pines that pines beholding food;
"To see the salve doth make the wound ache more;
"Great grief grieves most at that would do it good;
"Deep woes roll forward like a gentle flood,
 Who, being stopped, the bounding banks o'erflows;
1120 Grief dallied with nor law nor limit knows.

'You mocking birds,' quoth she, 'your tunes entomb
Within your hollow-swelling featheréd breasts,
And in my hearing be you mute and dumb.
My restless discord loves no stops nor rests;
1125 "A woeful hostess brooks not merry guests.
 Relish your nimble notes to pleasing ears;
 "Distress likes dumps when time is kept with tears.

'Come, Philomel, that sing'st of ravishment,
Make thy sad grove in my dishevelled hair.
As the dank earth weeps at thy languishment,   1130
So I at each sad strain will strain a tear,
And with deep groans the diapason bear;
    For burden-wise I'll hum on Tarquin still,
    While thou on Tereus descants better skill.

'And whiles against a thorn thou bear'st thy part   1135
To keep thy sharp woes waking, wretched I,
To imitate thee well, against my heart
Will fix a sharp knife to affright mine eye;
Who, if it wink, shall thereon fall and die.
    These means, as frets upon an instrument,   1140
    Shall tune our heart-strings to true languishment.

'And for, poor bird, thou sing'st not in the day,
As shaming any eye should thee behold,
Some dark deep desert, seated from the way,
That knows not parching heat nor freezing cold,   1145
Will we find out; and there we will unfold
    To creatures stern sad tunes, to change their kinds.
    Since men prove beasts, let beasts bear gentle minds.'

As the poor frighted deer, that stands at gaze,
Wildly determining which way to fly,   1150
Or one encompassed with a winding maze
That cannot tread the way out readily;
So with herself is she in mutiny,
    To live or die which of the twain were better,
    When life is shamed and death reproach's debtor.   1155

'To kill myself,' quoth she, 'alack, what were it,
But with my body my poor soul's pollution?
They that lose half with greater patience bear it

Than they whose whole is swallowed in confusion.
1160 That mother tries a merciless conclusion
    Who, having two sweet babes, when death takes one,
    Will slay the other and be nurse to none.

'My body or my soul, which was the dearer,
When the one pure, the other made divine?
1165 Whose love of either to myself was nearer,
When both were kept for heaven and Collatine?
Ay me! the bark pilled from the lofty pine,
    His leaves will wither and his sap decay;
    So must my soul, her bark being pilled away.

1170 'Her house is sacked, her quiet interrupted,
Her mansion battered by the enemy;
Her sacred temple spotted, spoiled, corrupted,
Grossly engirt with daring infamy;
Then let it not be called impiety
1175   If in this blemished fort I make some hole
    Through which I may convey this troubled soul.

'Yet die I will not till my Collatine
Have heard the cause of my untimely death,
That he may vow, in that sad hour of mine,
1180 Revenge on him that made me stop my breath.
My stainéd blood to Tarquin I'll bequeath,
    Which by him tainted shall for him be spent,
    And as his due writ in my testament.

'My honour I'll bequeath unto the knife
1185 That wounds my body so dishonouréd.
'Tis honour to deprive dishonoured life;
The one will live, the other being dead.
So of shame's ashes shall my fame be bred;
    For in my death I murder shameful scorn.
1190   My shame so dead, mine honour is new born.

'Dear lord of that dear jewel I have lost,
What legacy shall I bequeath to thee?
My resolution, love, shall be thy boast,
By whose example thou revenged mayst be.
How Tarquin must be used, read it in me: 1195
    Myself, thy friend, will kill myself, thy foe,
    And, for my sake, serve thou false Tarquin so.

'This brief abridgement of my will I make:
My soul and body to the skies and ground;
My resolution, husband, do thou take;   1200
Mine honour be the knife's that makes my wound;
My shame be his that did my fame confound;
    And all my fame that lives disbursèd be
    To those that live and think no shame of me.

'Thou, Collatine, shalt oversee this will;   1205
How was I overseen that thou shalt see it!
My blood shall wash the slander of mine ill;
My life's foul deed, my life's fair end shall free it.
Faint not, faint heart, but stoutly say "So be it".
    Yield to my hand; my hand shall conquer thee;   1210
    Thou dead, both die and both shall victors be.'

This plot of death when sadly she had laid,
And wiped the brinish pearl from her bright eyes,
With untuned tongue she hoarsely calls her maid,
Whose swift obedience to her mistress hies;   1215
"For fleet-winged duty with thought's feathers flies.
    Poor Lucrece' cheeks unto her maid seem so
    As winter meads when sun doth melt their snow.

Her mistress she doth give demure good-morrow
With soft slow tongue, true mark of modesty,   1220
And sorts a sad look to her lady's sorrow,

For why her face wore sorrow's livery,
But durst not ask of her audaciously
   Why her two suns were cloud-eclipséd so,
1225   Nor why her fair cheeks over-washed with woe.

But as the earth doth weep, the sun being set,
Each flower moist'ned like a melting eye,
Even so the maid with swelling drops 'gan wet
Her circled eyne, enforced by sympathy
1230 Of those fair suns set in her mistress' sky,
   Who in a salt-waved ocean quench their light,
   Which makes the maid weep like the dewy night.

A pretty while these pretty creatures stand,
Like ivory conduits coral cisterns filling.
1235 One justly weeps; the other takes in hand
No cause but company of her drops spilling:
   Their gentle sex to weep are often willing,
     Grieving themselves to guess at others' smarts,
     And then they drown their eyes or break their hearts.

1240 For men have marble, women waxen, minds,
And therefore are they formed as marble will;
The weak oppressed, th'impression of strange kinds
Is formed in them by force, by fraud, or skill.
Then call them not the authors of their ill,
1245   No more than wax shall be accounted evil
   Wherein is stamped the semblance of a devil.

Their smoothness, like a goodly champaign plain,
Lays open all the little worms that creep;
In men, as in a rough-grown grove, remain
1250 Cave-keeping evils that obscurely sleep.
   Through crystal walls each little mote will peep.
     Though men can cover crimes with bold stern looks,
     Poor women's faces are their own faults' books.

No man inveigh against the witheréd flower,
But chide rough winter that the flower hath killed.   1255
Not that devoured, but that which doth devour,
Is worthy blame. O, let it not be hild
Poor women's faults that they are so fulfilled
    With men's abuses: those proud lords to blame
    Make weak-made women tenants to their shame.   1260

The precedent whereof in Lucrece view,
Assailed by night with circumstances strong
Of present death, and shame that might ensue
By that her death, to do her husband wrong.
Such danger to resistance did belong,   1265
    That dying fear through all her body spread;
    And who cannot abuse a body dead?

By this, mild patience bid fair Lucrece speak
To the poor counterfeit of her complaining.
'My girl,' quoth she, 'on what occasion break   1270
Those tears from thee that down thy cheeks are raining?
If thou dost weep for grief of my sustaining,
    Know, gentle wench, it small avails my mood;
    If tears could help, mine own would do me good.

'But tell me, girl, when went'—and there she stayed   1275
Till after a deep groan—'Tarquin from hence?'
'Madam, ere I was up,' replied the maid,
'The more to blame my sluggard negligence.
Yet with the fault I thus far can dispense:
    Myself was stirring ere the break of day,   1280
    And ere I rose was Tarquin gone away.

'But, lady, if your maid may be so bold,
She would request to know your heaviness.'
'O, peace!' quoth Lucrece: 'if it should be told,

1285 The repetition cannot make it less,
For more it is than I can well express;
And that deep torture may be called a hell
When more is felt than one hath power to tell.

'Go, get me hither paper, ink and pen;
1290 Yet save that labour, for I have them here.
What should I say? One of my husband's men
Bid thou be ready by and by to bear
A letter to my lord, my love, my dear.
Bid him with speed prepare to carry it;
1295 The cause craves haste and it will soon be writ.'

Her maid is gone, and she prepares to write,
First hovering o'er the paper with her quill.
Conceit and grief an eager combat fight;
What wit sets down is blotted straight with will;
1300 This is too curious-good, this blunt and ill:
Much like a press of people at a door,
Throng her inventions, which shall go before.

At last she thus begins: 'Thou worthy lord
Of that unworthy wife that greeteth thee,
1305 Health to thy person! next vouchsafe t'afford—
If ever, love, thy Lucrece thou wilt see—
Some present speed to come and visit me.
So I commend me, from our house in grief;
My woes are tedious, though my words are brief.'

1310 Here folds she up the tenor of her woe,
Her certain sorrow writ uncertainly.
By this short schedule Collatine may know
Her grief, but not her grief's true quality;
She dares not thereof make discovery,
1315 Lest he should hold it her own gross abuse,
Ere she with blood had stained her stained excuse.

Besides, the life and feeling of her passion
She hoards, to spend when he is by to hear her,
When sighs and groans and tears may grace the fashion
Of her disgrace, the better so to clear her   1320
From that suspicion which the world might bear her.
    To shun this blot, she would not blot the letter
    With words, till action might become them better.

To see sad sights moves more than hear them told;
For then the eye interprets to the ear   1325
The heavy motion that it doth behold,
When every part a part of woe doth bear.
'Tis but a part of sorrow that we hear:
    Deep sounds make lesser noise than shallow fords,
    And sorrow ebbs, being blown with wind of words. 1330

Her letter now is sealed and on it writ
'At Ardea to my lord with more than haste.'
The post attends, and she delivers it,
Charging the sour-faced groom to hie as fast
As lagging fowls before the northern blast.   1335
    Speed more than speed but dull and slow she deems:
    Extremity still urgeth such extremes.

The homely villain curtsies to her low,
And blushing on her, with a steadfast eye
Receives the scroll without or yea or no,   1340
And forth with bashful innocence doth hie.
But they whose guilt within their bosoms lie
    Imagine every eye beholds their blame;
    For Lucrece thought he blushed to see her shame:

When, silly groom, God wot, it was defect   1345
Of spirit, life and bold audacity.

To talk in deeds, while others saucily
Promise more speed but do it leisurely.
1350 Even so this pattern of the worn-out age
Pawned honest looks, but laid no words to gage.

His kindled duty kindled her mistrust,
That two red fires in both their faces blazéd;
She thought he blushed, as knowing Tarquin's lust,
1355 And blushing with him, wistly on him gazéd;
Her earnest eye did make him more amazéd;
The more she saw the blood his cheeks replenish,
The more she thought he spied in her some blemish.

But long she thinks till he return again,
1360 And yet the duteous vassal scarce is gone.
The weary time she cannot entertain,
For now 'tis stale to sigh, to weep and groan;
So woe hath wearied woe, moan tiréd moan,
That she her plaints a little while doth stay,
1365 Pausing for means to mourn some newer way.

At last she calls to mind where hangs a piece
Of skilful painting, made for Priam's Troy,
Before the which is drawn the power of Greece,
For Helen's rape the city to destroy,
1370 Threat'ning cloud-kissing Ilion with annoy;
Which the conceited painter drew so proud
As heaven, it seemed, to kiss the turrets bowed.

A thousand lamentable objects there,
In scorn of nature, art gave lifeless life:
1375 Many a dry drop seemed a weeping tear,
Shed for the slaught'red husband by the wife;
The red blood reeked, to show the painter's strife;
And dying eyes gleamed forth their ashy lights,
Like dying coals burnt out in tedious nights.

There might you see the labouring pioneer   1380
Begrimed with sweat and smearéd all with dust;
And from the towers of Troy there would appear
The very eyes of men through loop-holes thrust,
Gazing upon the Greeks with little lust.
    Such sweet observance in this work was had   1385
    That one might see those far-off eyes look sad.

In great commanders grace and majesty
You might behold, triumphing in their faces;
In youth, quick bearing and dexterity;
And here and there the painter interlaces   1390
Pale cowards marching on with trembling paces,
    Which heartless peasants did so well resemble
    That one would swear he saw them quake
      and tremble.

In Ajax and Ulysses, O what art
Of physiognomy might one behold!   1395
The face of either ciphered either's heart;
Their face their manners most expressly told:
In Ajax' eyes blunt rage and rigour rolled;
    But the mild glance that sly Ulysses lent
    Showed deep regard and smiling government.   1400

There pleading might you see grave Nestor stand,
As 'twere encouraging the Greeks to fight,
Making such sober action with his hand
That it beguiled attention, charmed the sight.
In speech, it seemed, his beard all silver white   1405
    Wagged up and down, and from his lips did fly
    Thin winding breath which purled up to the sky.

About him were a press of gaping faces,
Which seemed to swallow up his sound advice,
All jointly list'ning, but with several graces,   1410

As if some mermaid did their ears entice,
Some high, some low, the painter was so nice;
   The scalps of many, almost hid behind,
    To jump up higher seemed, to mock the mind.

1415 Here one man's hand leaned on another's head,
His nose being shadowéd by his neighbour's ear;
Here one being thronged bears back, all boll'n and red;
Another smothered seems to pelt and swear;
And in their rage such signs of rage they bear
1420   As, but for loss of Nestor's golden words,
    It seemed they would debate with angry swords.

For much imaginary work was there;
Conceit deceitful, so compact, so kind,
That for Achilles' image stood his spear
1425 Griped in an arméd hand; himself behind
Was left unseen, save to the eye of mind:
   A hand, a foot, a face, a leg, a head,
    Stood for the whole to be imaginéd.

And from the walls of strong-besiegéd Troy
1430 When their brave hope, bold Hector, marched to field,
Stood many Trojan mothers sharing joy
To see their youthful sons bright weapons wield;
And to their hope they such odd action yield
   That through their light joy seeméd to appear,
1435   Like bright things stained, a kind of heavy fear.

And from the strand of Dardan where they fought
To Simois' reedy banks the red blood ran,
Whose waves to imitate the battle sought
With swelling ridges; and their ranks began
1440 To break upon the galléd shore, and than
   Retire again, till meeting greater ranks
    They join and shoot their foam at Simois' banks.

To this well-painted piece is Lucrece come,
To find a face where all distress is stelled.
Many she sees where cares have carvéd some,   1445
But none where all distress and dolour dwelled,
Till she despairing Hecuba beheld,
    Staring on Priam's wounds with her old eyes,
    Which bleeding under Pyrrhus' proud foot lies.

In her the painter had anatomized   1450
Time's ruin, beauty's wrack, and grim care's reign;
Her cheeks with chaps and wrinkles were disguised;
Of what she was no semblance did remain;
Her blue blood changed to black in every vein,
    Wanting the spring that those shrunk pipes had fed, 1455
    Showed life imprisoned in a body dead.

On this sad shadow Lucrece spends her eyes,
And shapes her sorrow to the beldam's woes,
Who nothing wants to answer her but cries,
And bitter words to ban her cruel foes: 1460
The painter was no god to lend her those;
    And therefore Lucrece swears he did her wrong,
    To give her so much grief and not a tongue.

'Poor instrument', quoth she, 'without a sound,
I'll tune thy woes with my lamenting tongue,   1465
And drop sweet balm in Priam's painted wound,
And rail on Pyrrhus that hath done him wrong,
And with my tears quench Troy that burns so long,
    And with my knife scratch out the angry eyes
    Of all the Greeks that are thine enemies.   1470

'Show me the strumpet that began this stir,
That with my nails her beauty I may tear.
Thy heat of lust, fond Paris, did incur

This load of wrath that burning Troy doth bear.
1475 Thy eye kindled the fire that burneth here;
    And here in Troy, for trespass of thine eye,
    The sire, the son, the dame and daughter die.

'Why should the private pleasure of some one
Become the public plague of many moe?
1480 Let sin, alone committed, light alone
Upon his head that hath transgresséd so;
Let guiltless souls be freed from guilty woe.
    For one's offence why should so many fall,
    To plague a private sin in general?

1485 'Lo, here weeps Hecuba, here Priam dies,
Here manly Hector faints, here Troilus swounds,
Here friend by friend in bloody channel lies,
And friend to friend gives unadviséd wounds,
And one man's lust these many lives confounds.
1490   Had doting Priam checked his son's desire,
    Troy had been bright with fame and not with fire.'

Here feelingly she weeps Troy's painted woes;
For sorrow, like a heavy-hanging bell
Once set on ringing, with his own weight goes;
1495 Then little strength rings out the dolefull knell;
So Lucrece, set a-work, sad tales doth tell
    To pencilled pensiveness and coloured sorrow;
    She lends them words, and she their looks
        doth borrow.

She throws her eyes about the painting round,
1500 And who she finds forlorn she doth lament.
At last she sees a wretched image bound
That piteous looks to Phrygian shepherds lent;
His face, though full of cares, yet showed content;
    Onward to Troy with the blunt swains he goes,
1505   So mild that Patience seemed to scorn his woes.

In him the painter laboured with his skill
To hide deceit and give the harmless show
An humble gait, calm looks, eyes wailing still,
A brow unbent that seemed to welcome woe;
Cheeks neither red nor pale, but mingled so   1510
   That blushing red no guilty instance gave,
   Nor ashy pale the fear that false hearts have.

But, like a constant and confirméd devil,
He entertained a show so seeming just,
And therein so ensconced his secret evil,   1515
That jealousy itself could not mistrust
False creeping craft and perjury should thrust
   Into so bright a day such black-faced storms,
   Or blot with hell-born sin such saint-like forms.

The well-skilled workman this mild image drew   1520
For perjured Sinon, whose enchanting story
The credulous old Priam after slew;
Whose words, like wildfire, burnt the shining glory
Of rich-built Ilion, that the skies were sorry,
   And little stars shot from their fixéd places,   1525
   When their glass fell wherein they viewed their faces.

This picture she advisedly perused,
And chid the painter for his wondrous skill,
Saying, some shape in Sinon's was abused;
So fair a form lodged not a mind so ill;   1530
And still on him she gazed, and gazing still
   Such signs of truth in his plain face she spied
   That she concludes the picture was belied.

'It cannot be', quoth she, 'that so much guile'—
She would have said 'can lurk in such a look';   1535
But Tarquin's shape came in her mind the while,

And from her tongue 'can lurk' from 'cannot' took;
'It cannot be' she in that sense forsook,
   And turned it thus, 'It cannot be, I find,
1540 But such a face should bear a wicked mind;

'For even as subtle Sinon here is painted,
So sober-sad, so weary and so mild,
As if with grief or travail he had fainted,
To me came Tarquin arméd to beguild
1545 With outward honesty, but yet defiled
   With inward vice. As Priam him did cherish,
   So did I Tarquin; so my Troy did perish.

'Look, look, how list'ning Priam wets his eyes,
To see those borrowéd tears that Sinon sheds.
1550 Priam, why art thou old and yet not wise?
For every tear he falls a Trojan bleeds;
His eye drops fire, no water thence proceeds;
   Those round clear pearls of his that move thy pity
   Are balls of quenchless fire to burn thy city.

1555 'Such devils steal effects from lightless hell;
For Sinon in his fire doth quake with cold,
And in that cold hot-burning fire doth dwell;
These contraries such unity do hold
Only to flatter fools and make them bold;
1560   So Priam's trust false Sinon's tears doth flatter
   That he finds means to burn his Troy with water.'

Here, all enraged, such passion her assails,
That patience is quite beaten from her breast.
She tears the senseless Sinon with her nails,
1565 Comparing him to that unhappy guest
Whose deed hath made herself herself detest.
   At last she smilingly with this gives o'er:
   'Fool, fool!' quoth she, 'his wounds will not be sore.'

Thus ebbs and flows the current of her sorrow,
And time doth weary time with her complaining.   1570
She looks for night, and then she longs for morrow,
And both she thinks too long with her remaining.
Short time seems long in sorrow's sharp sustaining;
 Though woe be heavy, yet it seldom sleeps,
  And they that watch see time how slow it creeps.   1575

Which all this time hath overslipped her thought
That she with painted images hath spent,
Being from the feeling of her own grief brought
By deep surmise of others' detriment,
Losing her woes in shows of discontent.   1580
 It easeth some, though none it ever curéd,
  To think their dolour others have enduréd.

But now the mindful messenger come back
Brings home his lord and other company;
Who finds his Lucrece clad in mourning black,   1585
And round about her tear-distainéd eye
Blue circles streamed, like rainbows in the sky.
 These water-galls in her dim element
  Foretell new storms to those already spent.

Which when her sad-beholding husband saw,   1590
Amazedly in her sad face he stares:
Her eyes, though sod in tears, looked red and raw,
Her lively colour killed with deadly cares.
He hath no power to ask her how she fares;
 Both stood, like old acquaintance in a trance,   1595
  Met far from home, wond'ring each other's chance.

At last he takes her by the bloodless hand,
And thus begins: 'What uncouth ill event
Hath thee befall'n, that thou dost trembling stand?

1600 Sweet love, what spite hath thy fair colour spent?
    Why art thou thus attired in discontent?
        Unmask, dear dear, this moody heaviness,
        And tell thy grief, that we may give redress.'

    Three times with sighs she gives her sorrow fire
1605 Ere once she can discharge one word of woe;
    At length addressed to answer his desire,
    She modestly prepares to let them know
    Her honour is ta'en prisoner by the foe;
        While Collatine and his consorted lords
1610   With sad attention long to hear her words.

    And now this pale swan in her wat'ry nest
    Begins the sad dirge of her certain ending.
    'Few words', quoth she, 'shall fit the trespass best,
    Where no excuse can give the fault amending:
1615 In me moe woes than words are now depending;
        And my laments would be drawn out too long,
        To tell them all with one poor tiréd tongue.

    'Then be this all the task it hath to say:
    Dear husband, in the interest of thy bed
1620 A stranger came, and on that pillow lay
    Where thou wast wont to rest thy weary head;
    And what wrong else may be imaginéd
        By foul enforcement might be done to me,
        From that, alas, thy Lucrece is not free.

1625 'For in the dreadful dead of dark midnight,
    With shining falchion in my chamber came
    A creeping creature with a flaming light,
    And softly cried "Awake, thou Roman dame,
    And entertain my love; else lasting shame
1630   On thee and thine this night I will inflict,
        If thou my love's desire do contradict.

'"For some hard-favoured groom of thine," quoth he,
"Unless thou yoke thy liking to my will,
I'll murder straight, and then I'll slaughter thee,
And swear I found you where you did fulfil   1635
The loathsome act of lust, and so did kill
    The lechers in their deed: this act will be
    My fame, and thy perpetual infamy."

'With this, I did begin to start and cry,
And then against my heart he set his sword,   1640
Swearing, unless I took all patiently,
I should not live to speak another word;
So should my shame still rest upon record,
    And never be forgot in mighty Rome
    Th'adulterate death of Lucrece and her groom.   1645

'Mine enemy was strong, my poor self weak,
And far the weaker with so strong a fear.
My bloody judge forbade my tongue to speak;
No rightful plea might plead for justice there.
His scarlet lust came evidence to swear   1650
    That my poor beauty had purloined his eyes,
    And when the judge is robbed, the prisoner dies.

'O, teach me how to make mine own excuse!
Or, at the least, this refuge let me find:
Though my gross blood be stained with this abuse,   1655
Immaculate and spotless is my mind;
That was not forced; that never was inclined
    To accessary yieldings, but still pure
    Doth in her poisoned closet yet endure.'

Lo, here, the hopeless merchant of this loss,   1660
With head declined, and voice dammed up with woe,
With sad-set eyes and wreathéd arms across,

From lips new waxen pale begins to blow
The grief away that stops his answer so;
1665   But, wretched as he is, he strives in vain;
What he breathes out his breath drinks up again.

As through an arch the violent roaring tide
Outruns the eye that doth behold his haste,
Yet in the eddy boundeth in his pride
1670 Back to the strait that forced him on so fast,
In rage sent out, recalled in rage, being past;
Even so his sighs, his sorrows, make a saw,
To push grief on and back the same grief draw.

Which speechless woe of his poor she attendeth
1675 And his untimely frenzy thus awaketh:
'Dear lord, thy sorrow to my sorrow lendeth
Another power; no flood by raining slaketh.
My woe too sensible thy passion maketh
More feeling-painful. Let it then suffice
1680   To drown one woe, one pair of weeping eyes.

'And for my sake, when I might charm thee so,
For she that was thy Lucrece, now attend me:
Be suddenly revengéd on my foe,
Thine, mine, his own; suppose thou dost defend me
1685 From what is past. The help that thou shalt lend me
Comes all too late, yet let the traitor die;
"For sparing justice feeds iniquity.

'But ere I name him, you fair lords', quoth she,
Speaking to those that came with Collatine,
1690 'Shall plight your honourable faiths to me,
With swift pursuit to venge this wrong of mine;
For 'tis a meritorious fair design
To chase injustice with revengeful arms:
Knights, by their oaths, should right poor
ladies' harms.'

At this request, with noble disposition   1695
Each present lord began to promise aid,
As bound in knighthood to her imposition,
Longing to hear the hateful foe bewrayed.
But she, that yet her sad task hath not said,
 The protestation stops. 'O, speak,' quoth she,   1700
 'How may this forcéd stain be wiped from me?

'What is the quality of my offence,
Being constrained with dreadful circumstance?
May my pure mind with the foul act dispense,
My low-declinéd honour to advance?   1705
May any terms acquit me from this chance?
 The poisonéd fountain clears itself again;
 And why not I from this compelléd stain?'

With this, they all at once began to say,
Her body's stain her mind untainted clears;   1710
While with a joyless smile she turns away
The face, that map which deep impression bears
Of hard misfortune, carved in it with tears.
 'No, no,' quoth she, 'no dame hereafter living
 By my excuse shall claim excuse's giving.'   1715

Here with a sigh, as if her heart would break,
She throws forth Tarquin's name: 'He, he,' she says,
But more than 'he' her poor tongue could not speak;
Till after many accents and delays,
Untimely breathings, sick and short assays,   1720
 She utters this: 'He, he, fair lords, 'tis he,
 That guides this hand to give this wound to me.'

Even here she sheathéd in her harmless breast
A harmful knife, that thence her soul unsheathéd:
That blow did bail it from the deep unrest   1725

Of that polluted prison where it breathéd.
Her contrite sighs unto the clouds bequeathéd
    Her wingéd sprite and through her wounds doth fly
    Life's lasting date from cancelled destiny.

1730 Stone-still, astonished with this deadly deed,
Stood Collatine and all his lordly crew;
Till Lucrece' father, that beholds her bleed,
Himself on her self-slaught'red body threw;
And from the purple fountain Brutus drew
1735   The murd'rous knife, and, as it left the place,
    Her blood, in poor revenge, held it in chase;

And bubbling from her breast, it doth divide
In two slow rivers, that the crimson blood
Circles her body in on every side,
1740 Who like a late-sacked island vastly stood
Bare and unpeopled in this fearful flood.
    Some of her blood still pure and red remained,
    And some looked black, and that false
        Tarquin stained.

About the mourning and congealéd face
1745 Of that black blood a wat'ry rigol goes,
Which seems to weep upon the tainted place;
And ever since, as pitying Lucrece' woes,
Corrupted blood some watery token shows;
    And blood untainted still doth red abide,
1750   Blushing at that which is so putrified.

'Daughter, dear daughter,' old Lucretius cries,
'That life was mine which thou hast here deprivéd.
If in the child the father's image lies,
Where shall I live now Lucrece is unlivéd?
1755 Thou wast not to this end from me derivéd.
    If children predecease progenitors,
    We are their offspring, and they none of ours.

'Poor broken glass, I often did behold
In thy sweet semblance my old age new born;   1760
But now that fair fresh mirror, dim and old,
Shows me a bare-boned death by time outworn;
O, from thy cheeks my image thou hast torn,
  And shivered all the beauty of my glass,
  That I no more can see what once I was.

'O time, cease thou thy course and last no longer,   1765
If they surcease to be that should survive.
Shall rotten death make conquest of the stronger,
And leave the falt'ring feeble souls alive?
The old bees die, the young possess their hive.
  Then live, sweet Lucrece, live again, and see   1770
  Thy father die, and not thy father thee.'

By this, starts Collatine as from a dream,
And bids Lucretius give his sorrow place;
And then in key-cold Lucrece' bleeding stream
He falls, and bathes the pale fear in his face,   1775
And counterfeits to die with her a space;
  Till manly shame bids him possess his breath,
  And live to be revengéd on her death.

The deep vexation of his inward soul
Hath served a dumb arrest upon his tongue;   1780
Who, mad that sorrow should his use control
Or keep him from heart-easing words so long,
Begins to talk; but through his lips do throng
  Weak words, so thick come in his poor heart's aid
  That no man could distinguish what he said.   1785

Yet sometime 'Tarquin' was pronouncéd plain,
But through his teeth, as if the name he tore.
This windy tempest, till it blow up rain,

Held back his sorrow's tide, to make it more;
1790 At last it rains, and busy winds give o'er;
    Then son and father weep with equal strife
    Who should weep most, for daughter or for
       wife.

The one doth call her his, the other his,
Yet neither may possess the claim they lay.
1795 The father says 'She's mine'. 'O, mine she is,'
Replies her husband: 'do not take away
My sorrow's interest; let no mourner say
    He weeps for her, for she was only mine,
    And only must be wailed by Collatine.'

1800 'O,' quoth Lucretius, 'I did give that life
Which she too early and too late hath spilled.'
'Woe, woe,' quoth Collatine, 'she was my wife;
I owed her, and 'tis mine that she hath killed.'
'My daughter' and 'my wife' with clamours filled
1805   The dispersed air, who, holding Lucrece' life,
    Answered their cries, 'my daughter' and 'my
       wife'.

Brutus, who plucked the knife from Lucrece' side,
Seeing such emulation in their woe,
Began to clothe his wit in state and pride,
1810 Burying in Lucrece' wound his folly's show.
He with the Romans was esteeméd so
    As silly jeering idiots are with kings,
    For sportive words and utt'ring foolish things.

But now he throws that shallow habit by
1815 Wherein deep policy did him disguise,
And armed his long-hid wits advisedly
To check the tears in Collatinus' eyes.
'Thou wrongéd lord of Rome,' quoth he, 'arise;

Let my unsounded self, supposed a fool,
Now set thy long-experienced wit to school.   1820

'Why, Collatine, is woe the cure for woe?
Do wounds help wounds, or grief help grievous
    deeds?
Is it revenge to give thyself a blow
For his foul act by whom thy fair wife bleeds?
Such childish humour from weak minds proceeds.   1825
    Thy wretched wife mistook the matter so
    To slay herself, that should have slain her foe.

'Courageous Roman, do not steep thy heart
In such relenting dew of lamentations,
But kneel with me and help to bear thy part   1830
To rouse our Roman gods with invocations
That they will suffer these abominations,
    Since Rome herself in them doth stand disgracéd,
    By our strong arms from forth her fair streets chaséd.

'Now by the Capitol that we adore,   1835
And by this chaste blood so unjustly stainéd,
By heaven's fair sun that breeds the fat earth's store,
By all our country rights in Rome maintainéd,
And by chaste Lucrece' soul that late complainéd
    Her wrongs to us, and by this bloody knife,   1840
    We will revenge the death of this true wife.'

This said, he struck his hand upon his breast,
And kissed the fatal knife to end his vow,
And to his protestation urged the rest,
Who, wond'ring at him, did his words allow;   1845
Then jointly to the ground their knees they bow,
    And that deep vow which Brutus made before
    He doth again repeat, and that they swore.

When they had sworn to this advisèd doom,.
1850 They did conclude to bear dead Lucrece thence,
To show her bleeding body thorough Rome,
And so to publish Tarquin's foul offence;
Which being done with speedy diligence,
　　The Romans plausibly did give consent
1855　To Tarquin's everlasting banishment.

THE PASSIONATE
PILGRIM

THE PASSIONATE PILGRIM

1

WHEN my love swears that she is made of truth,
I do believe her, though I know she lies,
That she might think me some untutored youth,
Unskilful in the world's false forgeries.
Thus vainly thinking that she thinks me young, 5
Although I know my years be past the best,
I smiling credit her false-speaking tongue,
Outfacing faults in love with love's ill rest.
But wherefore says my love that she is young?
And wherefore say not I that I am old? 10
O, love's best habit's in a soothing tongue,
And age in love loves not to have years told.
   Therefore I'll lie with love, and love with me,
   Since that our faults in love thus smothered be.

2

Two loves I have, of comfort and despair,
That like two spirits do suggest me still;
My better angel is a man right fair,
My worser spirit a woman coloured ill.
To win me soon to hell, my female evil 5
Tempteth my better angel from my side,
And would corrupt my saint to be a devil,
Wooing his purity with her fair pride.
And whether that my angel be turned fiend,
Suspect I may, yet not directly tell; 10

For being both to me, both to each friend,
I guess one angel in another's hell.
 The truth I shall not know, but live in doubt,
 Till my bad angel fire my good one out.

3

Did not the heavenly rhetoric of thine eye,
'Gainst whom the world could not hold argument,
Persuade my heart to this false perjury?
Vows for thee broke deserve not punishment.
5 A woman I forswore; but I will prove,
Thou being a goddess, I forswore not thee:
My vow was earthly, thou a heavenly love;
Thy grace being gained cures all disgrace in me.
My vow was breath, and breath a vapour is;
10 Then, thou fair sun, that on this earth doth shine,
Exhal'st this vapour vow; in thee it is:
If broken, then it is no fault of mine.
 If by me broke, what fool is not so wise
 To break an oath, to win a paradise?

4

Sweet Cytherea, sitting by a brook
With young Adonis, lovely, fresh and green,
Did court the lad with many a lovely look,
Such looks as none could look but beauty's queen.
5 She told him stories to delight his ear;
She showed him favours to allure his eye;
To win his heart, she touched him here and there;
Touches so soft still conquer chastity.
But whether unripe years did want conceit,
10 Or he refused to take her figuréd proffer,

The tender nibbler would not touch the bait,
But smile and jest at every gentle offer:
  Then fell she on her back, fair queen, and toward:
  He rose and ran away; ah, fool too froward.

5

If love make me forsworn, how shall I swear to love?
O never faith could hold, if not to beauty vowéd:
Though to myself forsworn, to thee I'll constant prove;
Those thoughts, to me like oaks, to thee like
     osiers bowéd.
Study his bias leaves, and makes his book thine eyes,   5
Where all those pleasures live that art can comprehend.
If knowledge be the mark, to know thee shall suffice;
Well learnéd is that tongue that well can thee commend:
All ignorant that soul that sees thee without wonder;
Which is to me some praise, that I thy parts admire.   10
Thine eye Jove's lightning seems, thy voice his
     dreadful thunder,
Which, not to anger bent, is music and sweet fire.
  Celestial as thou art, O do not love that wrong,
  To sing heaven's praise with such an earthly tongue.

6

Scarce had the sun dried up the dewy morn,
And scarce the herd gone to the hedge for shade,
When Cytherea, all in love forlorn,
A longing tarriance for Adonis made
Under an osier growing by a brook,   5
A brook where Adon used to cool his spleen.
Hot was the day; she hotter that did look
For his approach, that often there had been.

Anon he comes, and throws his mantle by,
10 And stood stark naked on the brook's green brim:
The sun looked on the world with glorious eye,
Yet not so wistly as this queen on him.
    He, spying her, bounced in whereas he stood;
    'O Jove,' quoth she, 'why was not I a flood!'

7

Fair is my love, but not so fair as fickle;
Mild as a dove, but neither true nor trusty;
Brighter than glass, and yet, as glass is, brittle;
Softer than wax, and yet as iron rusty;
5   A lily pale, with damask dye to grace her;
    None fairer, nor none falser to deface her.

Her lips to mine how often hath she joinéd,
Between each kiss her oaths of true love swearing!
How many tales to please me hath she coinéd,
10 Dreading my love, the loss thereof still fearing!
    Yet in the midst of all her pure protestings,
    Her faith, her oaths, her tears, and all were jestings.

She burned with love, as straw with fire flameth;
She burned out love, as soon as straw out-burneth;
15 She framed the love, and yet she foiled the framing;
She bade love last, and yet she fell a-turning.
    Was this a lover, or a lecher whether?
    Bad in the best, though excellent in neither.

8

If music and sweet poetry agree,
As they must needs, the sister and the brother,
Then must the love be great 'twixt thee and me,
Because thou lov'st the one and I the other.

Dowland to thee is dear, whose heavenly touch   5
Upon the lute doth ravish human sense;
Spenser to me, whose deep conceit is such
As passing all conceit needs no defence.
Thou lov'st to hear the sweet melodious sound
That Phoebus' lute, the queen of music, makes;   10
And I in deep delight am chiefly drowned
When as himself to singing he betakes.
   One god is god of both, as poets feign;
   One knight loves both, and both in thee remain.

9

Fair was the morn, when the fair queen of love,

  .   .   .   .

Paler for sorrow than her milk-white dove,
For Adon's sake, a youngster proud and wild,
Her stand she takes upon a steep-up hill,   5
Anon Adonis comes with horn and hounds;
She, silly queen, with more than love's good will,
Forbade the boy he should not pass those grounds.
'Once', quoth she, 'did I see a fair sweet youth
Here in these brakes deep-wounded with a boar,   10
Deep in the thigh, a spectacle of ruth!
See, in my thigh,' quoth she, 'here was the sore.'
   She showéd hers; he saw more wounds than one,
   And blushing fled, and left her all alone.

10

Sweet rose, fair flower, untimely plucked, soon vaded,
Plucked in the bud and vaded in the spring!
Bright orient pearl, alack, too timely shaded!
Fair creature, killed too soon by death's sharp sting!

5   Like a green plum that hangs upon a tree,
     And falls through wind before the fall should be.

I weep for thee and yet no cause I have;
For why thou left'st me nothing in thy will.
And yet thou left'st me more than I did crave,
10 For why I cravéd nothing of thee still:
     O yes, dear friend, I pardon crave of thee,
     Thy discontent thou didst bequeath to me.

11

Venus with young Adonis sitting by her
Under a myrtle shade began to woo him;
She told the youngling how god Mars did try her,
And as he fell to her, so fell she to him.
5 'Even thus', quoth she, 'the warlike god embraced me',
And then she clipped Adonis in her arms;
'Even thus', quoth she, 'the warlike god unlaced me',
As if the boy should use like loving charms;
'Even thus', quoth she, 'he seizéd on my lips',
10 And with her lips on his did act the seizure;
And as she fetchéd breath, away he skips,
And would not take her meaning nor her pleasure.
     Ah, that I had my lady at this bay,
     To kiss and clip me till I run away!

12

Crabbéd age and youth cannot live together:
Youth is full of pleasance, age is full of care;
Youth like summer morn, age like winter weather;
Youth like summer brave, age like winter bare.
5 Youth is full of sport, age's breath is short;
     Youth is nimble, age is lame;

Youth is hot and bold, age is weak and cold;
  Youth is wild and age is tame.
Age, I do abhor thee; youth, I do adore thee;
  O, my love, my love is young!   10
Age, I do defy thee. O, sweet shepherd, hie thee,
  For methinks thou stays too long.

13

Beauty is but a vain and doubtful good,
A shining gloss that vadeth suddenly,
A flower that dies when first it 'gins to bud,
A brittle glass that's broken presently;
  A doubtful good, a gloss, a glass, a flower,   5
  Lost, vaded, broken, dead within an hour.

And as goods lost are seld or never found,
As vaded gloss no rubbing will refresh,
As flowers dead lie witheréd on the ground,
As broken glass no cement can redress: 10
  So beauty blemished once, for ever lost,
  In spite of physic, painting, pain and cost.

14

Good night, good rest: ah, neither be my share;
She bade good night that kept my rest away;
And daffed me to a cabin hanged with care,
To descant on the doubts of my decay.
  'Farewell,' quoth she, 'and come again to-morrow';   5
  Fare well I could not, for I supped with sorrow.

Yet at my parting sweetly did she smile,
In scorn or friendship nill I conster whether;

'T may be, she joyed to jest at my exile,
10 'T may be, again to make me wander thither:
　　'Wander', a word for shadows like myself,
　　As take the pain, but cannot pluck the pelf.

Lord, how mine eyes throw gazes to the east!
My heart doth charge the watch; the morning rise
15 Doth cite each moving sense from idle rest,
Not daring trust the office of mine eyes.
　　While Philomela sings, I sit and mark,
　　And wish her lays were tunéd like the lark.

For she doth welcome daylight with her ditty,
20 And drives away dark dreaming night:
The night so packed, I post unto my pretty;
Heart hath his hope and eyes their wishéd sight;
　　Sorrow changed to solace and solace mixed
　　　　with sorrow;
　　For why, she sighed, and bade me come to-morrow.

25 Were I with her, the night would post too soon,
But now are minutes added to the hours;
To spite me now, each minute seems a moon;
Yet not for me, shine sun to succour flowers!
　　Pack night, peep day; good day, of night now borrow;
30　　Short night, to-night, and length thyself to-morrow.

15

It was a lording's daughter, the fairest one of three,
That likéd of her master as well as well might be,
Till looking on an Englishman, the fairest that eye
　　could see,
　　Her fancy fell a-turning.
Long was the combat doubtful that love with love
5　　did fight,

To leave the master loveless, or kill the gallant knight;
To put in practice either, alas, it was a spite
   Unto the silly damsel!
But one must be refuséd; more mickle was the pain
That nothing could be uséd to turn them both to gain, 10
For of the two the trusty knight was wounded
    with disdain:
  Alas, she could not help it!
Thus art with arms contending was victor of the day,
Which by a gift of learning did bear the maid away:
Then, lullaby, the learnéd man hath got the lady gay; 15
  For now my song is ended.

16

On a day, alack the day!
Love, whose month was ever May,
Spied a blossom passing fair,
Playing in the wanton air.
Through the velvet leaves the wind   5
All unseen 'gan passage find,
That the lover, sick to death,
Wished himself the heaven's breath,
'Air', quoth he, 'thy cheeks may blow;
Air, would I might triumph so!   10
But, alas! my hand hath sworn
Ne'er to pluck thee from thy thorn;
Vow, alack! for youth unmeet,
Youth, so apt to pluck a sweet.
Thou for whom Jove would swear   15
Juno but an Ethiope were;
And deny himself for Jove,
Turning mortal for thy love.'

17

My flocks feed not, my ewes breed not,
My rams speed not, all is amiss;
Love is dying, faith's defying,
Heart's denying, causer of this.
5　All my merry jigs are quite forgot,
All my lady's love is lost, God wot;
Where her faith was firmly fixed in love,
There a nay is placed without remove.
　　One silly cross wrought all my loss;
10　　O frowning Fortune, cursèd fickle dame!
　　For now I see inconstancy
　　More in women than in men remain.

In black mourn I, all fears scorn I,
Love hath forlorn me, living in thrall:
15 Heart is bleeding, all help needing,
O cruel speeding, fraughted with gall.
My shepherd's pipe can sound no deal;
My wether's bell rings doleful knell;
My curtal dog that wont to have played,
20 Plays not at all, but seems afraid;
　　My sighs so deep procures to weep,
　　In howling wise, to see my doleful plight.
　　How sighs resound through heartless ground,
　　Like a thousand vanquished men in bloody fight!

25 Clear wells spring not, sweet birds sing not,
Green plants bring not forth their dye;
Herds stand weeping, flocks all sleeping,
Nymphs back peeping fearfully.
All our pleasure known to us poor swains,
30 All our merry meetings on the plains,

All our evening sport from us is fled,
All our love is lost, for Love is dead.
    Farewell, sweet lass, thy like ne'er was
    For a sweet content, the cause of all my moan:
    Poor Corydon must live alone;   35
    Other help for him I see that there is none.

18

When as thine eye hath chose the dame,
And stalled the deer that thou shouldst strike,
Let reason rule things worthy blame,
As well as fancy, partial might;
    Take counsel of some wiser head,   5
    Neither too young nor yet unwed.

And when thou com'st thy tale to tell,
Smooth not thy tongue with filéd talk,
Lest she some subtle practice smell—
A cripple soon can find a halt—   10
    But plainly say thou lov'st her well,
    And set thy person forth to sell.

And to her will frame all thy ways;
Spare not to spend, and chiefly there
Where thy desert may merit praise,   15
By ringing in thy lady's ear:
    The strongest castle, tower and town,
    The golden bullet beats it down.

Serve always with assuréd trust,
And in thy suit be humble true;   20
Unless thy lady prove unjust,
Press never thou to choose anew:
    When time shall serve, be thou not slack
    To proffer, though she put thee back.

25 What though her frowning brows be bent,
Her cloudy looks will calm ere night,
And then too late she will repent
That thus dissembled her delight;
 And twice desire, ere it be day,
30 That which with scorn she put away.

What though she strive to try her strength,
And ban and brawl, and say thee nay,
Her feeble force will yield at length,
When craft hath taught her thus to say:
35 'Had women been so strong as men,
 In faith, you had not had it then.'

The wiles and guiles that women work,
Dissembled with an outward show,
The tricks and toys that in them lurk,
40 The cock that treads them shall not know.
 Have you not heard it said full oft,
 A woman's nay doth stand for nought?

Think women still to strive with men,
To sin and never for to saint:
45 There is no heaven, by holy then,
When time with age shall them attaint.
 Were kisses all the joys in bed,
 One woman would another wed.

But, soft, enough, too much I fear,
50 Lest that my mistress hear my song;
She will not stick to round me on th'ear,
To teach my tongue to be so long,
 Yet will she blush, here be it said,
 To hear her secrets so bewrayed.

19

Live with me, and be my love,
And we will all the pleasures prove
That hills and valleys, dales and fields,
And all the craggy mountains yield.

There will we sit upon the rocks,   5
And see the shepherds feed their flocks,
By shallow rivers, by whose falls
Melodious birds sing madrigals.

There will I make thee a bed of roses,
With a thousand fragrant posies,   10
A cap of flowers, and a kirtle
Embroider'd all with leaves of myrtle.

A belt of straw and ivy buds,
With coral clasps and amber studs;
And if these pleasures may thee move,   15
Then live with me and be my love.

LOVE'S ANSWER

If that the world and love were young,
And truth in every shepherd's tongue,
These pretty pleasures might me move
To live with thee and be thy love.   20

20

As it fell upon a day
In the merry month of May,
Sitting in a pleasant shade
Which a grove of myrtles made,
Beasts did leap and birds did sing,   5
Trees did grow and plants did spring;

Every thing did banish moan,
Save the nightingale alone:
She, poor bird, as all forlorn,
10 Leaned her breast up-till a thorn,
And there sung the dolefull'st ditty,
That to hear it was great pity:
'Fie, fie, fie', now would she cry;
'Tereu, Tereu!' by and by;
15 That to hear her so complain,
Scarce I could from tears refrain;
For her griefs so lively shown
Made me think upon mine own.
Ah, thought I, thou mourn'st in vain!
20 None takes pity on thy pain:
Senseless trees they cannot hear thee;
Ruthless beasts they will not cheer thee:
King Pandion he is dead;
All thy friends are lapped in lead;
25 All thy fellow birds do sing,
Careless of thy sorrowing.
Whilst as fickle Fortune smiled,
Thou and I were both beguiled.
    Every one that flatters thee
30 Is no friend in misery.
Words are easy, like the wind;
Faithful friends are hard to find:
Every man will be thy friend
Whilst thou hast wherewith to spend;
35 But if store of crowns be scant,
No man will supply thy want.
If that one be prodigal,
Bountiful they will him call,
And with such-like flattering,
40 'Pity but he were a king';

If he be addict to vice,
Quickly him they will entice;
If to women he be bent,
They have at commandment.
But if Fortune once do frown,   45
Then farewell his great renown;
They that fawned on him before
Use his company no more.
He that is thy friend indeed,
He will help thee in thy need: 50
If thou sorrow, he will weep;
If thou wake, he cannot sleep;
Thus of every grief in heart
He with thee doth bear a part.
These are certain signs to know   55
Faithful friend from flatt'ring foe.

THE PHOENIX AND
THE TURTLE

THE PHOENIX AND
THE TURTLE

LET the bird of loudest lay,
On the sole Arabian tree,
Herald sad and trumpet be,
To whose sound chaste wings obey.

But thou shrieking harbinger,   **5**
Foul precurrer of the fiend,
Augur of the fever's end,   *i.e. life? (but also death info)*
To this troop come thou not near!

From this session interdict
Every fowl of tyrant wing,   **10**
Save the eagle, feath'red king:
Keep the obsequy so strict.

Let the priest in surplice white,
That defunctive music can,
Be the death-divining swan,   **15**
Lest the requiem lack his right.

And thou treble-dated crow,
That thy sable gender mak'st
With the breath thou giv'st and tak'st,
'Mongst our mourners shalt thou go.   **20**

Here the anthem doth commence:
Love and constancy is dead;
Phoenix and the turtle fled
In a mutual flame from hence.

25   So they loved, as love in twain
    Had the essence but in one;
    Two distincts, division none:
    Number there in love was slain.

    Hearts remote, yet not asunder;
30   Distance, and no space was seen
    'Twixt this turtle and his queen:
    But in them it were a wonder.

    So between them love did shine,
    That the turtle saw his right
35   Flaming in the phoenix' sight;
    Either was the other's mine.

    Property was thus appalléd,
    That the self was not the same;
    Single nature's double name
40   Neither two nor one was calléd.

    Reason, in itself confounded,
    Saw division grow together,
    To themselves yet either neither,
    Simple were so well compounded;

45   That it cried, How true a twain
    Seemeth this concordant one!
    Love hath reason, reason none,
    If what parts can so remain.

    Whereupon it made this threne
50   To the phoenix and the dove,
    Co-supremes and stars of love,
    As chorus to their tragic scene.

Threnos

Beauty, truth, and rarity,
Grace in all simplicity,
Here enclosed, in cinders lie.   55

Death is now the phoenix' nest;
And the turtle's loyal breast
To eternity doth rest.

Leaving no posterity,
'Twas not their infirmity,   60
It was married chastity.

Truth may seem, but cannot be;
Beauty brag, but 'tis not she;
Truth and beauty buried be.

To this urn let those repair   65
That are either true or fair;
For these dead birds sigh a prayer.

A LOVER'S COMPLAINT

A LOVER'S COMPLAINT

From off a hill whose concave womb reworded
A plaintful story from a sist'ring vale,
My spirits t'attend this double voice accorded,
And down I laid to list the sad-tuned tale,
Ere long espied a fickle maid full pale,   5
Tearing of papers, breaking rings atwain,
Storming her world with sorrow's wind and rain.

Upon her head a platted hive of straw,
Which fortified her visage from the sun,
Whereon the thought might think sometime it saw   10
The carcase of a beauty spent and done.
Time had not scythéd all that youth begun,
Nor youth all quit, but spite of heaven's fell rage
Some beauty peeped through lattice of seared age.

Oft did she heave her napkin to her eyne,   15
Which on it had conceited characters,
Laund'ring the silken figures in the brine
That seasonéd woe had pelleted in tears,
And often reading what contents it bears;
As often shrieking undistinguished woe,   20
In clamours of all size, both high and low.

Sometimes her levelled eyes their carriage ride,
As they did batt'ry to the spheres intend;
Sometime diverted their poor balls are tied
To th'orbéd earth; sometimes they do extend   25
Their view right on; anon their gazes lend
To every place at once, and nowhere fixed,
The mind and sight distractedly commixed.

Her hair, nor loose nor tied in formal plat,
30 Proclaimed in her a careless hand of pride;
For some, untucked, descended her sheaved hat,
Hanging her pale and pinéd cheek beside;
Some in her threaden fillet still did bide,
And, true to bondage, would not break from thence,
35 Though slackly braided in loose negligence.

A thousand favours from a maund she drew
Of amber, crystal, and of beaded jet,
Which one by one she in a river threw,
Upon whose weeping margent she was set;
40 Like usury applying wet to wet,
Or monarchs' hands that lets not bounty fall
Where want cries some, but where excess begs all.

Of folded schedules had she many a one,
Which she perused, sighed, tore, and gave the flood;
45 Cracked many a ring of posied gold and bone,
Bidding them find their sepulchres in mud;
Found yet moe letters sadly penned in blood,
With sleided silk feat and affectedly
Enswathed and sealed to curious secrecy.

50 These often bathed she in her fluxive eyes,
And often kissed, and often 'gan to tear;
Cried, 'O false blood, thou register of lies,
What unapprovéd witness dost thou bear!
Ink would have seemed more black and damnéd here!'
55 This said, in top of rage the lines she rents,
Big discontent so breaking their contents.

A reverend man that grazed his cattle nigh,
Sometime a blusterer that the ruffle knew

Of court, of city, and had let go by
The swiftest hours observéd as they flew,   60
Towards this afflicted fancy fastly drew;
And, privileged by age, desires to know
In brief the grounds and motives of her woe.

So slides he down upon his grainéd bat,
And comely distant sits he by her side;   65
When he again desires her, being sat,
Her grievance with his hearing to divide.
If that from him there may be aught applied
Which may her suffering ecstasy assuage,
'Tis promised in the charity of age.   70

'Father,' she says, 'though in me you behold
The injury of many a blasting hour,
Let it not tell your judgement I am old:
Not age, but sorrow, over me hath power.
I might as yet have been a spreading flower,   75
Fresh to myself, if I had self-applied
Love to myself, and to no love beside.

'But woe is me! too early I attended
A youthful suit—it was to gain my grace—
O, one by nature's outwards so commended   80
That maidens' eyes stuck over all his face.
Love lacked a dwelling and made him her place;
And when in his fair parts she did abide,
She was new lodged and newly deified.

'His browny locks did hang in crookéd curls;   85
And every light occasion of the wind
Upon his lips their silken parcels hurls.
What's sweet to do, to do will aptly find:
Each eye that saw him did enchant the mind;

90 For on his visage was in little drawn
What largeness thinks in Paradise was sawn.

'Small show of man was yet upon his chin;
His phoenix down began but to appear,
Like unshorn velvet, on that termless skin,
95 Whose bare out-bragged the web it seemed to wear;
Yet showed his visage by that cost more dear;
And nice affections wavering stood in doubt
If best were as it was, or best without.

'His qualities were beauteous as his form,
100 For maiden-tongued he was, and thereof free;
Yet if men moved him, was he such a storm
As oft 'twixt May and April is to see,
When winds breathe sweet, unruly though they be.
His rudeness so with his authorized youth
105 Did livery falseness in a pride of truth.

'Well could he ride, and often men would say,
"That horse his mettle from his rider takes:
Proud of subjection, noble by the sway,
What rounds, what bounds, what course, what stop
        he makes!"
110 And controversy hence a question takes,
Whether the horse by him became his deed,
Or he his manage by th'well-doing steed.

'But quickly on this side the verdict went:
His real habitude gave life and grace
115 To appertainings and to ornament,
Accomplished in himself, not in his case.
All aids, themselves made fairer by their place,
Came for additions; yet their purposed trim
Pieced not his grace, but were all graced by him.

'So on the tip of his subduing tongue   120
All kind of arguments and question deep,
All replication prompt, and reason strong,
For his advantage still did wake and sleep.
To make the weeper laugh, the laugher weep,
He had the dialect and different skill,   125
Catching all passions in his craft of will,

'That he did in the general bosom reign
Of young, of old, and sexes both enchanted,
To dwell with him in thoughts, or to remain
In personal duty, following where he haunted.   130
Consents bewitched, ere he desire, have granted,
And dialogued for him what he would say,
Asked their own wills, and made their wills obey.

'Many there were that did his picture get,
To serve their eyes, and in it put their mind;   135
Like fools that in th'imagination set
The goodly objects which abroad they find
Of lands and mansions, theirs in thought assigned;
And labouring in moe pleasures to bestow them
Than the true gouty landlord which doth owe them.   140

'So many have, that never touched his hand,
Sweetly supposed them mistress of his heart.
My woeful self, that did in freedom stand,
And was my own fee-simple, not in part,
What with his art in youth, and youth in art,   145
Threw my affections in his charméd power
Reserved-the stalk and gave him all my flower.

'Yet did I not, as some my equals did,
Demand of him, nor being desiréd yielded;

150 Finding myself in honour so forbid,
    With safest distance I mine honour shielded.
    Experience for me many bulwarks builded
    Of proofs new-bleeding, which remained the foil
    Of this false jewel, and his amorous spoil.

155 'But ah, who ever shunned by precedent
    The destined ill she must herself assay?
    Or forced examples, 'gainst her own content,
    To put the by-past perils in her way?
    Counsel may stop awhile what will not stay;
160 For when we rage, advice is often seen
    By blunting us to make our wills more keen.

    'Nor gives it satisfaction to our blood
    That we must curb it upon others' proof,
    To be forbod the sweets that seems so good
165 For fear of harms that preach in our behoof.
    O appetite, from judgment stand aloof!
    The one a palate hath that needs will taste,
    Though Reason weep, and cry it is thy last.

    'For further I could say this man's untrue,
170 And knew the patterns of his foul beguiling;
    Heard where his plants in others' orchards grew;
    Saw how deceits were gilded in his smiling;
    Knew vows were ever brokers to defiling;
    Thought characters and words merely but art,
175 And bastards of his foul adulterate heart.

    'And long upon these terms I held my city,
    Till thus he 'gan besiege me: "Gentle maid,
    Have of my suffering youth some feeling pity,
    And be not of my holy vows afraid.
180 That's to ye sworn to none was ever said;

For feasts of love I have been called unto,
Till now did ne'er invite nor never woo.

'"All my offences that abroad you see
Are errors of the blood, none of the mind;
Love made them not; with acture they may be,   18
Where neither party is nor true nor kind.
They sought their shame that so their shame did find;
And so much less of shame in me remains
By how much of me their reproach contains.

'"Among the many that mine eyes have seen,   19
Not one whose flame my heart so much as warméd,
Or my affection put to th'smallest teen,
Or any of my leisures ever charméd.
Harm have I done to them, but ne'er was harméd;
Kept hearts in liveries, but mine own was free,   195
And reigned commanding in his monarchy.

'"Look here what tributes wounded fancies sent me,
Of paléd pearls and rubies red as blood;
Figuring that they their passions likewise lent me
Of grief and blushes, aptly understood   200
In bloodless white and the encrimsoned mood—
Effects of terror and dear modesty,
Encamped in hearts, but fighting outwardly.

'"And, lo, behold these talents of their hair,
With twisted metal amorously empleached,   205
I have receiv'd from many a several fair,
Their kind acceptance weepingly beseeched,
With the annexions of fair gems enriched,
And deep-brained sonnets that did amplify
Each stone's dear nature, worth, and quality.   210

' "The diamond? why, 'twas beautiful and hard,
Whereto his invised properties did tend;
The deep-green em'rald, in whose fresh regard
Weak sights their sickly radiance do amend;
215 The heaven-hued sapphire and the opal blend
With objects manifold; each several stone,
With wit well blazoned, smiled, or made some moan.

' "Lo, all these trophies of affections hot,
Of pensived and subdued desires the tender,
220 Nature hath charged me that I hoard them not,
But yield them up where I myself must render—
That is, to you, my origin and ender;
For these, of force, must your oblations be,
Since I their altar, you enpatron me.

225 ' "O then advance of yours that phraseless hand
Whose white weighs down the airy scale of praise;
Take all these similes to your own command,
Hallowéd with sighs that burning lungs did raise;
What me your minister for you obeys
230 Works under you; and to your audit comes
Their distract parcels in combinéd sums.

' "Lo, this device was sent me from a nun,
Or sister sanctified, of holiest note,
Which late her noble suit in court did shun,
235 Whose rarest havings made the blossoms dote;
For she was sought by spirits of richest coat,
But kept cold distance, and did thence remove
To spend her living in eternal love.

' "But, O my sweet, what labour is't to leave
240 The thing we have not, mast'ring what not strives,

†Playing the place which did no form receive,
Playing patient sports in unconstrainéd gyves!
She that her fame so to herself contrives,
The scars of battle scapeth by the flight,
And makes her absence valiant, not her might.   245

'"O pardon me in that my boast is true!
The accident which brought me to her eye
Upon the moment did her force subdue,
And now she would the cagéd cloister fly.
Religious love put out religion's eye.   250
Not to be tempted, would she be immuréd,
And now to tempt all liberty procuréd.

'"How mighty then you are, O hear me tell!
The broken bosoms that to me belong
Have emptied all their fountains in my well,   255
And mine I pour your ocean all among.
I strong o'er them, and you o'er me being strong,
Must for your victory us all congest,
As compound love to physic your cold breast.

' "My parts had pow'r to charm a sacred nun,   260
Who, disciplined, ay, dieted in grace,
Believed her eyes when they t'assail begun,
All vows and consecrations giving place,
O most potential love, vow, bond, nor space,
In thee hath neither sting, knot, nor confine,   265
For thou art all, and all things else are thine.

'"When thou impressest, what are precepts worth
Of stale example? When thou wilt inflame,
How coldly those impediments stand forth,
Of wealth, of filial fear, law, kindred, fame!   270

Love's arms are peace, 'gainst rule, 'gainst sense,
  'gainst shame.
And sweetens, in the suff'ring pangs it bears,
The aloes of all forces, shocks and fears.

 ' "Now all these hearts that do on mine depend,
275 Feeling it break, with bleeding groans they pine,
And supplicant their sighs to you extend,
To leave the batt'ry that you make 'gainst mine,.
Lending soft audience to my sweet design,
And credent soul to that strong-bonded oath,
280 That shall prefer and undertake my troth."

 'This said, his wat'ry eyes he did dismount,
Whose sights till then were levelled on my face;
Each cheek a river running from a fount
With brinish current downward flowed apace.
285 O, how the channel to the stream gave grace!
Who glazed with crystal gate the glowing roses
That flame through water which their hue encloses.

 'O father, what a hell of witchcraft lies
In the small orb of one particular tear!
290 But with the inundation of the eyes
What rocky heart to water will not wear?
What breast so cold that is not warméd here?
O cleft effect! cold modesty, hot wrath,
Both fire from hence and chill extincture hath.

295 'For lo, his passion, but an art of craft,
Even there resolved my reason into tears;
There my white stole of chastity I daffed,
Shook off my sober guards and civil fears;
Appear to him as he to me appears,

All melting; though our drops this diff'rence bore: 300
His poisoned me, and mine did him restore.

'In him a plenitude of subtle matter,
Applied to cautels, all strange forms receives,
Of burning blushes or of weeping water,
Or swooning paleness; and he takes and leaves,   305
In either's aptness, as it best deceives,
To blush at speeches rank, to weep at woes,
Or to turn white and swoon at tragic shows;

'That not a heart which in his level came
Could scape the hail of his all-hurting aim,   310
Showing fair nature is both kind and tame;
And, veiled in them, did win whom he would maim.
Against the thing he sought he would exclaim;
When he most burned in heart-wished luxury,
He preached pure maid and praised cold chastity.   315

'Thus merely with the garment of a Grace
The naked and concealéd fiend he covered,
That th'unexperient gave the tempter place,
Which, like a cherubin, above them hovered.
Who, young and simple, would not be so lovered?   320
Ay me, I fell, and yet do question make
What I should do again for such a sake.

'O, that infected moisture of his eye,
O, that false fire which in his cheek so glowéd,
O, that forced thunder from his heart did fly,   325
O, that sad breath his spongy lungs bestowéd,
O, all that borrowéd motion, seeming owéd,
Would yet again betray the fore-betrayed,
And new pervert a reconciléd maid.'

THE COPY FOR
THE POEMS

Though some curious views about the printing of the two narrative poems have been held, and may be studied in H. E. Rollins's *New Variorum* edition (1938), pp. 369–74 and 406–8, little serious disagreement is now possible. Both poems were printed by Shakespeare's fellow-townsman Richard Field, and it is clear that this very competent printer took pains to produce an accurate text. The variations in spelling, contrary to what Sidney Lee supposed, are perfectly normal for the period, and the degree of normalization that Field habitually introduced can be studied by comparison of manuscript and printed texts of Harington's *Orlando Furioso* (1591), discussed by Sir Walter Greg in *The Library*, 4 ser. IV (1923–4), 102–18, who notes that Field's spelling is 'more consistently modern than that of most printers of the time' (p. 114).

It has been customary to talk of Shakespeare 'seeing' the poems 'through the press', and it is easy to believe that he took an interest in the progress of the first heir of his invention, and of its more ambitious successor. But to argue from the fewness of misprints to his having personally corrected the proofs is perhaps to exaggerate his probable proficiency in this specialized skill. For *Lucrece*, there is positive evidence against authorial proof-correction; see below. But whatever the reasons, the task of the textual editor is easier here than anywhere else in the corpus.

I. Venus and Adonis, 1593

The only text of any authority is the Quarto of 1593,
surviving in a single copy, of which the later Quartos
and Octavos are a mere series of reprints, with the usual
accumulating errors.[1] Its substantive errors are very
few, and mostly trivial—turned letters and the like.
There is, in my view, a certain error at l. 466, and at
l. 873 a misleading apostrophe which has caused most
editors to accept an unnecessary emendation from Q7.
At l. 1031, a slight emendation seems unavoidable, and
also at l. 1054, though here an authorial slip is possible.
There are occasional odd spellings, especially in eye-
rhymes,[2] and a few places where the punctuation is
misleading (e.g. l. 1003).

II. The Rape of Lucrece, 1594

Here again the only authority is the Quarto of 1594.
There are eleven known copies, two imperfect, and
there are a number of press-variants, of which only the
following involve substantive readings. In sig. B, the
corrected state (uncorrected in brackets) is as follows:
l. 50, Colatia...arriued (Colatium...ariued); ll. 125–
6, themselues betake...wake (himselfe betakes...
wakes). The most significant of these changes is that at
l. 50, where the form of the name in the uncorrected
state is to be preferred—it is that used in the Argument
and in l. 4—though the corrected gives the true Latin

[1] These are analysed for both poems by F. T. Prince in
the *Arden* edition (1960), pp. xiii–xx.

[2] Greg (*Library*, 4 ser. IV (1923–4)) notes a few reten-
tions by Field of eye-rhymes in Harington's manuscript
(p. 116), as well as one elimination, where 'sens', rhymed
with 'offence', is altered to the more orthodox 'since'
(p. 109).

form. The correction, it appears, was called for in the first instance by the anomalous spelling 'ariued', and a press-corrector with some classical knowledge took the opportunity to make the pedantic correction as well. By the same token, the correction at l. 31 was made because of the spelling of 'Appologie', and it is reasonable to assume that the addition of the 's' is an example of the introduction of a new error in correcting the first. Hence, with C. J. Sisson, *New Readings in Shakespeare* (1956), 1, 208, I retain the singular, and I also follow Sisson in supposing that at ll. 125–6 the corrected reading arises from 'a grammatical protest against *minds that wakes*, with consequent changes'. I am more hesitant about l. 24, but there too an adjectival 'morning' seems acceptable, in spite of the compound adjective following, while it would certainly have been exposed to tampering at the hands of the type of corrector postulated.

This interference seems to have been confined to sig. B. In sig. I, the corrected readings are to be accepted: l. 1182 by him (uncorr. 'for him', caught from the latter part of the line), and l. 1335 blast (blasts). Finally in sig. K, l. 1350, there is the single variant 'this patterne of the' | 'the patterne of this', the former being presumably the correction, and certainly the right reading.

Thus the proof-corrector has done rather more harm than good to the text of *Lucrece*, in so far as we can identify his work. The other errors, as in *Venus and Adonis*, are few and slight. I regard W. S. Walker's 'wreathed' for 'wretched' at l. 1662 as palmary. Beyond this, the only substantive errors seem to be 'it in' for 'in it' at l. 1713, and perhaps 'cherish' at l. 950, for which no convincing emendation has been produced.

III. The Passionate Pilgrim, ?1599

For *The Passionate Pilgrim*, a miscellaneous collection published (and no doubt named) by William Jaggard, there are, by the accidents of preservation, two authoritative texts: an imperfect Octavo, lacking title-page,[1] which is the substantive text for the poems it contains (1–5 and 16–18), and an Octavo of 1599, described on the title-page as 'By W. Shakespeare', which has been shown to be the later of the two,[2] which we must fall back on for the other poems. This second Octavo, surviving in two complete copies, plus the sheets of the made-up Folger copy, has trivial press-variants, all involving turned letters, at three places (18. 7, 28, 36). Apart from a couple of readings (1. 11; 17. 4), the most important contribution of the undated Octavo is the correct order of stanzas in 18. This edition is probably of 1599, and cannot be more than a year earlier, as 8 and 20[3] depend on Barnfield's *Poems: In diuers humors* (1598).

Both editions are carelessly printed, and the texts, where they can be checked, are inaccurate. The only real Shakespearian interest lies in the text of 1, where (in spite of weighty opinion to the contrary) it does seem that Jaggard had access to an earlier version of the sonnet than appears in the 1609 collection, and not just an inaccurate transcript (as, for instance, with 2 (probably), 3, 5 and 16). One peculiarity of the 1599 text is the insertion before 15 of a second title-page, also dated

[1] The unique copy, in the Folger library, is made up from sheets of the 1599 edition where the earlier edition is deficient.

[2] See the edition by J. Q. Adams (1939).

[3] These poems are not in the undated fragment, but there is no reason to doubt that they were present in the edition.

1599 but not repeating Shakespeare's name, describing the remaining poems as 'Sonnets To sundry notes of Musicke'.

IV. THE PHOENIX AND THE TURTLE, 1601

The only authority for this poem is Chester's *Love's Martyr* (1601), in which it appears on Z 3^v–4^v, with the name 'William Shake-speare' at the end. There are no textual difficulties, though editors have unnecessarily altered the punctuation at the end of ll. 58 and 59 (see notes).

V. A LOVER'S COMPLAINT, 1609

Like the *Sonnets* which precede it, *A Lover's Complaint* is less well printed than the two major narrative poems. There are a number of literals (see notes on ll. 28, 78, 192; and such odd forms as *mannad'g*, 112), and the punctuation is often misleading or clearly incorrect (see notes on ll. 7, 123–4, 126, 270, 287, 319–20; at other places, editorial alterations of anomalous punctuation have been silently accepted). I have agreed with almost all editors in finding substantive errors in ll. 51, 118, 182, 241, 251, 252, 260, and suspect the text also in ll. 61, 161, 212, 233. This is about as many errors as one would expect to find in the same number of lines of a reasonably good dramatic text.[1] There are some odd spellings and forms, some of which can be paralleled in other Shakespeare texts (see notes on ll. 14, 20, 37, 112, 197, 204, 228, 305–8). There is nothing to rule out a reasonably clear manuscript in Shakespeare's hand, if that is what we are inclined to believe in on other grounds.

[1] C. S. Lewis's 'corrupt in text' (*English Literature in the Sixteenth Century*, 1954, p. 502) is an unargued aside.

NOTES

All significant departures from the original editions are recorded, the source of the accepted reading being indicated in brackets. Square brackets about an author's name mean that he is responsible for the substance of the note that precedes; round brackets a verbatim quotation from him.

In *Venus and Adonis*, Q stands for the First Quarto, 1593; Qq 2–10 for the editions of 1594, 1595?, 1596, 1599 (twice), 1602?, 1602 (twice), 1617, Qq 3–10 being in fact Octavos.

In *The Rape of Lucrece*, Q stands for the First Quarto, 1594; Qq 2–6 for the editions of 1598, 1600 (twice), 1607, 1616, all in fact Octavos.

In *The Passionate Pilgrim*, O stands for the imperfect First Octavo, 1599?; O 2 for the Second Octavo (the first surviving complete edition), 1599; O 3 for the Third Octavo, 1612.

The only early edition of *The Phoenix and the Turtle* is in *Love's Martyr*, 1601.

In *A Lover's Complaint*, Q stands for the 1609 edition of the *Sonnets*.

G stands for Glossary; O.E.D. for the Oxford English Dictionary; Sh. for Shakespeare or Shakespearian. Common words are also usually abbreviated: e.g. sp.=spelling or spelt, prob.=probable or probably, om.=omitted, etc.

The following is a list of other works cited in abridged forms:

Abbott=*A Shakespearian Grammar*, by E. A. Abbott (3rd ed. 1870).

Adams=ed. of *The Passionate Pilgrim*, by J. Q. Adams, 1939.

Alvarez = 'Sh.'s *The Phoenix and the Turtle*', by A. Alvarez, in *Interpretations*, ed. J. Wain, 1955.

Anders = *Sh.'s Books*, by H. R. D. Anders, 1904.

Baldwin = *The Literary Genetics of Sh.'s Poems & Sonnets*, by T. W. Baldwin, 1950.

Baynes = 'What Sh. Learnt at School', by T. S. Baynes, in *Fraser's Magazine*, N.S. XXI, 1880.

Brown = ed. by Carleton Brown (*Tudor Sh.*), 1913.

Bullough = *Narrative and Dramatic Sources of Sh.*, by G. Bullough, vol. 1, 1957.

Bush[1] = 'Notes on Sh.'s Classical Mythology' by D. Bush, in *Philological Quarterly*, VI, 1927.

Bush[2] = *Mythology and the Renaissance Tradition in English Poetry*, by D. Bush, 1932.

Camb. = *The Cambridge Sh.*, 1866, 1893.

Collier[1] = ed. of Sh. by J. P. Collier, 1843.

Collier[2] = ed. of Sh. by J. P. Collier, 1858.

Craig = ed. by W. J. Craig, 1905.

Daniel = *Poems and A Defence of Ryme*, by S. Daniel, ed. A. C. Sprague, 1930.

Delius = ed. of Sh. by N. Delius (3rd ed. 1872).

Dürnhöfer = *Sh.'s Venus und Adonis im Verhältnis zu Ovids Metamorphosen und Constables Schäfergesang*, by M. Dürnhöfer, 1890.

Dyce = ed. of Sh. by A. Dyce, 1857.

E.L.H. = *ELH: A Journal of English Literary History*.

E.Studien = *Englische Studien*.

Ewig = 'Sh.'s Lucrece', by W. Ewig, in *Anglia*, XXII, 1899.

Fairchild = 'The Phoenix and the Turtle', by A. H. R. Fairchild, in *Englische Studien*, XXXIII, 1904.

Franz = *Die Sprache Shakespeares*, by W. Franz (4th ed. of *Shakespeare-Grammatik*), 1939.

Fripp = *Sh. Studies*, by E. I. Fripp, 1930.

Gardner = ed. of *The Phoenix and the Turtle* in *The Metaphysical Poets*, ed. H. Gardner, 1957.

Gildon¹=ed. by C. Gildon, 1710.

Gildon²=ed. by C. Gildon, 1714.

Globe=ed. of Sh. by W. G. Clark and W. A. Wright (*Globe*), 1864.

Googe=*The Zodiacke of Life*, by B. Googe (1565), ed. 1576 cited, from facsimile reprint, ed. R. Tuve, 1947.

Grant White=ed. of Sh. by R. G. White, 1865.

Hankins=*Sh.'s Derived Imagery*, by J. E. Hankins, 1953.

Herf.=ed. of Sh. by C. H. Herford (*Eversley Sh.*), 1899.

Honigmann=*The Stability of Sh.'s Text*, by E. A. J. Honigmann, 1965.

Hudson=ed. of Sh. by H. N. Hudson (*Harvard Ed.*), 1881.

J.E.G.P.=*Journal of English and Germanic Philology*.

Knight=ed. of Sh. by C. Knight, 1841.

Kökeritz=*Sh.'s Pronunciation*, by H. Kökeritz, 1953.

Lee=ed. of Sh. by S. Lee (*Renaissance Sh.*), 1907.

Lintott=ed. by B. Lintott, 1709, 1711.

Mal.¹=ed. by E. Malone in *Supplement to Ed. of Sh.'s Plays Published in 1778*, 1780.

Mal²=ed. of Sh. by E. Malone, 1790.

M L.R.=*Modern Language Review*.

MSH=*The Manuscript of Sh.'s 'Hamlet'*, by J. D. Wilson, 1934, 1963.

Muir='"A Lover's Complaint": A Reconsideration', by K. Muir, in *Shakespeare 1564–1964: A Collection of Modern Essays by Various Hands*, ed. by E. A. Bloom, 1964.

Nashe=*Works of Thomas Nashe*, ed. by R. B. McKerrow, 1904–10.

N. & Q.=*Notes and Queries*.

O.D.E.P.=*Oxford Dictionary of English Proverbs* (2nd ed. 1948).

On.=*A Sh. Glossary*, by C. T. Onions, 1911 (last corrected impression, 1946).

Painter=*The Palace of Pleasure*, by W. Painter, ed. by J. Jacobs, 1890.

Parrott='Sh.'s Revision of *Titus Andronicus*', by T. M. Parrott, in *M.L.R.* xiv, 1919.

Pool.=ed. by C. K. Pooler (*Arden Sh.*), 1911.

Porter=ed. by C. Porter (*First Folio Sh.*), 1912.

P.Q.=Philological Quarterly.

Prince=ed. by F. T. Prince (*Arden Sh.*), 1960.

R.E.S.=Review of English Studies.

Roll.=ed. by H. E. Rollins (*New Variorum*), 1938.

Root=*Classical Mythology in Sh.*, by R. K. Root, 1903.

Sarrazin=*Sh.'s Lehrjahre*, by G. Sarrazin, 1897.

Schmidt=*Sh.-Lexicon*, by A. Schmidt (3rd ed. 1902).

Sewell[1]=ed. by G. Sewell, 1725.

Sewell[2]=ed. by G. Sewell, 1728.

Sh.Jb.=Jahrbuch der Deutschen Sh.-Gesellschaft, later *Shakespeare Jahrbuch*.

Sh.Q.=Shakespeare Quarterly.

S.P.=Studies in Philology.

Staunton=ed. by H. Staunton [1860].

Steev.=notes by G. Steevens in Mal.[1]

Tilley=*A Dictionary of the Proverbs in England in the Sixteenth and Seventeenth Centuries*, by M. P. Tilley, 1950.

Var.=Variorum ed. of Sh., ed. by J. Boswell, 1821.

Verity=ed. by A. W. Verity (*Henry Irving Sh.*), 1890.

Wynd.=ed. by G. Wyndham, 1898.

Yale=ed. by A. Feuillerat (*Yale Sh.*), 1927.

The above list does not contain a number of names occasionally cited from the Cambridge Shakespeare critical apparatus, or from Rollins's *New Variorum* edition.

Note on Compound Words

These poems are unusually rich in compounds, especially compound epithets. As it is of very little interest to record who first introduced a hyphen, I have omitted all such material from the notes, and simply give a list here of all the passages where the present text has a hyphen not found in the original. The exceptional cases where the original has a single word instead of two are recorded.

Venus and Adonis: ll. 6, 14, 76, 86 (one word), 110, 133 (wrinkled-old), 177 (one word), 236, 271, 290, 295 (twice), 324 (out stripping...ouerfly), 328 (one word), 354, 366, 432 (twice), 448, 548 (one word), 678, 818, 825, 844 (twice), 858, 920 (one word), 931, 985, 1151 (twice), 1178.

The Rape of Lucrece: ll. 19, 24, 41, 48, 84, 101, 140, 175 (one word), 179 (one word), 188, 231 (one word), 247, 360, 372, 446, 452, 482, 537, 540, 638, 786, 789 (one word), 799, 846, 858, 874, 928 (one word), 959, 1009 (one word), 1018, 1029, 1073, 1077, 1100, 1122, 1224, 1231, 1250, 1300, 1386, 1429, 1443, 1493, 1496, 1518 (one word), 1542, 1557, 1588 (one word), 1590, 1662, 1679, 1705, 1730, 1740, 1816, 1820.

The Passionate Pilgrim: 1. 7; 7. 14, 16; 9. 3, 5, 10; 15. 4.

The Phoenix and the Turtle: l. 17.

A Lover's Complaint: ll. 4, 76, 100, 112, 144, 153, 209, 213, 215, 279, 310.

VENUS AND ADONIS

Epigraph. Ovid, *Amores*, I. xv. 35–6.

1–4. *Even...scorn* Prince notes that the sun as lover (instead of Tithonus) is Sh.'s modification; so in ll. 855–6. Sarrazin, *E.Studien*, XIX (1894), 353–4, compared *3 H.VI*, 2. 2. 21–2; see n. in this ed., quoting Spenser, *F.Q.* I. v. 2 as source, and Baldwin, pp. 4–7. R. K. Root, *J.E.G.P.* IV (1902), 459, traces the idea as far back as Chaucer, *Troilus*, III, 1464–7, and suggests a confusion of the names *Titan* (used there by Chaucer) and *Tithonus*.

1. *purple-coloured* For 'purple' in relation to the dawn, Pool. cites Spenser, *F.Q.* I. ii. 7, I. iv. 16; so 'purpureus' in the Latin poets.

3. *Rose-cheeked Adonis* So Marlowe, *Hero and Leander*, I, 93 [Mal.²]. It is uncertain which poem is the earlier.

7. *Thrice fairer...began* Venus's opening speech s modelled on that of Salmacis to Hermaphroditus in Ovid, *Met.* IV, 320 ff. [Baldwin, pp. 10–11].

9. *Stain* See G. So Marina 'did distain' Philoten (*Per.* 4. 3. 31) [Herf.].

11–12. *Nature...life* It is difficult to render the sense in modern punctuation; 'with...strife' describes the conditions of the making—'striving to surpass herself' [Pool.]—and the meaning is virtually 'Nature that was in strife with herself when she made thee'. Most edd. (< Q 7) put a comma after 'thee' as well as after 'strife'. Pool. follows Q in putting one only after 'strife'. It seems clearer to cut out both.

16–18. *A...kisses* For parallels in Googe, pp. 30, 42–4, see Hankins, pp. 238–40.

19. *satiety* Q 'societie', as often.

20. *famish...plenty* Cf. *Ant.* 2. 2. 235–8 [Mal.¹].

25. *sweating palm* Sign of an amorous disposition in

l. 143, and in *Ant.* 1. 2. 51 ('oily') [Steev.], and *Oth.* 3. 4. 38 ff. [Mal.²]; 'here merely a sign of youthful vigor' (Brown), but surely Sh. means that it is natural for Venus to interpret it in the light of her wishes.

26. *precedent* Q 'president', as usual in Sh.

30. *Courageously* See G. In view of 'courage', in l. 276, this sense, suggested by Roll., is plausible, but not certain.

42. *lust* See G.

46–8. *And...open* Cf. *Ado*, 2. 1. 290–1, 'stop his mouth with a kiss'.

47. *kissing...broken* Cf. Ovid, *Met.* x. 559 'Sic ait, ac mediis interserit oscula verbis' [Root]. Here Golding would not have helped: 'She thus began: and in her tale shee bussed him among'.

47–8. *broken...open* Imperfect rhymes also in ll. 137–8, 434–6, 451–3, 565–7.

54. *murders* Q 'murthers', so in 906, *Lucr.* 766, 885, 909, 918, 929, 1189, 1634.

55. *empty eagle* Also in *2 H.VI*, 3. 1. 248, *3 H.VI*, 1. 1. 268, *Edw.III*, 3. 1. 88 [Verity].

61. *content* See G.; less naturally taken by some edd. as sb.

66. *distilling* 'falling gently like dew' (Kittredge *ap.* Roll.).

67. *Look how* See G.

69. *awed resistance* 'the fact that he feared to resist' (Pool.).

70. *bred...eyes* Cf. *Tw.N.* 3. 1. 147–8, 'O, what a deal of scorn looks beautiful | In the contempt and anger of his lip!' [Mal.²].

72. *Perforce...force* Cf. the compound adv. 'force perforce', as in *2 H.VI*, 1. 1. 256; *K.J.* 3. 1. 142 [Prince].

73–5. *entreats...frets* For rhyme, cf. ll. 91–3, 277–9, 449–50, 635–6, and Kökeritz, pp. 201–2.

84. *countless* Q 'comptlesse'.

89. *his pay* 'what he is to pay her' (Prince).

90. *winks* Word-play on the very rare O.E.D. *wink²*=wince [Wynd., Prince] is unlikely. For a poss. link with Donne's *Extasie*, see K. Gustav Cross, *M.L.N.* LXXI (1956), 480–2.

91–3 *heat...get* Cf. ll. 73–5 n.

92. *good turn* The noun is common in erotic connexions: cf. *Tit.* 2. 1. 96, *Ant.* 2. 5. 59.

109. *he* Cf. *Lucr.* 1682, Abbott, §207.

110. *Leading...chain* W. *ap.* Mal.² cited Ronsard (*Œuvres* (1914–19), II, 360), 'Les Muses lierent vn iour | De chaisnes de Roses, Amour'; cf. Bush¹, p. 300; Prince doubts if there is a precise 'debt'.

118. *What...ground?* 'What is there in what you are looking at (the ground) that is worth your attention?' (Kittredge *ap.* Roll.).

131–2. *Fair...time* For this omnipresent conceit, Wynd. cited Ovid *A.A.* II. 115–16.

133–6. *Were...juice* For this catalogue, cf. *Err.* 4. 2. 19–22 [Sarrazin, p. 114].

135. *rheumatic* Stressed on first syllable also in *M.N.D.* 2. 1. 105 [Grant White].

136. *juice* Kökeritz, p. 217, notes that Butler (1634) and Hodges (1643) treat 'juice' and 'joice' as homonyms.

140. *grey* Regarded as attractive also in *Rom.* 2. 4. 42, *Gent.* 4. 4. 190; Mal.² refers to his note (*ap.* Var. VI, 100) on the *Rom.* passage.

143. *moist hand* See l. 25 n.   *with* by.

145–7. *ear...hair* (Q 'eare...heare') For [ɛ:] pronunciation in *ear*, see Kökeritz, p. 209.

149–50. *Love...aspire* For the sequence 'Love', 'sink', 'light', cf. *Err.* 3. 2. 52, where Mal. cited this passage.

156. *should* Already changed to 'shouldst' in Q 2, but cf. *2 H.VI*, 5. 1. 21, and Franz, §152.

158. *seize love upon* win love by seizing.

160. *on* Used after 'complain' also in l. 544, and *Shr.* 4. 1. 27, and after 'exclaim' in *Lucr.* 741.

161–2. *Narcissus...brook* Not in the Ovidian story (*Met.* III, 370–510), in which he was turned into a flower, but in Lydgate, *Reson and Sensuallyte* (*E.E.T.S.* (1901)), ll. 3847 ff., 4258 ff., Warner, *Albion's England*, IX, 46 [Bush¹, p. 297]. R. K. Root, *J.E.G.P.* IV (1902), 454–5, notes that Marlowe, *Hero and Leander*, I, 74–6, follows this version, as does Sh. in *Lucr.* 265–6. As an immediate source for the *Lucr.* lines, he proposed John Clapham's Latin poem *Narcissus* (1591), dedicated to the Earl of Southampton.

166. *to themselves* only for their own sakes; cf. l. 1180 and *Son.* 94. 10, 'Though to it self, it only live and die' [Mal.¹].

168. *it* The rhetoric of the line suggests that this is a (redundant) subject of 'is' rather than object of 'get', meaning 'beauty'. The sentiment, as often noted, is that of the *Sonnets*, esp. 13. Pool. notes also Sidney, *Arcadia*, Bk. III (*Works*, ed. Feuillerat, II. 80): 'The father justly may of thee complaine, | If thou doo not repay his deeds for thee, | In granting unto him a grandsires gaine'. See also Hankins, pp. 233–5, quoting Googe, pp. 72–3.

177. *Titan* See G.; for the history of the identification, see W. Kranz, *Philologus*, CV (1961), 290–5. *tiréd* Almost certainly 'weary', rather than, as Boswell thought, for 'attired'.

185. *Souring* Q 'So wring'; a mere error of spacing.   *Souring his cheeks* See G. 'sour'; cf. *R.II*, 2. 1. 169, 'made me sour my patient cheek' [Delius].

186. *face;* (Mal.¹) Q 'face' Q 2 'face,'.

187. *young...unkind* Cf. *Lr.* 1. 1. 105, 'So young, and so untender'. [Steev.].   *unkind!* (Q 7) Q 'vnkinde,'.

188. *bare* lit. 'threadbare', hence fig. 'shamelessly inadequate' (Pool.).   *gone!* (Q 7) Q 'gon?'.

199. *obdurate, flinty* So also *3 H.VI*, 1. 4. 142 [Sarrazin, *E.Studien*, xix (1894), 354]; 'obdúrate' is invariably the stress in Sh.

200. *stone...relenteth* Cf. Tilley, D 618, 'Constant dripping will wear the stone'.

204. *unkind* without relenting to her lover (your father) [Case *ap.* Pool.]; cf. l. 310 [Roll.]. Other suggested senses of 'unkind' are much less apt. For the sentiment, Tilley, M 1196, cites Lyly, *Euphues*, 'If thy Mother had bene of that minde when shee was a mayden, thou haddest not nowe bene borne to bee of this minde to bee a virginne'. See also New Arden (1959) note on *All's*, 1. 1. 126–7 (=129–30 in this ed.), which Mal.² here cited, and Baldwin, pp. 194–6, quoting *Arcadia*.

205. *this* Perh., as most edd. and O.E.D. suppose, an archaic form of 'thus', but Mal.¹'s 'contemptuously refuse this favour that I ask' would give a use of 'contemn' that has a Sh. ring.

208. *Speak,* (Q 7) Q 'Speake'. There can be little doubt that this is the meaning: to take 'fair' adverbially after 'Speak' would substitute tautology for word-play.

211. *lifeless* Q 'liuelesse', a frequent spelling, e.g. *Lucr.* 1374, *Err.* 1. 1. 158, *2 H.VI,* 4. 1. 142 [Kittredge *ap.* Roll.].

212. *Well painted* painted so as to look well; not quite the sense of mod. 'well-painted', which edd. since Gildon have usually printed.

216. *even...direction* even without being instructed (as I am instructing you).

220. *Being cause* I.e. because one cannot be judge in one's own cause, cf. Tilley, M 341 [White, *Commentaries on the Law in Sh.* (1911), p. 493]. This is more plausible than Pool.'s view that 'Being...love' is concessive in force.

229. *Fondling* See G.

231. *deer* Q 'deare'; so l. 239, and also l. 689 (where no pun is involved): the common pun, as in *Tit.* 3. 1. 89–91.

235. *Within* (Q 2) Q 'Witin'. *relief* See G.

236. *bottom-grass* Here only in O.E.D., but recorded in the *Dictionary of American English* (1938) from 1850 on. The similar 'bottom ground','bottom land', are noted as prob. of American origin. R. Chester's *Love's Martyr* (1601), p. 81, has 'deep bottome plaines'.

239. *park;* (Mal.¹) Q 'park,': Pool. notes that this punctuation would make it possible to construe, 'such a park that no dog etc.', but this is unlikely.

240. *rouse* See G.

243. *if himself* in order that if he himself (Love = Cupid).

259. *copse* Q 'copp's'.

272. *stand* Plural, because the mane is thought of 'as composed of many hairs' (Mal. *ap.* Var.).

273. *drink the air* So *Tim.* 1. 1. 86 [Mal.¹], and elsewhere.

276. *courage* See G.

277–9. *steps...leaps* Cf. ll. 73–5 n.

285. *What...spur* Cf. Virgil, *Georg.* iii, 252–3: 'Ac neque eos iam frena virum neque verbera saeva | ...retardant' [Pool.; with Baldwin, pp. 24–5, on reference to Venus in Virgil's l. 267].

289. *Look when* Originally 'whenever', but here virtually = 'as when'.

291. *art...strife* A Renaissance commonplace; cf.

Tim. I. I. 40 [Steev.]. Q gives capitals to 'Art' and 'Natures'.

293–4. *one...bone* Cf. Kökeritz, p. 232, noting [oːn] as apparently the regular pronunciation.

295–8. *Round-hoofed...hide* Sh. agrees in general with the standard treatments of the subject, such as Thomas Blundeville's *Arte of Ryding*. Further references in Roll., and Baldwin, pp. 23–6.

299. *Look what* See G.

301. *and* (Q2) Q 'aud'.

302. *starts...feather* Cf. *All's*, 5. 3. 231, 'every feather starts you' [Craig]. Cf. *R.III*, 3. 5. 7, for the commoner proverbial form (Tilley, W 5), 'at wagging of a straw' [Mal.²].

304. *whe'er* Q 'where'; cf. *Tp.* 5. 1. 111.

310. *strangeness* aloofness; cf. l. 524, and the phrase 'make it strange' = 'seem to be shocked' (*Tit.* 2. 1. 81; *Gent.* 1. 2. 102).

311–12. *scorns...heels* Cf. *Ado*, G. 'scorn'.

321. *Jealous of catching* 'fearing to be caught' (Brown).

329–30. *the...tongue* Cf. *Mac.* 4. 3. 209–10, 'the grief that does not speak | Whispers the o'erfraught heart and bids it break' [Steev.]. See Tilley, G 449. The ultimate source is Seneca, *Phaedra*, 615, 'Curae leves loquuntur, ingentes stupent', more literally rendered in Tilley, S 664.

331–3. *An...said* Proverbial (Tilley, F 265, S 929), but particularly close to *Tit.* 2. 4. 36–7 [Verity]; see Baldwin, pp. 26–9.

334. *fire* Disyllabic.

335–6. *attorney...client* Cf. *R.III*, 4. 4. 127, 'Windy attorneys to their client woes' [Steev.].

343. *wistly* See G., and New Arden (1956) note on *R.II*, 5. 4. 7.

346. *How...destroy* Cf. *Shr.* 4. 5. 30, 'war of white

and red' [W. *ap.* Mal.²]; *Lucr.* 71 [Roll.], and Sh.'s
application to the Wars of the Roses in *3 H.VI*, 2. 5.
97–102 [Sarrazin, *E.Studien*, XIX (1894), 354].

347. *by and by* the next moment; this sense, refer-
ring to the immediate future, survives locally, e.g. in
Cornwall.

359–60. *dumb...rain* Cf. *Ham.* 3. 2. 244, with n.
in this ed.

359. *his* its.

362–3. *A...band* Cf. Ovid, *Met.* IV. 354–5 (of
Salmacis) [Lee, facsimile ed. (1905), p. 19].

363. *alabaster* Q 'allablaster', as always in Sh.

366. *Showed* Q 'Showed'—one of the few places
in the poem where an '-ed' spelling is not syllabic; but
not uncommon after 'w' or 'u' cf. *Lucr.* 111 n.

367. *engine...thoughts* her tongue; so in *Tit.* 3. 1. 82
[Verity].

370. *my wound* I.e. it is not merely wounded, it is
nothing but a wound. Pool. compares *Tp.* 5. 1. 287–
8, 'I am not Stephano, but a cramp'.

385–7. *should...cooled* Cf. Kökeritz, pp. 310–12.

392. *Servilely* Q 'Seruilly', reflecting the pro-
nunciation; so Donne, *Sermons*, ed. G. R. Potter and
E. M. Simpson, 1 (1953), 7. 16, has 'hostilly'.

393. *But* (Q 2) Q 'Bnt'.   *his...fee* the 'due
reward, something really owed to his youth' (Roll.).

397. *in her naked bed* Common in 16th c. for
'naked in bed'.

398. *Teaching...white* Cf. *Cym.* 2. 2. 16, 'whiter
than the sheets' [Mal.¹].

399. *glutton eye* Brown notes that these words
occur in Constable's *Diana* (1592), III. iii. 5, l. 11
(*Poems*, ed. J. Grundy (1960), p. 175).

411. *'Tis much* it is a serious matter, i.e. not to be
undertaken lightly; cf. *R.III*, 3. 7. 93 (with G.),
where Q substitutes ''tis hard'.   *owe* After 'borrow',

the primary sense here is presumably 'incur such an obligation', though Roll.,without dissent,cites Schmidt's 'have, possess'.

412. *My...it* 'my inclination towards love is only a desire to render it contemptible' (Mal.[1]).

414. *with a breath* in the same breath; cf. *H.VIII*, 1. 4. 30.

426. *batt'ry* (successful) assault [Brown].

429. *mermaid's* Q 'marmaides', so l. 777, *Lucr.* 1411; cf. Kökeritz, p. 250.

431. *harsh sounding* sounding harshly; I do not think modern usage demands the hyphen of *Poems on Affairs of State* (1707), and most editors (not Alexander).

432. *Ears'* (Prince) Q 'Eares' Var. 'Ear's', but cf. l. 433.

449–50. *guest...feast* Cf. ll. 73–5 n.

453. *red morn* Cf. Tilley, M 1175; originally biblical, Matt. xvi. 2–3, as noted by T. F. T. Dyer (*Folk Lore of Sh.* (1884), p. 62).

458. *wind...raineth* Cf. Tilley, R 16, *Lucr.* 1790.

461. *of* from.

466. *bankrupt* Q 'bankrout'; so *Lucr.* 140, 711, *R.II* (Q), 2. 1. 257.   *loss* S. Walker Q 'loue', presumably caught from l. 464. The rhetoric of the passage demands this correction: the whole point is the paradox of her situation. The alternative emendation 'looks' (Kinnear) is very pedestrian.

472. *Fair fall* may good befall.

474. *Till...again* Cf. Marlowe, *Hero and Leander*, II, 3, 'He kiss'd her, and breath'd life into her lips' [Anders], on which Bullen cited *Rom.* 5. 1. 8, 'And breathed such life with kisses in my lips'.

478. *To mend...marred* A conflation of 'to mend the hurt he caused' and 'to mend what his unkindness marred' [Pool. after Craig]; cf. *Err.* 2. 1. 96–7, 'What

ruins are in me that can be found, | By him not ruined?'
[Brown]; and, for the 'mend/mar' antithesis, *Lucr.* 578.

479. *by...will* if she can have her way.

482. *windows* See G.

490. *brow's* (Collier¹) Q 'browes' Capell MS., and
a minority of edd. 'brows''. Sh.'s usage where the
brow is indicative of emotion strongly favours the
singular.

491-2. *But...night* Cf. *L.L.L.* 4. 3. 28-31
[Mal.²]

493. *where...heaven* Cf. *Err.* 2. 2. 212, 'Am I in
earth, in heaven, or in hell?' [Sarrazin, p. 112].

497. *death's annoy* deathlike sorrow.

500. *eyes'* (Mal.¹) Q 'eyes'.

507. *verdure* See G. Q 'verdour'.

510. *plague* Though the allusion is commonplace,
it may be noted that *Ven.* does belong to the plague
years 1592-3 [Wynd.].

511. *seals* Cf. the 'seals of love' in *Meas.* 4. 1. 56
[Mal.¹], though there 'seal'='impression' and here
'stamp' (the implement).

511-13. *imprinted...contented* For lowering of 'ī'
to 'ĕ', see Kökeritz, p. 212; cf. *Lucr.* 113-15; *P.P.*
14. 8-10.

515. *slips* A play on the sense 'counterfeit money'
(which Steev. took to be the primary sense) is possible
but does not seem to have much point.

517. *buys* Cf. Franz, §§155, 671-3. The sing. is
specially natural here, as 'a thousand kisses' is thought
of as a sum.

524. *strangeness* Cf. l. 310 n.

529-34. *Look...good night* Baldwin, pp. 30-1,
compares this *chronographia* with Ovid, *Met.* x, 446-54
(on Myrrha, the mother of Adonis).

531. *shrieks* (Collier²) Q 'shreeks,', the comma
being quite normal before a dependent clause.

540. *Incorporate...to face* Cf. *H.VIII*, 1. 1. 9–10 [Steev.], with note in this ed., and, for the source, Ovid, *Met*. iv, 373–5 [Fripp, p. 114], on Salmacis and Hermaphroditus.

541–6. *Till...earth* Bush¹, p. 299, cites a similarly luscious account of the kissing of Venus and Adonis from A. Fraunce's *Third Part of the Countesse of Pembroke's Ivychurch* (1592), sig. M 2, which Sh. may have read.

544. *on* Cf. l. 160 n.

565. *wax...temp'ring* Cf. *2 H.VI*, 4. 3. 126–7 [Steev.].

565–7. *temp'ring...vent'ring* Cf. ll. 47–8 n.

568. *whose...commission* 'which intemperately exceeds its instructions' (Pool.).

570. *choice* Some take this to mean 'object of choice', citing *Wint*. 5. 1. 214 [Pool.], but the abstract gives good sense: to choose one who is unwilling is to make a perverse choice.

574. *rose...prickles* Cf. Tilley, R 182, 'No rose without a thorn'; variants on this are common in Sh.

575–6. *Were...last* Cf. [Prince] the proverb, 'Love laughs at locksmiths', for which O.D.E.P.'s first reference in that form, and the next after this, is dated 1803.

597. *All...prove* 'all that she experiences is mere imagination' (Kittredge *ap*. Roll.).

598. *manage* See G.

601. *so* Q 10, and many edd., 'as'. One might suppose this was correct, and that 'so' was caught from l. 603, were the 'so' there not answered by 'as' in l. 604. Note too that Q punctuates heavily, with a colon, at the end of l. 602. *birds...grapes* Zeuxis' painted grapes (Pliny, *N.H.* xxxv. 36) were well known to the Elizabethans. Roll. refers to *Tottel's*

Miscellany (ed. Rollins), I, 168; *Rosalynde* (Hunterian Club ed.), p. 80. Further references in Pool.

608. *assayed*...*proved* Metaph. from testing metal [Yale]; but see also G. 'prove'.

612. *reason* See G.

616. *javelin's* Q 'iauelings'; cf. Kökeritz, pp. 313–14.

619. *battle* See G.

619–21. *On*...*shine* Mal. *ap.* Var. thought Sh. here indebted to the description of the Calydonian boar in Golding's translation of the *Metamorphoses*, VIII, 376–80 (=Ovid's 284–6): 'His eyes did glister blud and fire: right dredfull was to see | His brawned necke, right dredful was his haire which grew as thicke | With pricking points as one of them could well by other sticke. | And like a front of armed Pikes set close in battell ray | The sturdy bristles on his back stood staring vp alway.' See also Baldwin, pp. 33–6, claiming that Sh. also used Brooke's *Romeus and Juliet*.

626. *better proof* more thoroughly impenetrable; with E. Hubler, *Sh.'s Songs and Poems* (1959), I take 'proof' as adj. (with 'better' adv.); not, with Schmidt and others, as sb.

628. *venter* The Q sp., required for the rhyme, represents the normal pronunciation in Sh.'s time: cf. Kökeritz, p. 271.

631–3. *Alas*...*eyne* Cf. Ovid, *Met.* x, 547–9, 'non movet aetas | Nec facies nec quae Venerem movere, leones | Saetigerosque sues oculosque animosque ferarum' [Baynes, p. 632]. Golding, ll. 634–6, translates, 'Thy tender youth, thy beauty bryght, thy countnance fayre and braue | Although they had the force too win the hart of *Venus*, haue | No powre ageinst the Lyons, nor ageinst the bristled swyne.'

632. *pays* Cf. l. 517 n.

635–6. *dread*...*mead* Cf. ll. 73–5 n.

635. *dread* Schmidt and On. refer to boar, 'one deeply revered', but surely just 'a dreadful situation'.

639. *danger* See G., and cf. *M.V.* 4. 1. 177 [Knight] (and G.).

644. *Saw'st* (Q 11) Q, exceptionally, fails to represent the pronunciation and prints 'Sawest'; cf. l. 366 n.

645. *downright* Two words in Q; On. is uncertain whether this is local ('straight down') or temporal ('forthwith')—the former seems more probable.

655–7. *This... Jealousy* There is a similar 'this'-catalogue in *Lucr.* 220–3, *Tit.* 2. 1. 21–3, *R.II.* 2. 1. 40–51 [A. K. Gray, *S.P.* xxv (1928), 303–4], and in *K.J.* 2. 1. 581–2, *L.L.L.* 3. 1. 178–9 [Introd. to *Tit.*, in this ed., p. xxiii].

665–6. *Whose...head* Cf. *Tit.* 2. 3. 199–201 [Parrott, p. 28].

667. *indeed* in actuality; play on this sense and on the weakened sense is frequent; cf. *Ant.* 1. 5. 14–16.

674–6. *Uncouple...dare* Cf. Ovid, *Met.* x, 537–9, 'Hortaturque canes tutaeque animalia praedae, | Aut pronos lepores aut celsum in cornua cervum, | Aut agitat dammas' [Dürnhöfer, p. 26]; Golding, ll. 621–3, translates, 'shee cheerd the hounds with hallowing like a hunt, | Pursewing game of hurtlesse sort, as Hares made lowe before, | Or stagges with loftye heades, or bucks.' There are also verbal similarities [Sarrazin, p. 143], to Sidney, *Arcadia* (1593), Ecl. 1. 9, ll. 123–5, on which W. Ringler, *Poems of Sidney* (1962), p. 388, cites Ovid, *Remedia Amoris,* where ll. 201–4 bear some resemblance to our passage.

680. *overshoot* (Steev.) Q 'ouer-shut', an obsolete form: see O.E.D.

685–8. *Sometime...yell* There is a similar description in G. Turberville, *Arte of Venerie* (1576), ed. 1908, p. 165 [Pool.].

694. *fault* See G.

695–6. *Then...skies* Cf. *Tit.* 2. 3. 17–19 [Pool.].

695. *spend* See G.

698–9. *Stands...still* A similar description is cited by Pool. from Topsell's *Historie of Foure-footed Beastes* (1607), sig. 2A3.

701–2. *And...bell* Topsell, sig. 2A2ᵛ, describes 'the Foxes presence' as 'like the voice of a passing bell' to the hare.

705. *do* For this 'confusion of proximity', see Abbott, §412.

710. *Nay...rise* Cf. Salmacis to Hermaphroditus in Ovid, *Met.* IV, 370–1, '"pugnes licet, improbe" dixit, | "Non tamen effugies" '; where Sh. is closer to the expanded version in Golding, ll. 459–60, 'Striue, struggle, wrest and writhe (she said) thou froward boy thy fill: | Doe what thou canst thou shalt not scape' [Brown].

712. *moralize* Like Jaques in *A.Y.L.* 2. 1. 45 ff.

720. *In...all* Cf. *Rom.* 3. 2. 8–9 [Steev.].

724. *Rich...thieves* The notion is proverbial: Tilley, P 570, 'The prey entices the thief'.   *true men* Q 'true-men'; often thus, or as single word, in the sense 'honest men' as opposed to thieves.

725. *cloudy* See G.

729–30. *Till...divine* Probably imitated from Daniel's *Complaint of Rosamond* (1592), 143–4, 'Treason, to counterfeit the seale of nature, | The stamp of heauen, impressed by the hiest' [Brown]. But the image continues to be popular with Sh.: cf. *Meas.* 2. 4. 45 n.

748. *th'* (Q 2) Q 'the th''.

749. *thawed* Q 'thawed'; cf. l. 366 n.

754. *sons* Q 'suns'.

755–6. *the...light* For the notion of the lamp, or candle, that 'lights others and consumes itself', cf. Tilley, C 39.

760. *If...obscurity* A twelve-syllable line, as if the rhyme were on '-urity', not on '-ty'; so in *Lucr.* 352–4, 'resolútión | absolútión' [S. Walker]. This type of rhyme is less harsh than, but akin to, the stressed-unstressed rhymes common in Chapman and occasional in Donne and others, discussed by G. C. Moore Smith, *M.L.R.* xv (1920), 300–3, and P. Simpson, *M.L.R.* xxxviii (1943), 127–9. See also R. N. Dodge, in Univ. of Wisconsin *Sh.Studies* (1916), pp. 174–200.

766. *butcher...life* A notion that haunted Sh.; cf. *R.III*, 5. 5. 25–6 [Sarrazin, p. 178], and *3 H.VI*, 2. 5. 55 ff.

768. *gold...begets* For the notion of interest as offspring (Gk. τόκος) and the condemnation of it as unnatural, cf. Tilley, M 1053, *M.V.* 1. 3. 131 n.

769. *will* 'are determined to' (Brown).

770. *over-handled theme* Cf. *Tit.* 3. 2. 29, 'O, handle not the theme'.

772. *strive...stream* Cf. Tilley, S 927

787. *reprove* See G.

789. *I...love* Contrary to what he has said at ll. 409 ff. [Roll.].

792. *When...abuse* Cf. *Ham.* 3. 4. 88, 'reason pandars will' [Steev.].

804. *Love...lies* Brown quotes Greene, *Perimedes the Blacke-Smith* (ed. Grosart, vii, 92), 'lust had lies, but loue quoth he sayes truth'.

809–10. *Mine...offended* Cf. *Cym.* 1. 6. 140–1, 'I do condemn mine ears that have | So long attended thee' [Steev.].

815–16. *Look...eye* Bush[2], p. 141, cites Golding's translation of the *Metamorphoses* (1567), ii, 404–6 (=Ovid's 319–22), 'But Phaeton (fire yet blasing still among his yellow haire) | Shot headlong downe, and glid along the Region of the Ayre, | Like to [a] Starre in Winter nightes (the wether cleare and fayre).'

828. *discovery...way* 'him...by whose light she perceived her way' (Schmidt). Comparable abstracts for concretes are cited by Mal.² from *Cor.* 4. 6. 54 ('information') and by Pool. from l. 932 ('divorce'). Perh. 'means of discovery' would convey how the usage developed.

829–40. *And...so* These stanzas, and ll. 847 ff., have been thought indebted to Lodge's *Scillaes Metamorphosis* (1589) [cited, though sceptically (p. 146), by Sarrazin, p. 145]; and the treatment of the echo to Ovid, *Met.* iii, 495–501 [Pool. p. xxx].

832 *deeply* S. Walker's 'doubly' would give an appropriate expression (he cited *Mac.* 1. 2. 39, 'Doubly redoubled' and Grant White added *R.II*, 1. 3. 80), but it is hard to see how the corruption could have arisen.

838. *foolish witty* Mal.¹ hyphenated, but the sense seems to be 'foolish when witty', an antithesis to wise in folly'.

848. *parasites* Q 'parasits', giving a perfect rhyme; cf. *L.L.L.* 5. 2. 264–5, Kökeritz, p. 219.

849. *tapsters...call* As in *1 H.IV*, 2. 4. 43 ff. [Steev.].

855–6. *And...majesty* See ll. 1–2 n.

862. *him* it.

863. *sucked...mother* Not literally true; the mother of Adonis, Myrrha, was changed to a myrtle before his birth—Ovid, *Met.* x, 503–14 [Roll.].

869. *it* For the redundant use, cf. Abbott, §226.

873. *twind* (Q 4) Q 'twin'd' Q 7 'twine'; see G. and *2 H.IV*, 2. 4. 195, 'Untwind'. The form is not uncommon; cf. Kökeritz, p. 300.

878–9. *like...way* A. K. Gray, *S.P.* xxv (1928), 305, compares *Tit.* 2. 3. 35–6, 'Even as an adder when she doth unroll | To do some fatal execution'.

878–80. *adder...shudder* Cf. Kökeritz, p. 241, who describes the rhyme as 'inexact'.

882. *spirit* Monosyllabic, as in *Comp.* 3, 236.

888. *strain court'sy* See G. 'courtesy'.

891–4. *Who...field* According to the old physiology, 'in Fear, as in Grief, the heart contracted, and became weakened. Heat was withdrawn from the rest of the body to comfort the heart, blood and spirits were drawn to it' (J. B. Bamborough, *The Little World of Man* (1952), p. 122). The figure of the surrendering captain links up with l. 890, but is not wholly integrated with the physiology. Sh. seems to move from a captured fortress to a lost battle.

902. *together* Q 'togither', making the rhyme perfect; cf. Kökeritz, pp. 186–7.

903. *spread* Perh. pr. tense, attracted into the plur. by 'sinews', rather than an isolated pa. tense (for which, however, as the late C. B. Young pointed out to me, cf. l. 900, 'spied').

906. *murther* See l. 54 n.

909. *more than haste* So *Lucr.* 1332.   *mated* See G.

925. *Look how* (Q 3) Q 'Looke how,', apparently a mere slip; cf. l. 815.

928. *Infusing* See G. It seems more natural to take this with 'people', as a metaphor for reading prophecies into the apparitions, or possibly to take 'them' as reflexive = 'themselves', than to take it with 'apparitions', making l. 927 parenthetical, as Pool. does.

930. *on* Cf. l. 160 n.

932. *divorce* Cf. l. 828 n., and *Tim.* 4. 3. 383 [Brown].

933. *Grim-grinning* Cf. *1 H.VI*, 5. 3. 59, 'grinning honour'.   *earth's worm* Q 'earths-worme'.

940. *random* Q 'randon'; so *1H VI* (F) 5. 3. 85.

944. *his* its.

946. *bid* Past tense, as perh. is 'pluck'st': cf. Franz, §152.

947. *Love's...fled* Cf. Marlowe, *Hero and Leander*, I, 161, 'Thence flew Love's arrow with the golden head' [C. A. Herpich, *N. & Q.* 10, ser. 1 (1904), 12]. But both are Ovidian (*Met*. 1, 470). There may be a hint of the story of the exchange of arrows between Love and Death [S. C. Chew, *The Pilgrimage of Life* (1962), pp. 190–1].   *fled* See G. 'flee'; but the anon. conj. *ap*. Camb. 'sped' is not unattractive.

956. *who* which (as in l. 984).

963. *crystals* With allusion to magic crystals 'in which one in sympathy with another could see the scene of his distress' (Wynd.).

973–4. *By...well* Cf. *Tit*. 2. 3. 27–9 [Sarrazin, p. 33].

973. *holla* Q 'hallow'; cf. *Tw.N.* 1. 5. 276.

980. *eye* (Q 5) Q 'eye:'.

985–6. *O...credulous* Cf. Marlowe, *Hero and Leander*, II 221–2 'Love is too full of faith, too credulous, | With folly and false hope deluding us' [Brown].

988. *makes* Sing. because 'it is the rapid interchange...which produces this effect' (Herf.).

993. *called...nought* See G. 'call'.

996. *supreme* Stressed 'súpreme' by Sh., except in the one place where it is used predicatively: *Cor*. 3. 1. 110; see Schmidt, pp. 1413–15.

998. *me*, Dyce deleted the comma, treating 'I... fear' as a dependent clause (cf. l. 531 n.). A fair number of edd. have followed him, but I think it more likely that 'pardon me' is parenthetical.

1002. *decease* Q 'decesse'; cf. the rhyme 'bless | cesse' in *All's*, 5. 3. 71–2; Kökeritz, p. 202.

1006. *author...slander* responsible for your being slandered.

1007. *yet* '[ĭ] remained the accepted pronunciation down to the end of the 18th century' (Kökeritz,

p. 187); though according to E. J. Dobson, *English Pronunciation 1500–1700* (1957), 77, 'ĕ' seems to have been the more common variant in educated St[andard] E[nglish]'.

1010. *extenuate* See G.

1012. *insinuate* See G.

1013. *stories* (Theobald *ap.* Jortin, *Miscellaneous Observations*, II (1732), 244) Q 'stories,'. See G.; attempts to defend 'stories' as sb. are fruitless. The comma is no more anomalous than those which Q prints at the end of ll. 541 and 1175; Q's end-of-line commas are often contrary to modern usage.

1018. *mutual* See G.

1023–4. *Trifles...grieves* Prob. the sing. vb. is due to 'confusion of proximity'—cf. l. 705 n.—but perh. 'heart' is the subject and 'grieves' = 'grieves over'.

1028. *The...light* Cf. Virgil, *Aen.* VII, 808–9 [Steev.]; Ovid, *Met.* x. 655, from the story of Atalanta which Venus tells to Adonis [Baldwin, p. 42].

1031. *as* (Q 3) Q 'are'. The ease of this corruption, with no preceding comma, is shown by the fact that Q 12 re-introduced it.

1032. *of* at the approach of.

1033. *whose...being* Conflation of 'who, his... being' and 'whose...are'. *tender horns* Also in *L.L.L.* 4. 3. 335 [Pool.].

1041. *consort with...night* So again *M.N.D.* 3. 2. 387 [Pool.].

1043. *perplexèd* A much stronger word than in mod. Eng., cf. *Oth.* 5. 2. 348 (cited by Staunton on *Lucr.* 733), and F. P. Wilson, *Proceedings of the British Academy*, XXVII (1941), 173; rptd. *Sh. Criticism 1935–1960*, ed. A. Ridler (1963), p. 97.

1046–7. *As...shakes* The traditional (Aristotelian) belief about the cause of earthquakes; cf. *1 H.IV*, 3. 1 27–32 [Steev.].

1054. *was* (Q 7) Q 'had', which may be an author's slip [Roll., p. 371], as if he had written 'The purple tears', or may have been caught from the rhyming line 1052.

1062. *that...now* 'that they have wasted their tears on inferior "hints of woe"' (Rolfe); perh., more specifically, that they have used up some of their capacity for weeping.

1064. *That...three* Cf. *3 H.VI*, 2. 1. 25, 'Dazzle mine eyes, or do I see three suns?' [Sarrazin, *E.Studien*, XIX (1894), 355].

1082. *Nor...wind* Cf. Marlowe, *Hero and Leander*, I, 27–8, 'neither sun nor wind | Would burn or parch her hands' [Anders]. This rivalry of sun and wind may echo the fable of their contest to remove the man's cloak.

1083. *fair...fear* Mal.¹ noted the jingle, which also occurs in Lyly, *Sapho and Phao*, 2. 1. 5–6, *Gallathea*, 1. 3. 1 [Kökeritz, p. 106].

1095. *sung* Q 'song', cf. Kökeritz, pp. 242–3; so l. 1171, 'new-sprong'.

1099. *shadow* See G.; the 'substance/shadow' contrast is very common; and cf. *Rom.* 5. 3. 103, 'unsubstantial Death'.

1110–16. *He...groin* So [Theocritus], *Id.* xxx [Mal.²]. Sh. could have read this in E.D.'s translation (1588); see Roll. for other versions.

1115–16. *swine...groin* A good rhyme down to the 18th c.: cf. Kökeritz, pp. 216–18.

1116. *in...groin* Cf. Ovid, *Met.* x, 715, 'sub inguine' [Dürnhöfer, pp. 37–8, who notes that Golding, l. 839, has 'in his codds', so that Sh. must have used the original].

1127–8. *She...lies* Cf. *Lucr.* 1378–9 [Verity].

1128. *lies* Cf. l. 517 n.; the interchange of sing. and plur. forms is particularly normal with rhyme-words.

1130. *more*, (J.C.M.) Q 'more'. Theobald (*ap.* Jortin, *Miscellaneous Observations*, II (1732), 245) saw there was something wrong with the traditional text, and proposed 'times and more,' for 'times, and now'. I take 'reflect' as past pple. If it is to be pres. indic., 'and' = 'and which', which is awkward.

1136–40. *Sorrow…woe* Cf. *M.N.D.* I. I. 134–40 [Steev.], Tilley, L 510, 513.

1158. *courage…coward* Cf. Tilley, D 216.

1168. *purple flower* Cf. Ovid, *Met.* x, 735–7, 'flos de sanguine concolor ortus | Qualem quae lento celant sub cortice granum, | Punica ferre solent'; Golding, ll. 858–60, 'Of all one colour with the blood a flowre she there did fynd | Euen like the flowre of that same tree whose frute in tender rynde | Haue pleasant graynes inclosde'. Cooper's *Thesaurus*, s.v. *Adonis*, has 'purple flower' [Bullough, p. 159]. Ovid, l. 739, identifies it as the anemone, 'excutiunt idem qui praestant nomina venti', but this could not be gathered from Golding, who translates the corrupt text 'perflant omnia' for 'praestant nomina': 'the windes that all things perce'. But the anemone is mentioned in current commentaries [Baldwin, p. 86; H. T. Price, *Papers of the Michigan Academy*, xxxi (1945), 288–9].

1177. *guise* See G.

1180. *unto himself* Cf. l. 166 n.

1193. *Paphos* Seat of Venus in Cyprus. In Ovid, because of Adonis, 'To *Cythera* Ile no mynd at all shee had, | Nor vnto *Paphos* where the sea beats round about the shore' (Golding, x, 611–12 = 529–30 of Latin).

THE RAPE OF LUCRECE

1. *all in post* Cf. Painter, 1, 22, 'they roode to Rome in post' [Mal.²].

3. *Lust-breathèd* See G.

4. *lightless* Cf. the application to 'hell' in l. 1555.

5. *aspire* Q indicates that this is trans. (as in *Rom.* 3. 1. 116) by commas after 'aspire' and 'flames'.

8. *Haply...unhapp'ly* Q 'Hap'ly...vnhap'ly', emphasizing the word-play.   *name of chaste* word 'chaste'; cf. *Tit.* 3. 2. 26, 'name of hands'; Sh. is closer to Livy, 'spectata castitas incitat', than to Ovid [Ewig, p. 20]; but commentaries on Ovid use the word 'castitas' [Baldwin, p. 100].

10. *let* See G.

14. *aspects* The technical sense 'relative positions of heavenly bodies' may be glanced at, but the primary meaning is simply 'looks'.   *peculiar duties* See G.

16. *treasure* Prob. fig. use of the sense 'treasure-house', as 'treasury' in *Tit.* 2. 1. 131.

22–5. *O...sun* Cf. Daniel, *Delia* (1592), 50, 1–4 [Sarrazin, p. 161].

24. *morning* (Q uncorr.) Q corr. 'mornings'. See Note on the Copy, p. 148.

26. *date* See G.; and for association with 'cancelled', ll. 934–5, 1729 [Prince].

29–30. *Beauty...orator* Cf. Daniel, *Complaint of Rosamond* (1592), ll. 122–3, 'Dombe eloquence, whose powre doth moue the blood, | More then the words, or wisedome of the wise' [Steev.].

31. *apology* Q uncorr. 'Appologie' Q corr. 'Apologies'. See Note on the Copy, p. 148.

47. *liver* 'supposed to be the seat of love' (Mal.¹); cf. *Ado*, G., *Tw.N.* G.

50. *Collatium* Q uncorr. 'Colatium' Q corr. 'Colatia'. See Note on the Copy, pp. 147–8.

56. *o'er* (*Poems on Affairs of State*, 1707) Q 'ore'
Mal.¹ 'or'. Mal.'s conj. with 'or' = 'gold', as a heraldic
term, is attractive. It gives a straightforward phrase 'that
or', whereas, with 'o'er', 'that' loosely takes up 'blushes',
and Sh. uses 'ore' = 'gold' (not heraldically) in *Ham.* 4.
1. 25. But as 'or' = 'yellow', not 'red', the word is not
really apt, even though 'red gold' is a traditional phrase;
cf. also ll. 59–60 [Mal.¹]. (Wynd. treats 'or' as arising
from an admixture of Virtue's *white* with Beauty's *red*,
but if we read 'or', 'that or' must be identified with the
blush of beauty.) All in all, it seems safest to retain the
traditional text, the natural modernization of Q's 'ore',
though the possibility of at least a word-play on 'or'
cannot be ruled out.

58–61. *field...gild...shield* See Kökeritz, p. 192.

67. *from...minority* from the 'golden age' (l. 60),
when the world was young [Wynd., Pool.].

71–7. *This...foe* An elaboration of the simple
notion of being caught between two fires.

71. *war...roses* Cf. *Shr.* 4. 5. 30, 'war of white
and red' [Steev.].

72–5. *field...killed...yield* Cf. ll. 58–61 n.

74. *killed,* (Q 2) Q 'kild.'.

80. *wrong,* (Q 7) Q 'wrong.' Q 3 'wrong:'.

83. *answers* See G.; cf. *1 H.IV*, 1. 3. 185
[Pool.].

87–8. "*For...*"*Birds* On inverted commas to
single out sententious utterances, see *Meas.* 2. 4. 185 n.,
and the full discussion by G. K. Hunter, *Library*,
5 ser. vi (1951–2), 171–88.

88. *Birds...fear* For the converse, cf. *3 H.VI*, 5.
6. 13–14 [Steev.], and Tilley, B 394, 'Birds once
snared (limed) fear all bushes'.

90. *reverend* Interchangeable with 'reverent' in Sh.

92. *that* the 'inward ill'.

97. *wanteth...store* One of the variations on the

popular Ovidian tag, 'inopem me copia fecit' (*Met.* III, 466).

98. *cloyed...more* Cf. 'Much would have more' (Tilley, M 1287, for which F. P. Wilson, *The Proverbial Wisdom of Sh.* (1961), p. 21, cites Barclay's *Ship of Fools*, and O.D.E.P. a MS. of *c.* 1350).

102. *Writ...books* Referring to marginal glosses; cf. *Rom.* 1. 3. 6–7 [Mal.¹].

104. *moralize* See G.

105. *More than* more than to the extent that.

106–12. *He...success* So Gower, *Conf.Am.* VII, 4926–34 [Pool. p. lvi]. Sh. may have recalled this in the tactics of Jachimo in *Cym.*

110. *bruiséd...victory* Cf. *R.III*, 1. 1. 5–6, 'Now are our brows bound with victorious wreaths; | Our bruiséd arms hung up for monuments' [Mal.¹].

111. *heaved-up* Q 'heaued-vp', with '-ed' not representing a separate syllable; this tends to occur after 'u' (cf. *Ven.* 366 n.); but contrast l. 638, 'heau'd vp'.

113–15. *thither...weather* Cf. *Ven.* 511–13 n.

117. *mother...fear* Cf. Daniel, *Complaint of Rosamond* (1592), 432, 'the night, mother of sleepe and feare' [Mal.²].

121. *Intending* See G.

125–6. *himself betakes...wakes* Q uncorr. 'himselfe betakes...wakes' Q corr. 'themselues betake... wake'. See Note on the Copy, p. 148.

128. *will's obtaining* For this rather unusual possessive cf. l. 1573, 'sorrow's sharp sustaining', l. 1715, 'excuse's giving'.

130. *weak-built hopes* 'the fact that his hopes have no sure foundation' (Pool.).

135–6. *that...bond* Evidently an anacoluthon: Sh. begins as if about to say, 'what they have not, they are so eager to obtain that they scatter what they possess', but hastens on to the final clause without expressing what comes between. The notion which Gildon (with the excuse of reading 'oft' (Q 6) for 'what') and others (without that excuse) have detected, that the covetous man does not really have what he possesses, has no relevance to the context. Knight interpreted correctly.

138. *profit of excess* 'only advantage of having more than enough' (Pool.).

140. *bankrupt* Q 'bāckrout'; cf. *Ven.* 466 n.

147. *all together* (Q 8) Q 'altogether'. The two forms are not consistently differentiated in Sh.'s Eng.; cf. *Tim.* 5. 4. 44 n.

151–2. *defect...have* Perh. simply 'the inadequacy of what we have', but Pool.'s rather more complicated 'the absence of what is really present' may be right. It would introduce the proverbial notion wrongly detected in ll. 135–6 (see note), on which Gildon quoted Publilius Syrus, 694, 'Tam deest avaro quod habet quam quod non habet'.

161. *sland'rous* Q 'sclandrous'; cf. l. 1001. In Harington's *Orlando* (1591), Field once introduced the sp. 'sclander' for Harington's 'slawnder' (Greg, *Library*, 4 ser. IV (1923–4), 114).

162–8. *Now...kill* Cf. *Mac.* 2. 1. 49–56 [Mal.¹].

163. *sleep* (Q 2) Q 'sleeep'.

165–7. *wolves'...lambs* This comparison occurs in Ovid, *Fasti*, II, 800 (noted by Mal.¹ on l. 677), as well as in Gower, *Conf.Am.* VII, 4983–4, Chaucer, *L.G.W.* 1798 [Furnivall, 1885 facsimile, p. vi].

169. *lord,* (Herf.) Q 'Lord'. The comma brings out that 'leaped' is past pple.

170. *Throwing...arm* Cf. Gower, *Conf.Am.* VII, 4964–5, 'And upon himself he cast | A mantell' [Porter].

174. *retire* See G.; this must be a sb., as 'betake oneself to' plus infinitive is not recorded.

181. *As...fire* Cf. Tilley, F 371.

188. *naked...lust* 'His only armor in this enter-prise is lust—which is no real armor, for it is always slain (perishes, comes to naught) when it is satisfied' (Kittredge *ap.* Roll.).

194. *shrine* Cf. *Cym.* 5. 5. 164 n.

197–210 *O...been* Cf. Chaucer, *L.G.W.* 1822–4, 'Why hastow doon dispite to chevalrye? | Why hastow doon thys lady vylanye? | Allas, of the thys was a vilenous deede!' [Ewig, pp. 27–8].

198. *household's grave* family sepulchre. Intro-duces the heraldic images of the next stanza [Wynd.].

201. *a...have* Prob. 'should be rightly exercised' —valour in a false cause is no true valour; the literal meaning would then be something like 'look in the right direction'. Roll.'s 'a careful regard for that which is truly valorous' seems to me to make the sentence tautological.

206. *loathsome dash* Wynd. identifies with Guil-lim's 'abatements'—'accidentall markes annexed to Coate-Armour, denoting some ungentleman-like, dis-honorable, or disloyall demeanour...in the Bearer' (*Display of Heraldrie*, 1610).

210. *been* Q 'beene': as the normal pronunciation is 'ĭ', there is no need to follow Q 3 in spelling 'bin'.

212–14. *dream...toy* Hankins, p. 221, quotes 'dreames and toyes' from Googe, p. 192.

217. *strucken* (Q 6) Q 'strokē'; so *J.C.* (F) 3. 1. 210.

237. *as...friend* Cf. *Mac.* 1. 7. 13 [Steev.]. The two soliloquies are closely similar in spirit.

239–41. *Shameful...own* Cf. ll. 841–2, and the most famous example of this internal dialogue in the early drama, Kyd's *Spanish Tragedy*, 2. 1. 19–28 [Prince].

244. *sentence* See G.

245. *painted cloth* See G.; and cf. *Mac.* 2. 2. 54–5 n.

266. *Self-love…flood* Cf. *Ven.* 161–2 n.

269. *remorse…abuses* See G.

270. *shadows* See G.; very broadly used for anything that can be taken as real without being so—here it would include, e.g., sense of honour—'a word' for Tarquin as for Falstaff (*1 H.IV*, 5. 1. 134).

273. *coward fights* Cf. *Ven.* 1158 n.

275. *Respect and reason* Joined also in *Troil.* 2. 2. 49 [Mal.²].

295. *servile powers* The 'mortal instruments' of *J.C.* 2. 1. 66 [Pool.]; see n. in this ed.

303. *his* its.

305. *thief* Cf. Chaucer, *L.G.W.* 1781 (cited in 365 n.).

307. *weasels* On the unluckiness of meeting a weasel, which is also a sign 'of evil to those whose houses [it] infest[s]' (Alciati), see D. C. Allen, *Sh. Survey*, 15 (1962), 92.

312. *blows…face* There is a passage curiously similar to this in Prudentius, *Psychomachia*, 43–5, where 'Sodomita Libido' attacks Pudicitia: 'Adgreditur piceamque ardenti sulpure pinum, | Ingerit in faciem pudibundaque lumina flammis | Adpetit, et taetro temptat subfundere fumo.' For the 'smokie fire' of 'desire', cf. Sidney, 'Certaine Sonets' in 1598 *Arcadia* (*Works*, ed. Feuillerat, II, 322).

313. *conduct* See G.

319. *needle* Monosyllabic; often spelt 'neeld' or 'neele', cf. *M.N.D.* 3. 2. 204 n.

328–9. *Who…his…his* which…its…its.

334. *income* See G.

335. *rocks…winds…sands* For the collocation, cf. *M.V.* 1. 1. 22–34; Hankins, pp. 24–5, 55–6, links both passages with Googe, p. 100.

336. *merchant* Q 'marchant', cf. *Ven.* 429 n.

341. *So...wrought* Three interpretations have been put forward: (i) 'his sin has made him unlike himself' (Pool.); (ii) 'so unlike himself the impious one (i.e. Tarquin) has wrought' (Brown); (iii) 'so far has Impiety worked contrary to its nature' (Kittredge *ap.* Roll.). All have difficulties: (i) gives the aptest sense and is prob. right—the point is that Tarquin must be beside himself to pray in such a cause (cf., with J.D.W. *ad loc., Mac.* 2. 2. 32)—but the omission of the object 'him' is awkward; (ii) gives a very forced abstract for concrete, and the perfect tense has little point if 'has wrought' is intransitive; (iii) is also open to the last objection, and l. 343 suggests that the absurdity of Tarquin's conduct, and not the departure from what befits impiety, is the point.

347. *they* Appropriate to the 'powers' of l. 349 rather than to the 'power' of l. 345. Such transitions àre common: cf. *R.III*, 1. 3. 217–19, 'heaven... them' [Mal.²].

352–5. *resolution...absolution...dissolution* Cf. *Ven.* 760 n.

365. *stalks* Cf. Chaucer, *L.G.W.* 1781, 'And in the nyght ful thefly gan he stalke' [W. W. Skeat, *ad loc.* in ed. of *The Legend of Good Women* (1889)].

376. *that* the fact that; hence no comma after 'bright' (so Neilson and Hill, ed. of Sh., 1942).

384–5. *to...joy* must lose her joy because of their (her eyes') being seen. The expression is obscure, but I think this is rather more appropriate than to take 'sight' as the power of sight inhering in the eyes.

389. *Swelling* With play on metaph. sense 'being angry'.   *to want* at wanting (i.e. lacking).

391. *virtuous monument* 'figure representing some virtue' (Schmidt).

397. *marigolds* Cf. *Son.* 25. 6, *Wint.* 4. 4. 105–6 [Verity].

398. *canopied* So, in a similar context, *Cym.* 2. 2. 21 [Mal.¹].

402. *map* See G.

409. *Save...knew* Cf. Ovid, *Fasti*, ii, 804, 'Tunc primum externa pectora tacta manu' [Mal.¹].

417. *will...wilful* See G.

419. *alabaster* Q 'alablaster'; cf. *Ven.* 363 n.

425. *Slacked* (Q 2) Q 'Slakt'. This early change is one interesting example of the replacement of 'slake' (O.E.D. 9) by 'slack' (first recorded in this sense, O.E.D. 3, in 1589). Rhyme demands the older form in l. 1677.

440. *veins* Most edd. insert a comma after this, but the sense is 'and as his hand scaled their ranks, they left'. *scale,* (Q 3) Q 'scale.'.

443. *governess and lady* The mind (thought of as resident in the heart). The metaphor is not sustained, and in l. 446 'she' is simply Lucrece herself.

446. *amazed* See G.

460. "*Such* Cf. ll. 87–8 n. *weak brain's* (Q 6) Q 'weake-brains'.

461. *from...lights* Apparently a mannered way of saying 'from transmitting the light it is their task to transmit', or 'from exercising their power of sight' (see G. 'light').

468. *rage* See G.

476. *colour* For word-play cf. *2 H.IV*, 5. 5. 87–8 [Steev.].

489. *reproof...beat* Østerberg, *Sh.Jb.* lxv (1929), 60, cited *Edw.III*, 2. 1. 291–2: 'I must enjoy her; for I cannot beat | With reason and reproof fond love away.' He believed the scene to be by Sh.; cf. l. 1004 n.

492. *I...defends* Cf. *Ven.* 574 n.

493. *I...sting* Cf. Tilley, H 553, 'Honey is

sweet but the bee stings'. Other proverbs with the
same point are cited under H 556, 'No honey without
gall'.

495. *will* See G.

496. *Only* With 'on beauty'; the initial position
adds emphasis.

497. *looks* looks on; cf. Abbott, §394.

511 *falcons'* (Capell MS.) Q 'Faulcōs' *Poems on
Affairs of State*, 1707, 'falcon's'.

515. *slave of thine* So Chaucer, *L.G.W.* 1807, 'thy
knave'; the ownership of the slave is undetermined in
Ovid and Livy [Lee, facsimile ed. (1905), p. 15].
slay, (Q 2) Q 'slay.'.

522. *nameless* Perh. not simply 'because an illegiti-
mate child has no name by inheritance' (Mal.¹), but
because the putative children of a 'worthless slave'
would not have even such distinction as can attach to the
bastards of eminent fathers.

528–30. *"A..."The* Cf. ll. 87–8 n.

528–9. *A...enacted* Cf. *M.V.* 4. 1. 213, 'To do a
great right, do a little wrong'. Tilley, E 112, treats
these as variants of 'the end justifies the means'; for
which F. P. Wilson, *R.E.S.* n.s. III (1952), 196, has
a 1583 quotation in slightly different form.

529. *policy* Here and at l. 1815 with the usual
implication of Macchiavellian cunning.

535. *device* See G.

537. *slavish wipe* slave's brand.   *birth-hour's
blot* birthmark; cf. *M.N.D.* 5. 1. 407, 'blots of
Nature's hand' [Rolfe]. A reference to heraldic marks
of illegitimacy (mentioned, though rejected, by Mal.,
elaborated by Wynd., and favoured by Roll.) would be
beside the point, which is precisely to *contrast* natural
blemishes with the shame of bastardy.

540. *dead-killing* For the tautology, cf. *Tit.* 3. 1.
92, and for the powers of the cockatrice, Tilley, C 495.

544. *in...laws* A favourite notion of Sh., cf. *Tit.* G. 'wilderness'.

547. *But* Sewell 'As' (cf. 'So' in l. 552). But the slight irregularity is no doubt Sh.'s.

550. *blows* (Mal.¹) Q 'blow'; perh. Sh.'s slip.

552. *delays* The subj. is 'words'; cf. *Ven.* 1128 n.

554-5. *Yet...panteth* Cf. Tilley, C 127.

554-6. *dally...folly* For the rhyme (with un-rounded 'o'), cf. Kökeritz, pp. 223-6.

559. *penetrable entrance* It is usu. assumed that 'penetrable' is passive and 'entrance'='passage by which one enters'. But 'penetrable' may be active, as '-able' words often are in Sh. (Franz, §124), with 'entrance'='act of entering'—the commoner Sh. meaning of the word.

560. *marble...raining* Cf.*Ven.* 200 n.; ll. 592,959.

562. *wrinkles* See G., and cf. *R.II*, 2. 1. 170 [Prince].

567. *twice...speaks* Cf. l. 1604 n.

573. *make retire* A military phrase, as Craig notes. On military imagery, see H. T. Price, *Papers of the Michigan Academy*, xxxi (1945), 283-4.

576. *pretended* See G.

577. *Mud...thee* Cf. Tilley, D 345 (first clearly as proverb, 1678); *Tit.* 5. 2. 171 [Parrott, p. 35], with New Arden (1953) note.

592. *stones...convert* Cf. *Ven.* 200 n., l. 560 above, l. 959 below.   *convert* A perfect rhyme with 'heart'; cf. *Ven.* 429 n.

593-4. *if...compassionate* Cf. *Tit.* 3. 1. 37-47.

596-630. *In...way* Cf. Chaucer, *L.G.W.* 1819-21, 'Tarquinius, thou art a Kynges eyre, | And sholdest, as by lynage and by right, | Doon as a lorde and as a verray knyght' [Ewig, p. 27].

598. *host of heaven* Again as object of invocation in *Ham.* 1. 5. 92.

603. *seeded* See G.   *age* Prob., in contrast with 'before thy spring', maturity rather than old age.

605. *hope sc.* of being king; cf. l. 1003 [Prince].

609. *Then* The argument is *a fortiori*; cf. *Cor.* 3. 2. 38–9, 'I cannot do it to the gods; | Must I then do't to them?'.

612–13. *With...prove* A favourite theme of Sh.'s, as Tilley, F 107, indicates.

615. *glass...book* Cf. *2 H.IV*, 2. 3. 31 [Mal.¹], and Tilley, K 70, 'Like king, like people'.

629. *patterned...fault* With 'learned to sin', as the present punctuation tries to bring out. Q has comma after 'say'; edd., rightly omitting this, add commas after 'When' and 'fault', and omit Q's after 'sin'.

638–9. *To...relier* Recalls the appeal from Philip drunk to Philip sober [Tilley, P 252, citing].

639. *thy...relier* 'which confides too rashly in thy present disposition and does not foresee its necessary change' (Schmidt).

641. *flatt'ring* Flatterers are traditionally the worst enemies of kings.

642. *His...respect* due regard for him.

646. *swells...let* Cf. *Ven.* 331–3 n.

647–8. *Small...fret* Cf. Tilley, W 448a, where this is the first quotation.

650. *sovereign* For the image, cf. *K.J.* 5. 4. 57, 'to our ocean, to our great King John'.

654. *misgoverning* So 'misgovernment' at *Ado*, 4. 1. 98 [Clarendon ed., *ad loc.*].

664. *cedar...foot* A proverbial antithesis (Tilley, C 208), perh. going back to 1 Kings iv. 33 (cedar and hyssop as extremes).

677. *wolf...lamb* Cf. ll. 65–7 n.

688. *And...again* Cf. Ovid, *Fasti*, II. 811, 'Quid, victor, gaudes? haec te victoria perdet ' [Wynd.].

Ewig, p. 25, noted ll. 211–17, 692–714, as related to this sentiment; so, most succinctly, l. 730 [J. C. Collins, *Studies in Sh.* (1904), p. 17].

699. *taste...souring* Cf. *R.II*, 1. 3. 236 and Tilley, M 1265 (with F. P. Wilson, *R.E.S.* N.S. III (1952), 197).

702. *still* See G.; Schmidt cites under 'silent', but this is much less apt.

707. *Till...tire* Cf. *H.VIII*, 1. 1. 134, 'self-mettle tires him' [Steev.].

711. *bankrupt* Q 'banckrout'; cf. *Ven.* 466 n.

713. *it...that* desire...the flesh.

715–17. *Rome...doom* Cf. ll. 1644–5, 1849–51, *J.C.* 1. 2. 156 n.; Kökeritz, p. 141.

730. *A...gain* See l. 688 n.

732. *The...remain* Cf. Tilley, W 929.

733. *perplexed* Cf. *Ven.* 1043 n.

741. *on* Cf. *Ven.* 160 n.

747. *day...lay* The earliest quotation in Tilley, N 179. But Bush¹, p. 301, quotes the similar passage from Spenser, *F.Q.* III. iv. 59, 'For day discouers all dishonest wayes, | And sheweth each thing, as it is indeed'; also *2 H.VI*, 4. 1. 1, 'The gaudy, blabbing and remorseful day' [Steev.], where n. in this ed. cites *Lucr.* 806, as well as the present line.

755. *water...steel aqua fortis* [Porter].

764–70. *O...ravisher* 'In style and substance this is rather close to...*F.Q.* III. iv. 55, 58' (Bush¹, p. 301).

766. *Black...tragedies* Cf. *1 H.VI*, 1. 1. 1 [Hudson], with n. in this ed.

779. *unwholesome* Q 'vnholdsome', cf. *L.L.L.* (Q) 5. 2. 746, 'holdsome', Kökeritz, p. 300.

780. *The...purity* that which gives purity its very existence; like 'the supreme fair', refers to the sun. *supreme* See *Ven.* 996 n.

782. *musty* Many edd. accept the more conventional 'misty' (Q 3), which is used with 'vapours' in *Ven.* 184 [Dyce].

787. *handmaids* Cf. *Troil.* 5. 2. 92, 'Diana's waiting-women' [Mal.¹].

788. *Through...peep* J.D.W. cites this (and l. 801) in n. on *Mac.* 1. 5. 52, 'Nor heaven peep through the blanket of the dark'.

790. *fellowship...assuage* A very common proverb; Tilley, C 571.

793. *cross...arms* Cf. l. 1662·n.

803. *still* See l. 702 and G.; it could be adv., but reads more naturally as adj.

805. *sepulchred* Sh. regularly stresses the vb. on the second syllable.

807. *charactered* Sh. stresses the vb. sometimes on the first and sometimes on the second syllable.

812. *quote* Q 'cote'.

820. *senseless* The natural contrast would seem to be between her reputation which cannot feel and herself who can, but that does not seem a relevant point to make in the context. Hence Lee might be right in glossing 'free from, or irreconcilable with, sensual sin', though no comparable meaning is recorded.

828. *unfelt* not physically perceived.

831–2. "*How*..."*Alas* Cf. ll. 87–8 n.

836. *honey* So for chastity also in *Tit.* 2. 3. 131.

841–2. *Yet...Yet* The second line answers the contention of the first; Lucr. engages in internal dialogue; cf. ll. 239–41 n.: in the Kyd passage there cited, 'Ay, but' and 'Yet' alternate.

853. "*But* Cf. ll. 87–8 n.

855–9. *coffers up...barns* Baldwin, p. 135, links with a note on Luke xiii. 15, in the 1560 Geneva Bible, about 'the arrogancie of the riche worldelings, who as thogh they had God locked vp in their coffres

& barnes, set their whole felicitie in their goods'.

858. *Tantalus* The use of him as emblematic of a miser is current in Renaissance commentaries on Ovid, ultimately from Horace, *Sat.* 1. i. 68 ff. [Baldwin, pp. 134–5; on a further possible link between Horace and the Bible (ll. 855–8 n.), see K. Muir, *N. & Q.* CCI (1956), 424–5].

875. *quality* See G.

876–924. *O...doom* For a stock declamation on this theme, cf. R. Taverner, *Proverbes* (1539), sigs. C 8–8ᵛ [Bush¹, pp. 301–2; Erasmus original quoted in Baldwin, p. 136]. See also Tilley, O 70, 'Opportunity is whoredom's bawd', and the Bastard on 'Commodity', *K.J.* 2. 1. 561–99 [Prince].

878. *sets* Cf. Franz, § 152, *Tim.* 4. 1. 2 n.

879. *point'st* Q 'poinst', an alternative device for euphony to the omission of the final 't' in l. 878.

889. *honey...gall* Cf. Tilley, H 556, 'No honey without gall'.

894. *Thy...last* Cf. Tilley, N 321, 'Nothing violent can be permanent', and *Rom.* 2. 6. 9, 'These violent delights have violent ends' [Mal.¹].

910. *wait...pages* Cited by J.D.W. in n. on *Mac.* 1. 5. 40, 'tend on mortal thoughts'.

922. *accessary* Sh. always stresses on the first syllable.   *inclination* (Q 3) Q inclination.' Q 2 'inclination,'.

925–59. *Misshapen...water-drops* For classical sources, see Baldwin, pp. 212–16; for Renaissance images of Time, S. C. Chew, *The Pilgrimage of Life* (1962), ch. 2.

928. *watch of woes* Because recording woes like a clock-face; Schmidt links with *Mac.* 2. 1. 54, as 'anything regularly repeated within a certain period'—I think 'watchman's cry' (On.) is best there, but that here Time is actually figured as a time-piece.

937. *opinion* For the normal derogatory sense, see *Per.* 2. 2. 56 n.

940. *bring...light* Cf. Tilley, T 324.

944. *thy* She slips into direct address to Time.

950. *cherish* I can scarcely believe the text is sound, as one would expect some action hostile to springs, to balance 'To dry...sap'; but Warburton's 'tarish' would be too much a mere repetition of 'dry' and Johnson's 'perish' is also unconvincing. Perh. Sh. rather carelessly slipped in an example of the more beneficent side of Time's activity, which is more fully represented in the next stanza.

954. *the man a child* Cf. Tilley, M 570, 'Old men are twice children'.

959. *waste...water-drops* Cf. *Ven.* 200 n., ll. 560, 592 above.

962. *retiring* See G.

964. *bad debtors* This antedates O.E.D.'s earliest quotation for 'bad debt' (1622).

966. *prevent* See G.

968. *cross* See G.

973. *Shape...devil* Cf. Tilley, B 738.

975. *bedrid* Q 'bedred', cf. *Ant.* 3. 10. 10 n.

978. *hearts...stones* Cf. Tilley, H 311.

990–2. *Let...sport* For this commonplace, cf. *A.Y.L.* 3. 2. 305–29.

993. *unrecalling* For a similar formation, cf. *Tit.* 3. 1. 90, 'unrecuring' [Pool.], and Franz, §665 (e), Abbott, §372.

1001. *sland'rous* Q 'sclandrous', as in l. 161.

1003. *his hope* the hope centred on him.

1004. *The...thing* Cf. *Edw. III*, 2. 1. 434 ff. [Østerberg, *Sh. Jb.* LXV (1929), 58]; see l. 489 n.

1013–15. *kings...Gnats...eagles* The same collocation in *Tit.* 4. 4. 82–4 [A. K. Gray, *S.P.* XXV (1928), 307; quoted earlier by Sarrazin, p. 34].

1021. *force* See G.

1027. *smoke* Cf. *L.L.L.* 3. 1. 62.

1028. *indeed* Cf. *Ven.* 667 n.

1029. *foul-defilèd* The hyphen (S. Walker) makes the expression less tautological. Cf. *Ado*, 4. 1. 142 (where also Walker hyphenated 'foul-tainted'); with G. R. Trenery's note on l. 140 (Arden ed. 1924).

1039. *this no slaughterhouse* this place which is not a slaughterhouse.

1053. *To clear* by clearing.

1053–4. *give...livery* add to the livery of disgrace a badge of fame that will, in some measure, mitigate the disgrace. The image is deliberately paradoxical: normally a badge goes with the livery—here it contradicts it.

1081. *slow sad* Most edd. since Mal. hyphenate, but surely the adjj. are independent; so Prince.

1092. *do* do with.

1109–18. "*For*..."*Deep* Cf. ll. 87–8 n. It is notable that these lines contain only one proverb recognized by Tilley; cf. ll. 1118–20 n.

1109. *mirth...annoy* Cf. *Tit.* 2. 3. 262, 'Now to the bottom dost thou search my wound', and n. in this ed.

1113. *sympathized* See G.

1118–20. *Deep...knows* Cf. Tilley, S 929, *Ven.* 331–3 n.

1123. *mute and dumb* So *Ham.* 2. 2. 137 [Mal.¹].

1126. *Relish* Q 'Ralish'; cf. *Meas.* (F), 1. 2. 15, 'rallish', Kökeritz, p. 185. For meaning see G.

1133. *burden-wise* Q 'burthen-wise'.

1134. *descants* Cf. l. 878 n.

1135. *against a thorn* Cf. Barnfield's poem in *P.P.* 20, 10 [Round, *ap.* Furnivall facsimile (1885), p. xxvi], Tilley, N 183; and earlier quotations from J. Hall (1563) and others, in F. P. Wilson, *The Proverbial*

Wisdom of Sh. (1961), p. 21. Still earlier is the 'favourite old part song of King Henry VIII' (Naylor *ap.* Roll.), which occurs in B.M.Royal MSS., Appendix 58 (ed. E. Flügel, *Anglia*, XII (1889), 264; also in *Oxford Book of 16th c. Verse*, no. 17): 'She syngeth in the thyke | And under hur brest a p^rike | to kepe hur fro slepe'.

1139. *Who* The most natural antecedent is 'mine' in l. 1138.

1142. *sing'st...day* For this popular fallacy see *M.V.* 5. 1. 105 [Mal.²].

1155. *death...debtor* It is not quite clear whether this means that death will incur (additional) reproach, as the following stanza suggests, or merely that it will not wipe out the whole of the reproach. Still other interpretations have been offered, but they fail to satisfy the conditions (noted by Brown) that this phrase should refer to the case *against* death, as 'life is shamed' does to that against life.

1157. *body* body's.   *pollution* Q 'pollusion', giving a perfect rhyme; cf. *L.L.L.* (Q), 4. 2. 47, 'polusion'.

1160. *conclusion* See G., and cf. Gobbo's perversion 'try confusions' in *M.V.* 2. 2. 34 [Verity], where the 'Roberts' Q substituted 'conclusions'.

1167. *pilled* Q 'pild' edd. 'peeled'; see G., and cf. *M.V.* 1. 3. 81 n. (where 'pyled' is an error for 'pyld').

1180-1. *breath...bequeath* Cf. *Ven.* 1002 n.

1181-1204. *My...me* Roll. refers to E. C. Perrow, 'The Last Will and Testament as a Form of Literature' in *Trans. of the Wisconsin Academy*, XVII (1913), 682-753. Prob. the best-remembered example is Donne's 'The Will'.

1182. *by him* Q. uncorr. 'for him'. See Note on the Copy, p. 148.

1190. *new born* born anew (hence no hyphen, *pace* most edd. since Mal.[2] (first Lintott)).

1213. *pearl* Collective, as often.

1216. "*For* Cf. ll. 87–8 n.   *with…flies* Cf. Tilley, T 240, with earlier quotation in F. P. Wilson, *The Proverbial Wisdom of Sh.* (1961), p. 23.

1230. *Of* with.

1236. *drops*' (Prince) Q 'drops'; cf. l. 128 n.

1240–3. *For…skill* For this commonplace, E. Scott, *Athenaeum*, 7 July 1877, p. 15, cited Caxton, *Game…of the Chesse* (1474), ed. W. E. A. Axon (1883), pp. 123–4, 'For the women ben likened vnto softe waxe or softe ayer and therfor she is callid mulier whyche Is as moche to saye in latin as mollys aer. And in english soyfte ayer | And it happeth ofte tymes that the nature of them that ben softe and mole | taketh souner Inpression than the nature of men that is rude and stronge'. For the 'mollis aer' part of this, cf. *Cym.* 5. 5. 446 n.

1242. *strange kinds* 'natures alien to their own' (Hudson).

1245–6. *evil…devil* See Kökeritz, pp. 188–9.

1257. *hild* So Q for rhyme; cf. Kökeritz, p. 188.

1258. *faults* For plur., cf. *Tit.* 5. 3. 100, 'For their fell faults'.

1261. *precedent* Q 'president': see *Ven.* 26 n.

1266–7. *That…dead* Ewig, p. 28, suggested an imitation of Chaucer, *L.G.W.* 1814–18, in which (as also in Gower) Lucrece faints. He also saw a contradiction with ll. 677–86, which he explained by Sh.'s reading Chaucer in the meantime. But here she is not described as fainting, merely as being paralysed with fear [Prince]. Sh. is in fact half way between Chaucer on the one hand and Livy and Ovid on the other, in whose versions she yields to fear of Tarquin's threats, but is not represented as being physically incapacitated by fear.

1268. *bid* bade.

1272. *of my sustaining* which I undergo.

1273. *small* Adv. here only in this sense ('little')
in Sh.

1299. *will* passion; 'wit' and 'will' are traditional
terms in the opposition of intellect and emotion; cf.
Gent. 2. 6. 12, *L.L.L.* 2. 1. 49, and see R. Pruvost,
'Variations élisabéthaines sur *wit* et *will*' (*Mélanges
Fernand Mossé* (1959), pp. 423–36).

1301–2. *Much...before* Perh. Sh. recalls the
jostling of the rumours in Chaucer, *Hous of Fame*,
2088 ff. Cf. also *K.J.* 5. 7. 18–20 [Mal.¹], *H.VIII*,
2. 4. 185–6.

1302. *which...before* 'striving which shall enter
first' [Prince].

1308. *from our house* A customary way of ending a
letter [Mal.¹].

1310. *tenor* Q 'tenure'; a common sp.: cf.
Kökeritz, p. 271.

1311, *uncertainly* 'not so as to convey certain
knowledge' (Schmidt).

1312. *schedule* Q 'Cedule'.

1324. *To...told* Cf. Horace, *Ars Poetica*, 180–2
[Mal.¹].

1326. *motion* See G.

1327. *a...bear* Metaphor from part-song.

1329. *Deep...fords* Cf. Tilley, W 130, with
earlier quotations in F. P. Wilson, *The Proverbial
Wisdom of Sh.* (1961), p. 24; a metaphorical variant on
S 664 (see *Ven.* 329–30 n.).

1332. *with...haste* Cf. *Ven.* 909.

1335. *blast* Q uncorr. 'blasts'. See Note on the
Copy, p. 148.

1338. *curtsies* Q 'cursies'; cf. *Tit.* 5. 3. 74.

1342. *lie* Cf. *Ven.* 1128 n.

1345. *silly* Q 'seelie'.

1348. *talk in deeds* Cf. *Troil.* 4. 5. 98, 'Speaking in deeds' [Mal.²].

1350. *this...the* Some copies of Q have 'the... this'. See Note on the Copy, p. 148.

1355. *wistly* Cf. *Ven.* 343 n.

1357–8. *replenish...blemish* Cf. *Ven.* 47–8 n.

1366–1568. *At...sore* In spite of extensive speculation on possible pictorial originals (whether paintings, 'painted cloths', or tapestries), there is nothing in this description to suggest anything but a literary source. The classical example of such a description is Virgil, *Aen.* 1, 453 ff. [Lee, facsimile ed. (1905), p. 16]. For the relevance of the fall of Troy to *Lucr.* see Baldwin, pp. 144–5, D. C. Allen, *Sh. Survey*, 15 (1962), 94.

1367. *for* to represent.

1374. *lifeless* Q 'liuelesse'; see *Ven.* 211 n.

1377. *painter's strife* Cf. *Ven.* 291 n.

1380. *pioneer* Q 'Pyoner', with the usual Sh. ending.

1388. *triumphing* Sh. varies between 'tríumph' and 'triúmph' for the vb.

1394. *Ajax and Ulysses* A stock contrast since Ovid, *Met.* XIII [Root, p. 35]; used again by Sh. in *Troil.*, where Achilles rather than Ajax is the main representative of brute strength against intelligence.

1411. *mermaid* Q 'Marmaide'; cf. *Ven.* 429 n.

1414. *seemed,* (Mal.¹) Q 'seem'd'.

1420. *but...of* except that it would have made them lose; for the compression, cf. *Ant.* 2. 2. 216, 'but for vacancy'.

1422. *imaginary* Apparently a transferred epithet, 'appealing to the imagination'. Roll. quotes a happy phrase from Lamb, 'On...Hogarth', *Works*, ed. E. V. Lucas (1903), 1, 74, 'This he well calls *imaginary work*, where the spectator must meet the artist in his conceptions half way'. The rest of the stanza elaborates the notion. Neither 'fanciful' (Schmidt) nor 'of the nature of an image' (O.E.D.) is so appropriate. E. H. Gombrich, *Art and Illusion* (1960), pp. 211–12, cites as source the praise given by Philostratus, *Imagines*, I. 4, to the painter who depicted armed men 'so that some are seen in full figure, others with the legs hidden, others from the waist up, then only the busts of some, heads only, helmets only, and finally just spearpoints'.

1425. *Griped* Q 'Grip't'; Sh. never has the form 'grip'.

1433. *to...yield* they express their hope in such strange (equivocal) gestures. See G. 'action': a common meaning (see Schmidt), though often overlooked by edd. Sh. is constantly referring to significant gesture in this description. Some take 'hope' concretely=Hector, as in l. 1430.

1436. *strand* Q 'strond'.

1444. *all* nothing but; so in l. 1446.

1449. *Which...lies* As if 'Priam' were the antecedent. Pyrrhus treads on Priam's breast in Marlowe, *Dido*, 2. 1. 242, not in Virgil [Bush², p. 151 n.].

1450. *anatomized* Q 'anathomiz'd': similar spellings are common; cf. *L.L.L.* in this ed., p. 103.

1452. *chaps* Q 'chops'; cf. Kökeritz, p. 165; O.E.D. has a quotation as late as Wesley (1767).

1478–84. *Why...general* J. M. Tolbert, *N. & Q.* cxcviii (1953), 14–15, suggests as a source the Senecan quotations, with editorial comments, in Mirandula's *Illustrium Poetarum Flores* (Section 'De Scelere'), which T. W. Baldwin, *Sh.'s Small Latine and Lesse Greeke* (1944), II, 414, regards as probably though not certainly used by Sh. at school (cf. epigraph to *Ven.*).

1478–80. *one...alone* Cf. *Ven.* 293–4 n.

1486. *swounds* (Mal.¹) Q 'sounds', a common

form; cf. *Comp.* 305, 308, *Tit.* (Qq, F) 5. 1. 119, Kökeritz, pp. 246–7.

1497. *pencilled* See G.

1502. *Phrygian* Root, p. 107, thinks that the use of this word (not in Phaer's translation) shows a direct debt to Virgil, *Aen.* 11, 68.

1505. *So...woes* I think this means 'so mild that Patience did not seem to regard his woes as sufficient to be worth exercising herself upon'.

1507. *the...show* Either 'the harmless painted figure' (Mal.¹), or, perh. more pointedly, 'the appearance of harmlessness'.

1517. *False creeping* Hyphenated by Mal.², but surely the adjj. are independent.

1521. *Sinon* For the Sinon–Tarquin link, see Baldwin, pp. 144–6, quoting Baynes, pp. 638–9.

1525. *little...places* Cf. *M.N.D.* 2. 1. 153, 'certain stars shot madly from their spheres' [Mal.¹]; Virgil, *Aen.* 11, 693–4 [Wynd.].

1529. *some...abused* 'the painter had insulted [rather, 'misused'?] some other person's shape by painting it and calling the portrait Sinon' (Craig).

1542. *So...mild* A similar sequence in *2 H.IV*, 1. 1. 70–1, 'Even such a man, so faint, so spiritless, | So chill, so dead in look, so woe-begone', also in connexion with the fall of Troy.

1544. *arméd to beguild* (Q) Gildon, 'armed, so beguil'd'. But the original, as Munro (London ed. 1958) argues, is perfectly sound, if we suppose 'beguild' to be a twin of 'beguile' for the sake of the rhyme, like 'twind' in *Ven.* 873, where see note. (At *Ven.* 24, Q 5 reads 'time-beguilding' for 'time-beguiling' of Qq 1–4.) Pool. notes that he 'once thought' this, but follows Gildon in his text.

1549. *sheds* Q 'sheeds', giving a perfect rhyme: so *Son.* 34. 13–14 [Roll.], cf. Kökeritz, p. 187.

1550. *why...wise* Cf. *Lr.* 1. 4. 240 [Prince].

1560–1. *flatter...water* A normal rhyme at the time: see Kökeritz, p. 171.

1573. *sorrow's...sustaining* Cf. l. 128 n. This is even odder than the other instances, because of the interposition of the transposed epithet 'sharp', and some may prefer to take as 'sustaining sharp sorrows', with contorted word-order. Q's 'sorrowes', of course, is neutral between the two.

1576. *Which* I.e. the passage of time (l. 1575).

1577. *That* Antecedent, 'all this time' (l. 1576).

1581–2. *It...enduréd* Cited by Tilley, F 295, 'I am not the first and shall not be the last'.

1585. *Who* The 'other company' is passed over, as of subordinate importance.

1589. *to* in addition to.

1590. *sad-beholding* Prob.='seriously gazing at', with slight word-play on 'sad' (='sorrowful') in l. 1591; cf. *Tit.* 5. 3. 82, where S. Walker hyphenated 'sad-attending'.

1597–8. *At...begins* He asks the question also in Livy, quoted in Marsus's notes on Ovid [Baldwin, p. 101], and in Gower, not in Ovid or Chaucer [Ewig, p. 21].

1604. *Three times* Cf. Ovid, *Fasti*, 11, 823, 'ter conata loqui' [Round *ap.* Furnivall, 1885 facsimile, p. xxv]—a favourite tag—and l. 567.

1604–5. *gives...fire...discharge* Metaphor from 'discharging ancient fire-arms by means of a match' (Staunton).

1611–12. *And...ending* Sh. refers to the swan's dying song also in *Oth.* 5. 2. 250–1, *M.V.* 3. 2. 44–7, *K.J.* 5. 7. 21–4, *Phoen.* 14–15 [T. F. T. Dyer, *Folk Lore of Sh.* (1884), p. 147].

1619. *the...bed* An obscure phrase; perh. 'interest' is best taken concretely, 'that in which one has a right', and 'of thy bed' as defining the interest: hence 'into your bed, in which you (alone) have a legitimate interest'.

1632. *of thine* Cf. l. 515 n.

1644. *Rome* Q 'Roome'; cf. ll. 715–17 n.

1648. *forbade* Q 'forbod', as in *Comp.* 164; Q 3+ 'forbad'.

1650. *scarlet* Like a judge's robe [Wynd.]. Tarquin is judge, presumably, because of his status as the king's son, but the conceit remains unsatisfactory.

1655–6. *Though...mind* Cf. Livy, 1, 58, 'corpus est tantum violatum, animus insons' [Ewig, p. 22]; quoted in Marsus's notes on Ovid [Baldwin, p. 103].

1658. *accessary* 'that would make me an accessary' (Pool.). Sh. always stresses on the first syllable.

1660. *merchant* Q 'Marchant', cf. *Ven.* 429 n. *loss* Abstract for concrete, 'lost vessel'.

1662. *wreathéd* (S. Walker) Q 'wretched', but 'wreathéd arms' is a stock phrase for arms folded as a sign of sorrow; Walker cites *L.L.L.* 4. 3. 133, as well as Peele and Fletcher; so *Tit.* 3. 2. 4, 'sorrow-wreathen knot', with n. in this ed. The MS. may have had 'wrethed', misread 'wreched'.

1663. *new* anew; hence the hyphenated 'new-waxen' (Sewell) is out of place, as in l. 1190, though here Alexander and Prince accept it.

1671. *rage,* (Mal.1) Q 'rage'.   *being past* Apparently 'once it (the tide) has passed', but the phrase has the air of a rather unhappy stop-gap.

1677. *slaketh* Cf. l. 425 n.

1680. *one woe* (Q 3) Q 'on woe'.

1682. *she* Cf. *Ven.* 109 n.

1687. "*For* Cf. ll. 87–8 n.   *sparing...iniquity* Cf. *Meas.* 2. 1. 277–8, Tilley, P 50, and *Tim.* 3. 5. 3 n.

1706. *any terms* 'anything that I might do' (Schmidt); for Sh.'s vague use of 'terms', see Schmidt, On.

1709–10. *With...clears* Cf. Livy, I, 58, 'conso-
lantur aegram animi...mentem peccare, non corpus'
[Ewig, p. 22]; quoted in Marsus's notes on Ovid
[Baldwin, p. 102].

1713. *in it* (Capell MS.) Q 'it in'.

1714–15. *No...giving* Cf. Livy, I, 58, 'nec ulla
deinde impudica Lucretiae exemplo vivet' [Mal.¹, who
noted (1790) that the sentiment was also in Painter];
quoted in Marsus's notes on Ovid [Baldwin, p. 103].

1715. *excuse's giving* Cf. l. 128 n.

1723–4. *Even...unsheathéd* For the casuistry of
Lucrece's suicide (acceptable by Roman standards),
see Roll. on ll. 1707–8, esp. Augustine's condemnation,
De Civ. Dei, I, 19, summed up in the dilemma, 'Si
adulterata, cur laudata? si pudica, cur occisa?' An
interesting verdict concurring with Augustine ('laudis
avida') is that of Tyndale, *Obedience of a Christian
Man* (*Doctrinal Treatises*, Parker Society, 1848), pp.
183–4, who attributes her whole conduct to pride: 'She
sought her own glory in her chastity, and not God's.'

1729. *Life's...date* An obscure phrase; what one
would expect to fly through the wounds is simply 'life'
or 'the soul'; perh. the meaning is, 'life, which is
destined to be everlasting'.

1730–1. *Stone-still...Collatine* Cf. Spenser, *F.Q.*
II. vi. 31. 9, 'Wherewith astonisht, still he stood, as
senselesse stone' (E. I. Fripp, *Sh. Man and Artist*
(1930), p. 384).

1734–6. *And...chase* Sh. seems to have recalled
this in describing the deed of the other Brutus in *J.C.*
3. 2. 178–81 [Pool.].

1737–9. *And...side* Cf. *Tit.* 2. 4. 22–4 [Parrott,
p. 29].

1740. *vastly* See G.; adv. where mod. Eng. would
use an adj. predicatively; cf. *Cym.* 4. 2. 180 n.

1745. *rigol* I.e. the serum.

1768. *falt'ring* Q 'foultring'; cf. *Cor.* 4. 7. 55 n.

1774. *key-cold* For the proverbial comparison, cf. Tilley, K 23.

1790. *At...o'er* Cf. *Ven.* 458 n.

1794. *the...lay* what they lay claim to.

1801. *too late* When joined with 'too soon' in *3 H.VI,* 2. 5. 92–3 [Steev.] this means 'too recently', and Mal.¹ so interprets here. But the context suggests rather 'too late to save herself from dishonour' (Verity).

1821–2. *is...deeds* For the principle, cf. Tilley, G 446, 'The greater grief drives out the less'.

1822. *help...help* The repetition is rather feeble, and S. Walker's 'heal wounds' may be right.

1832–4. *suffer...chaséd* allow to be chased; cf. *All's,* 1. 3. 112–13, 'suffer her poor knight surprised'.

1832. *abominations,* (Q 3) Q 'abhominations.'.

1835. *Now...adore* Cf. *Tit.* 2. 1. 61, 'Now, by the gods that warlike Goths adore'.

1836. *by...blood* So Chaucer, *L.G.W.* 1862, 'by hir chaste blood'; and Livy, 1, 59, 'per hunc castissimum ante regiam iniuriam sanguinem' [Ewig, p. 23]; quoted in Marsus's note on Ovid [Baldwin, p. 103].

1838. *country* See G.

1839. *by...soul* Cf. Ovid, *Fasti,* 11, 842, 'perque tuos manes' [Ewig, p. 25].

1850–1. *They...Rome* So, as Furnivall noted (1885 facsimile, p. vii), Chaucer, *L.G.W.* 1866–7; he, however, like Gower, places her death in Rome. The idea of a journey from Collatium to Rome, followed by the display of the body in the market-place, is found in Barnaby Googe's *Prouerbes of...Sir Iohn Lopez de Mendoza* (1579), fo. 60ᵛ, cited by G. K. Hunter, *N. & Q.* cxcvii (1952), 46, who notes that this version also affords all that Sh. is usually thought to have got from Livy.

1851. *Rome* Q 'Roome', cf. ll. 715–17 n.

1855. *Tarquin's...banishment* It is curious that Sh. makes no mention here (though the Argument concludes with it) of the historical importance of this, as involving the abolition of the monarchy (unless 'everlasting' glances at it); this tells heavily against the view of E. P. Kuhl, *P.Q.* xx (1941), 352–60, that the popularity of the poem owed much to its bearing on political issues.

THE PASSIONATE PILGRIM

I

A version of *Sonn.* 138. Folger MS. 2071. 7, which also has versions of 4, 6, 7, 11 and 18, has a text almost identical with that of *P.P.* Most commentators treat the 1609 text as a revision of this, but Prince (following Brooke) thinks that 'the earlier readings are just of the kind that might be expected in an inaccurate report'. This is hard to believe when the poem is compared with 2, where the trifling variants *do* suggest merely an inaccurate report. In the more seriously discrepant lines, 'forgeries' is used in a sense for which O.E.D. has only one pre-Sh. quotation, and 'unskilful' and 'outfacing' are both Sh. words (though common enough elsewhere). The variants in ll. 9 and 11 are not so clearly authentic, but the presumption is in their favour. For comment on readings common to this and the 1609 text in both 1 and 2, see *Sonn.* volume.

4. *Unskilful...forgeries* 1609 'Vnlearned... subtilties'. As Prince notes, 'false forgeries' is tautological, but this is not enough to prove the reading a mere corruption.

6. *I know...years* 1609 'she knowes...dayes'. *be* 1609, Folger 'are'. Perh. a corruption, but 1609 may be a revision.

7. *I smiling* 1609 'Simply I'.

8. *Outfacing...rest* 1609 'On both sides thus is simple truth supprest'. The most puzzling line in the *P.P.* text, but also the hardest to attribute to mere misreporting. *Outfacing...love* 'dissembling (i.e. concealing any knowledge of) faults in love' (Case *ap.* Pool.). *with...rest* Obscure and perh. corrupt. The more plausible sense seems to me to be 'with (the help of) the ill-grounded sense of security that is characteristic of love'. To interpret 'rest' as 'remainder'

is less plausible. Dowden, facsimile ed. [1883], p. vii, glosses 'ill rest', by 'uneasy sleep'.

9. *my...young* 1609 'she not she is vniust'. The only indication in the poem that the beloved is not young. Even if we have here revision and not corruption, Dowd. is clearly right in saying that 'there should be one lie on each side, and that the lady's lie should be an assertion of fidelity, the man's lie an implied assertion of his youth', as in 1609.

11. *habit's in* (O) O 2 'habite is', which looks like a smoothing of a harsh expression, especially as 1609 has 'in'.   *habit's...tongue* 1609 'habit is in seeming trust'. Pool. glosses 'love is best clothed in flattery', which is prob. right, though Brown and Brooke (ed. of *Sonnets*, 1936), no doubt to soften the metaphor, would make 'habit'='demeanour, deportment'; so Schmidt for the 1609 text, but the clothing image is surely present there.   *soothing* Folger MS. 'smoothinge', re-introduced by Gildon[1].

12. *to have* 1609 't'haue'.

13. *I'll...and love* 1609 'I lye with her, and she'.

14. *Since that...in love thus smothered* 1609 'And in...by lyes we flattered'.

2

A version of *Sonn.* 144. As there is no sign that this is more than an ill-transmitted text (though it corrects an obvious 1609 error in l. 6), I give only collation; for commentary, see *Sonn.* volume.

2. *That* 1609 'Which'.

3. *My* 1609 'The'.

4. *My* 1609 'The'.

6. *side* 1609 'sight'.

8. *fair* 1609 'fowle'.

11. *For...to* 1609 'But...from'.

13. *The truth I shall not* 1609 'Yet this shal I nere'.

3

A version of *L.L.L.* 4. 3. 58–71. None of the corrup-
tions, here or in 5 and 16, seem significant. All *L.L.L.*
citations from Q 1.

2. *could not L.L.L.* 'cannot'.

9. *My vow was L.L.L.* 'Vowes are but'. Caught
from l. 7.

10. *that…this…doth L.L.L.* 'which…my…
doost'.

11. *Exhal'st (L.L.L.)* O 'Exhalt'; O 2 'Exhale'.

12. *broken, then L.L.L.* 'broken then,', which is
obviously right.

14. *break L.L.L.* 'loose'.

4

Other versions in Folger MSS. 2071.7 (see on 1) and
1.8 (which also contains 11). It seems reasonable to
attribute all four Venus and Adonis poems, 4, 6, 9 and
11, to Bartholomew Griffin, as 11 is a version of a
sonnet in his *Fidessa* (1596). All are dependent on
Venus and Adonis.

1. *Sweet* Folger 1.8 'ffaire'.

2. *green* Cf. *Ven.* 806 [Brown].

4. *could* Folger 1.8 'can'.

5. *ear* (Folger 1.8, Mal.[1]) O 'eares'.

8. *soft* Folger 2071.7 'sought'.

10. *refused* Folger 1.8 'did scorne'. *her* (O 2)
O 'his'. *figuréd* O 'figured' Folger MSS.
'figurd'.

11. *touch* Folger 1.8 'take'.

12. *smile…jest* Folger 1.8 'blusht…smild'.

13. *queen* om. Folger 1.8. *toward:* (Sew.[1] O 3
with comma) O 'toward'.

14. *rose…ah* Folger 1.8 'blusht…ô'.

5

A version of *L.L.L.* 4. 2. 112–25.

2. *O L.L.L.* 'Ah'.
3. *constant L.L.L.* 'faythfull'.
4. *me like L.L.L.* 'me were'.
6. *can L.L.L.* 'would'.
11. *Thine* (O 2) O 'Thin' *L.L.L.* 'Thy'. *seems L.L.L.* 'beares'.
13. *do not...that L.L.L.* 'pardon...this'.
14. *To sing L.L.L.* 'That singes'.

6

Version in Folger 2071.7. For the scene portrayed cf. *Shr.* Ind. ii. 50–1 [Pool.]. Root, p. 32, notes the indebtedness to Ovid's Salmacis and Hermaphroditus story, esp. *Met.* IV, 347–9.

6. *spleen* A word used in connexion with various passionate impulses. Here, the most obvious is sexual desire, so that this poem does not present the cold Adonis of *Ven.* Kittredge, *ap.* Roll., however, takes *spleen* to be 'literal'.

12. *this* Folger MS. 'the'.
13. *whereas he stood* Prince joins with l. 14, glossing 'and as he stood there'; more naturally, with most edd., 'jumped in from where he was standing'.
14. *O* Folger MS. 'Ah'.

7

Version in Folger MS. 2071.7. No evidence as to authorship. On Lee's claim for Barnfield of 7, 10, 13, 14, 17 and 18, see Harry Morris, *Richard Barnfield, Colin's Child* (1963), pp. 147–56. Morris confidently rejects 14, 17 and 18, and regards the other three, especially 13, as possibilities.

3. *brittle* The form *brickle*, required by rhyme, is found, e.g., in Spenser, *F.Q.* IV. x. 39.9 [Pool.].

10. *whereof* O 3 'thereof'.

11. *midst* (O 3, Folger MS.) O 'mids': see O.E.D. for this form, still found in the 1611 Bible.

13. *fire* Disyllabic.

8

By Richard Barnfield, in *Poems: In diuers humors*, added to *The Encomion of Lady Pecunia* (1598). The identification of the 'R.L.' to whom the poem is addressed as Richard Linche, author of *Diella* (1596), is shown to be very insecurely based by Harry Morris, *Richard Barnfield: Colin's Child* (1963), pp. 112–13.

7–8. *conceit...conceit* Word-play, though there are not two clearly distinct senses: conceit (understanding) in the reader responds to, but is transcended by, the conceit (imagination or invention) of the poet.

14. *One knight* 'Prob. Sir George Carey, K.G., to whom Dowland dedicated his first book of airs (1597). His wife, daughter of Sir John Spencer of Althorpe, was a great friend of Spenser' (L. *ap*. Herf.). But, as Harry Morris points out (*op. cit*. p. 115), the 'both' of 'loves both' is music and poetry, rather than Dowland and Spenser, and 'the identity of the knight becomes folly to speculate upon since the only clue left is his love for two of the arts'.

9

No other version. Mal.[1] first noted the omission of l. 2.

3–4. *dove,...wild,* In the absence of l. 2, it is impossible to determine the exact relationship of ll. 3–5, and consequently the appropriate punctuation. I retain that of O.

5. *steep-up* Also in *Sonn.* 7. 5; 'steep-down' in *Oth.* 5. 2. 283.

13–14. *one...alone* Cf. *Ven.* 293–4 n.

10

No other version. No evidence on authorship. Perh., as some have thought, 13 is by the same author.

8–10. *For why . . . For why* (Dyce) O 'For why:... For why:'. The meaning is 'because' (cf. Franz, §560), but it is often, as here, followed by strong punctuation in early texts.

8–9. *left'st . . . left'st* (Gild.²) O 'lefts . . . lefts', which is less unpronounceable; cf. *Lucr.* 878 n.

11

A version in Bartholomew Griffin's *Fidessa* (1596), and others, generally agreeing with *P.P.*, in Folger MSS. 2071.7 and 1.8.

1. *with* Griffin, Folger 1.8 'and'; Folger 2071.7 '&'   *young* om. Folger 2071.7.

3. *god* Folger 1.8 'great'.

4. *so fell she* (Griffin, Folger 1.8) O, Folger 2071.7 'she fell'. Edd. dispute whether 'fell to' is metaph.,='set to work on', or literal, ='fell towards'. I suspect a pun: in this instance the metaph. 'falling to' would involve literal falling.

5. *warlike* Griffin 'wanton'.

6. *clipped* Griffin 'clasp'd'; Folger 1.8 'tooke'.

7. *Even* Folger 2071.7 '&'   *warlike* Folger 1.8 'lusty'.

9–12. *Even . . . pleasure* Griffin, 'But he a wayward boy refusde her offer, | And ran away, the beautious Queene neglecting: | Shewing both folly to abuse her proffer, | And all his sex of cowardise detecting.' No evidence whether the *P.P.* variant comes from Griffin himself.

9. *Even* Folger 2071.7 'then'.

11. *And . . . fetchéd* Folger 1.8 'but . . . tooke hir'.

13. *Ah. . . . this* Griffin, Folger 1.8 'Oh. . . that'.

lady Griffin, Folger 'mistris'.　　*at this bay* Pool. fancifully thinks that 'the poet does not wish that he was hunting his lady, but that his lady was hunting him'. Rather, the hunting metaphor is somewhat worn, and the phrase means little more than 'at close quarters'.

14. *kiss...me* Folger 1.8 'clipp & kiss hir'.　　*run* Griffin, Folger 1.8 'ranne'.

12

The first stanza of 'A Maidens choice twixt Age and Youth' in Thomas Deloney's *Garland of Good Will* (earliest surviving ed. 1631, but referred to by Nashe (III, 84) in 1596). This may be the poem entered S.R. 26 Aug. 1591 as 'A pleasant *newe ballad Called the Maydens choyce*' [Mann's ed. of Deloney (1912), p. 579]. Not all the poems in the *Garland* are by Deloney (see Roll. p. 548), but at least he has a better claim to this than has Sh., the only argument for whom —a faint one—might be 'full of care' in l. 2, in a similar context to the same phrase in *Sonn.* 56. 13.

2. *pleasance* Deloney 'pleasure'.

3. *summer...winter* Deloney 'Summers...Winters'.

4. om. Deloney.

12. *stays* Deloney 'stay'st'.

13

No other versions, except in 18th c. periodicals, not collated here. No evidence of authorship: in an older manner than most of the collection—a typical 'Drab' poem, in C. S. Lewis's terminology (*English Literature in the Sixteenth Century* (1954), p. 64).

10. *cement* Stressed on the first syllable, as in Sh. O spells 'symant'.

11. *once* Some edd. insert an 'is'—Globe, gro-

tesquely, reading 'once's'—but the omission of the
finite verb is quite natural in such a gnomic expression:
cf. 14. 30.

14

No other version. Many edd. since Mal.¹ begin a new
poem with st. 3. No evidence on authorship.

8–10. *whether...thither* Cf. *Ven.* 511–13 n.

12. *As* such as.

14. *charge the watch* Disputed. Perh. 'accuse...
the watch [=timepiece] for marking the time too
slowly' (Rolfe).

14–16. *the morning...eyes* This has been thought
inconsistent with l. 19, since daylight there comes only
with the lark's song. But it seems natural to say that the
slightest sign of morning sets all the senses on the alert.

15–16. *rest,...eyes.* All edd. since Mal.¹, exc.
Kittredge (ed. of *Sh.* 1936), change the punctuation to
'rest....eyes,'. This is by no means an improvement:
l. 16 is loosely attached to what precedes, and the
meaning is, '*each* sense is summoned, since I cannot
trust my eyes alone (which would be the normal means
of deciding whether dawn is approaching)'. Joined to
ll. 17–18, l. 16 would have no appropriateness.

17. *sings* (Camb. conj.) O 'sits and sings'.

20. *And...night* The two lost syllables were prob.
an adj. between 'dark' and 'dreaming'.

24. *For why* Cf. 10. 8–10 n.   *sighed* O 'sight':
this form of the past tense originally belonged to the
obsolete 'siche' (see O.E.D.).

27. *a moon* (Steev. conj. *ap.* Mal.¹) O 'an houre'.

30. *Short night* I.e. 'let us have a short night'.
Mal.¹'s 'Short, Night,', whether he means 'Short' as a
verb or as='Be short', gives a most awkward effect;
'length' is addressed to night, not, as Pool. thinks, tc
to-morrow: night is to reimburse itself to-morrow.

15

This poem is preceded in O 2 by a new title-page (see pp. 149–50). No other version. No evidence on authorship. For the traditional *Disputatio inter militem et clericum* see W. A. Neilson, *Origin and Sources of the Court of Love* (1899) [Brown].

16

L.L.L. 4. 3. 99–118 (omitting 113–14). A version also (which I do not collate) in *England's Helicon* (1600), derived from *P.P.*, though it corrects the obvious error in l. 12 (present also in *L.L.L.* 1598). It is notable that, as Dowden observed (facsimile ed. [1883]), of the five poems from *P.P.* in *Eng.Hel.*, this, the only one by Sh., is also the only one there attributed to him.

2. *was* L.L.L. 'is'.
6. *'gan* L.L.L. 'can'.
8. *Wished* L.L.L. 'Wish' (wrongly).
11. *alas...hath* L.L.L. 'alacke...is'.
12. *thorn* (*Eng.Hel.*) O, L.L.L. 'throne'.

17

First in Thomas Weelkes's *Madrigals* (1597). Also in *England's Helicon* (1600) from *P.P.* (not here collated) and in Harl. MS. 6910 'perhaps a year or two older than' Weelkes (Rollins's ed. of *Eng.Hel.* 1935, II, 116). No evidence on authorship. The following poem, which is by Barnfield, is indeed printed in *Eng.Hel.* as 'Another of the same Sheepheards', but this is only because it is also from *P.P.*, and is no evidence (Roll. p. 552, following his ed. of *Eng.Hel.* II, 117).

1. *flocks feed...breed* Harl. 'flocke feedes... breeds'.

2. *speed...amiss* Harl. 'speedes not in their blis'.

3. *is dying*. This is also the text of Weelkes and Harl., and is presumably right, though most edd. follow Mal.[1]'s 'Love's denying', based on *Eng.Hel.*'s erroneous 'Loue is denying'. See Adams, pp. lii–iii, on ll. 3–4.   *faith's* Harl. 'fayth'.

4. *Heart's denying* Harl. 'her denyinge', which, with its 'fayth' in l. 3, may well be the true text. For 'denying', most edd. since Mal. have accepted 'renying' from *Eng.Hel.* But this is merely a conjectural emendation of the misprint 'nenying' in O 2, which must have been *Eng.Hel.*'s copy.

5. *my...quite* Weelkes 'our...cleane'.

6. *lady's love is* Harl. 'layes of Loue are'.

7. *her* Weelkes 'our' Harl. 'my'.   *faith was... fixed in* Harl. 'joyes were...linkt by'.

8. *a nay is* Weelkes 'annoy is' Harl. 'annoyes are'.

9. *One silly* Weelkes 'Our seely'.   *cross...my* Harl. 'poore crosse hath wrought me this'.

10. *frowning...cursèd fickle* Harl. 'fickle...cruell cursed'.

11. *For...see* Harl. 'Now you may see that'.

12. *More...remain* Harl. 'In women more than I my selfe haue found'   *men remain* Weelkes 'many men to be'.

13. *fears* Weelkes 'feare'.

14. *Love...living* Harl. 'lo how forlorne I, liue'.

15. *help* Harl. 'helpes'.

16. *cruel* Harl. 'cursed'.   *fraughted* Weelkes, Harl. 'fraught'.

17. *can* Weelkes, Harl. 'will'.

18. *bell rings* Harl. 'ringe a'.

19. *curtal* O 'curtaile' Weelkes 'curtall' Harl. 'curtail'd'.   *that wont to* Harl. 'wch would'.

20. *afraid* Harl. 'dismayd'.

21. *My...procures* (Weelkes) O 'With...procures' Harl. 'My sights so deepe, doth cause him'. I

accept 'My', as 'With' is a sheer blunder, but do not normalize the concord of 'procures'. The object, as Mal.[2] saw and as Harl. makes explicit, is 'him'.

22. *In...wise* Weelkes, Harl. 'With...noise'. *see...doleful* Harl. 'wayle...woefull'.

23. *How...ground* Harl. 'My shrikes resoundes, through Arcadia groundes'. *How* Weelkes 'Harke how'. *heartless* Weelkes 'harckless', of which O 'hartles' is probl. a corruption, though 'harkless' (=not listening) is not recorded elsewhere. If 'heartless' is correct, it may mean much the same: unsympathetic.

24. *a thousand...bloody* Harl. 'thousandes... deadly'.

26. *Green...dye* Weelkes 'Lowde bells ring not, cherefully'. *plants* Harl. 'palmes'. *their* Harl. 'yor', which would make 'spring', 'sing' and 'bring' all imperative. This is the point at which *P.P.* most clearly betrays dependence on a MS. occasionally closer to Harl. than to Weelkes, with whom it is normally in close agreement.

27. *stands* Weelkes 'stand'. *flocks all* Harl. 'ecchoes'.

28. *back* (Weelkes, *Eng. Hel.*) O 'blacke' Harl. 'looke'. *peeping* Weelkes 'creeping'. *fearfully* Harl. 'pittyfully'.

29. *our pleasure* Weelkes 'our pleasures' Harl. 'the pleasure'.

31. *sport...is* Weelkes, Harl. 'sportes...are'. *us* Harl. 'greenes'.

32. *our love is* Weelkes 'our loues are' Harl. 'alas is'. *for love* Harl. 'now Dolus'. Harl. ends here.

36. *see...is* Weelkes 'know...ther's'.

18

Versions in Lysons MS. (Folger 1. 112) and in Folger
MS. 2071.7. (Mere differences in spelling between
these two MSS. are not recorded.) No evidence on
authorship.

1–2. *When...strike* For the figure of the chase, cf.
Ovid *Ars.Am.* 1, 45–50 [Pool.].

1. *as* Folger MSS. 'y^t'.

2. *shouldst* Folger MSS. 'wouldest'.

4. *fancy...might* Folger 1.112 'fancye parcyall
like' Folger 2071.7 'parciall fancie like', which gives
sense and rhyme, and which a few edd. accept; 'partial
might' in the sense of 'partial being' [Steev.] or 'power'
is as good as the conj. 'wight' (Capell MS.), and
assonance for rhyme would not be too surprising.

5. *Take* Folger 2071.7 'aske'.   *wiser* Folger
MSS. 'other'.

6. *too young* Folger MSS. 'vnwise'.   *unwed*
Folger 1.112 'vnwayde'.

8. *Smooth* Folger MSS. 'Whett'.

10. *A...halt* Cf. Tilley, H 60, 'It is hard (ill)
halting before a cripple'.   *find* Folger 2071.7
'spie'.   *a* Folger 1.112 'one'.

11. *say* om. Folger 2071.7.

12. *thy...sell* (Folger MSS.) O 'her...sale'. The
meaning is, 'make the most of yourself' [Pool., citing
Ovid, *Ars Am.* 1, 595–6]. *person* Folger 2071.7 'body'.

13–24. *And...back* O 2 wrongly transferred these
stanzas to follow l. 36.

13. *And to* Folger 2071.7 'vnto'.

15. *desert...merit* Folger 1.112 'expences...
sounde thy' Folger 2071.7 'expence...sound thy'.

16. *By...in thy lady's* Folger 2071.7 'still be...
in in [sic] her'.   *in thy lady's* Folger 1.112 'all-
wayes in her'.

17. *castle, tower* Folger 2071.7 'towres fort'. *and* Folger MSS. 'or'.

18. *beats it* Folger 1.112 'hathe beat' Folger 2071.7 'beateth'.

20. *humble* (O 2) O 'hnmble' Folger 2071.7 'ever'.

21. *Unless* Folger 2071.7 'vntill'.

22. *Press* Folger 1.112 'seeke'.   *anew* Folger 1.112 'anewe' O 'anew' O 2 'a new' Folger 2071.7 'for newe'.

23. *shall...be thou* Folger 1.112 'dothe...then be' Folger 2071.7 'doth...thee be'.

24. *thee* Folger MSS. 'it'.

25. *though...frowning* Folger 2071.7 'if shee frowned w^th'.

26. *calm* Folger 1.112 'cleare'.   *ere* (Folger 1.112) O 'yer' (a common 16th c. sp.; again l. 29), Folger 2071.7 'at'.

27. *And...will* Folger 1.112 'And she perhappes will sone' Folger 2071.7 'when y^t perhaps shee will'.

28. *thus* Folger 1.112 'she', Folger 2071.7 'so'.

29. *ere it* (Folger 1.112) O 'yer it' Folger 2071.7 'it ere'.

30. *which with* Folger MSS. 'wth suche'.

31. *though...her* Folger 2071.7 'if...thy'.

32. *ban* Folger 1.112 'chide'.   *say* Folger 2071.7 'swere'.

34. *When* Folger MSS. '&'.   *hath taught* Folger 2071.7 'will cause'.

35. *so* Folger MSS. 'as'.

36. *In faith* Folger 2071.7 'by cock'.   *had it* Folger 1.112 'got it'.

37–42. *The...nought?* This stanza follows l. 48 in Folger MSS.

37. *The...work* Folger 2071.7 'A thousand wiles

in wantons lurkes'.   *women work* Folger 1.112 'in them lurkes'.

39. *that...lurk* Folger 1.112 '& meanes to woorke' Folger 207.7 'the meane to worke'.

40. *shall* Folger 2071.7 'doth'.

41. *Have you* Folger 2071.7 'hast y^u'.   *it* Folger 1.112 'that'.

42. *A...nought?* Cf. Tilley, W 660, 'A woman says nay (no) and means aye'.

43. *still to strive* Folger 1.112 'love to matche' Folger 2071.7 'seeke to match'. The *P.P.* text can be construed, but it is hard to think that the substitution of 'still' for a verb is more than an error.

44. *To...saint* Folger 1.112 'and not to live soe like a sainte' Folger 2071.7 'to liue in sinne & not to saint'. The *P.P.* text is again clumsy, but Folger 2071.7 confirms the unusual vb. 'saint'.

45. *There* Folger MSS. 'here'.   *by...then* Folger 1.112 'they...then' Folger 2071.7 'be...then'. This last is the obvious reading, and 'by' cannot be right, but the Folger 1.112 text of ll. 45–6 suggests some confusion at an earlier stage of the transmission.

46. *When...them* Folger 1.112 'beginne when age dothe them' Folger 2071.7 'till time shall thee w^{t}h age'.

47. *kisses* Folger MSS. 'kyssinge'.

49. *But, soft* Folger 1.112 'Nowe hoe' Folger 2071.7 'ho now'.   *too...fear* Folger 2071.7 '& more I feare'.   *enough,...fear,* O's punct. need not be changed (though the comma after 'fear' could be dropped). Collier[1] first introduced a comma after 'much', and made 'too...fear' a parenthetic correction of 'enough'.

50. *Lest...mistress* Folger 1.112 'for if my ladye' Folger 2071.7 'for if my m^{rs}'.   *hear my* Folger 1.112 'heare this' Folger 2071.7 'hard this'.

51. *will* Folger 2071.7 'would'.   *round...ear*

Folger 1.112 'ringe my eare' Folger 2071.7 'warme my eare'. The MSS. give the sense required; the normal meaning of 'round in [not 'on'] the ear' is 'whisper to', and this phrase seems to have been in the transcriber's mind, leading him to write nonsense.

53. *will* Folger MSS. 'would'. *blush* Folger 2071.7 'smile'.

54. *so* Folger MSS. 'thus'.

19

The first four stanzas by Marlowe, to whom the poem is attributed in *England's Helicon* (1600), which has a longer text independent of *P.P.* 'Love's Answer' is the first stanza of the reply attributed to Sir Walter Raleigh. There are several MS. copies of both, but I collate only *Eng.Hel.* Both were first published in *P.P.*

1. *Live Eng.Hel.* 'Come liue'.

3. *hills...dales Eng.Hel.* 'Vallies, groues, hills'.

4. *And...yield Eng.Hel.* 'Woods, or steepie mountaine yeeldes'.

5. *There will we Eng.Hel.* 'And wee will'.

6. *And see Eng.Hel.* 'Seeing'.

7–10. *By...posies* Sung by Sir Hugh Evans, *M.W.* 3. 1. 16–19.

7. *by Eng.Hel.* 'to'.

8. *sing Eng.Hel.* 'sings'.

9. *There will I...a bed Eng.Hel.* 'And I will... beds'.

10. *With Eng.Hel.* 'And'.

16. *Then Eng.Hel.* 'Come'.

17. LOVE'S ANSWER *Eng.Hel.* 'The Nimphs reply to the Sheepheard', as the title of a separate poem of six stanzas attributed to 'Ignoto'.

20

By Richard Barnfield, in his *Poems: In diuers humors* (1598). *England's Helicon* (1600) has a shorter version, dependent on *P.P.* except for a final couplet which replaces ll. 27–56. On possible sources, see Harry Morris, *Richard Barnfield, Colin's Child* (1963), pp. 124–7.

10. *Leaned...thorn* Cf. *Lucr.* 1135 n.

44. *commandment* O 'commaundement', giving the four-syllable scansion required.

THE PHOENIX AND THE TURTLE

1. *the...lay* Most edd. think that Sh. leaves the bird unidentified, prob. rightly. But as the contrasting 'shrieking harbinger' is identifiable, there is perh. something to be said for Fairchild's view that it is the crane, citing Chaucer, *P.F.* 344, 'The crane, the geaunt, with his trompes soun' [p. 363]. R. Bates, *Sh.Q.* VI (1955), argues for the cock, citing *Ham.* I. I. 150, 'The cock that is the trumpet to the morn'. But against any identification, see M. C. Bradbrook, *ibid.* p. 356.

2. *sole* One phoenix, one tree; cf. *Tp.* 3. 3. 23, 'one tree, the phoenix' throne' [Mal.¹].

5. *shrieking harbinger* screech-owl; cf. *M.N.D.* 5. I. 374–6 [Mal.¹].

10. *of...wing* of prey. Fairchild (p. 365) quotes Chaucer, *P.F.* p. 334–5, 'the tiraunt with his fetheres donne | And grey, I mene the goshauk', the eagle having been mentioned in l. 330. For background, see J. A. W. Bennett, *The Parlement of Foules* (1957), pp. 150–1.

15. *death-divining* presaging its own death (by its song).

16. *his right* its due.

17. *treble-dated* A vaguely intensive epithet for 'long-lived': prob. not three times any particular number of years, though Pliny talks of the crow as living '9 times as long as we' (*N.H.* VII, 48, p. 180 of Holland's tr. (1601)) [Pool.].

18–19. *That...tak'st* Halliwell–Phillipps (ed. 1865) quoted Swan's *Speculum Mundi* (1635), p. 397: 'Neither...doth the raven conceive by conjunction of male and female, but rather by a kinde of billing at the mouth, which Plinie [*N.H.* x. 12] mentioneth as an opinion of the common people.'   *sable gender* black offspring.

25–6. *So...one* Cf. *Sonn.* 36, 1–2 [K. Muir and
S. O'Loughlin, *The Voyage to Illyria* (1937), p. 133].
The idea, of course, is a commonplace.

25. *as* Sh. perh. leaves it open to us to choose
between the more extreme assertion 'that' and the more
guarded 'as if'.

27. *distincts* separate things (here only). The con-
trast between distinction and division inevitably recalls
the Athanasian creed, 'neither confounding the persons
nor dividing the substance', as Walter Whiter (with
some disquiet) noted (*Specimen of a Commentary on
Sh.* (1794), pp. 257–8). For the relation of *P.T.* to
scholastic tradition, see J. V. Cunningham, *E.L.H.*
XIX (1952), 265–76, esp. 273–6.

28. *Number...slain* Cf. the proverb 'One is no
number' (Tilley, O 54; *Sonn.* 136.8) [Adams *ap.*
Roll.].

32. *But* except.

34. *his right* what was due to him, viz. a return of
love [Pool.].

36. *mine* Edd. are sharply divided on whether this
is a noun ='source of wealth' (Schmidt) or a pronoun =
'self'. The latter fits in with the arguments on unity
and duality, but sounds to me indefinably wrong, at
least as the primary meaning. Perh. a pun (so Alvarez,
p. 12; Gardner), with the sense of the noun pre-
dominant.

37. *Property* selfhood (personified); 'what belongs
to an individual (*proprium*)' (Gardner).

38. *self...same* Normally synonymous in Sh.; but
the other sense of 'self' makes it poss. to state the
paradox without absolute self-contradiction.

41. *Reason...confounded* Reason here, though for
the opposite reason, suffers the same conflict as in
Troil. 5. 2. 142–52.

43–4. *To...compounded* Deliberately mysterious

syntax, with incantatory effect. A poss. paraphrase would be 'and yet to themselves neither of them was simply itself and not the other as well, so well were they compounded though each was simple'. What is perfectly simple is normally (*a*) indivisible, (*b*) incapable of entering into union without losing its simplicity. (Cunningham (p. 275) takes 'To themselves' in isolation as = 'each of the two was distinct'.)

45. *How...twain*. Word-play on 'true' = (*a*) how faithful a pair, (*b*) how truly are they two (in spite of also being one).

47. *Love...reason* These words 'owe all their importance to the fact that it is Reason who utters them' (C. S. Lewis, *English Literature in the Sixteenth Century* (1954), p. 509); cf. also J. M. Murry's reference to 'Reason's deliberate homage to a higher power' (*Discoveries* (1924), 1930 ed., p. 25). The gnomic form emphasizes the reversal of such proverbs as 'love is without reason' (Tilley, L 517).

48. *If...remain* '*If two that are disunited* from each other, can yet remain together and undivided' (Mal.¹).

55. *enclosed,* As Prince insists, the comma after this word should not be dropped: 'Here enclosed' = 'enclosed in this way'.

58-9. *rest....posterity,* Almost all edd. since Mal.¹ (not Gardner, or Harrison, Penguin ed. 1959) change the punctuation to make l. 59 go with l. 58. Straumann (*Phönix und Taube* (1953), p. 56) gives the right and natural explanation: 'that they left no posterity was not etc.'. The syntactical irregularity is slight compared with that in ll. 43-4.

67. *sigh* Dependent on 'let' (l. 65).

A LOVER'S COMPLAINT

2. *sist'ring* For the parallel with *Per.* 5, Prol. 7, 'That even her art sisters the natural roses', wh. edd. treat as first noted by Mal.[1], see Sewell[1], p. 442.

3. *spirits* Cf. *Ven.* 882 n.

4. *laid* If this is pa. indic., it='lay', as nowhere in Sh., and gives an awkward asyndeton between ll. 3 and 4, or ellipse of 'I' before 'espied'. (This is paralleled in l. 299.) To treat it as pa. pple gives a word-order which is perh. equally awkward, but to leave open the possibility I retain Q's comma after 'tale', instead of strengthening it to a semi-colon with most edd.

7. *world* I.e. the 'little world of man' (*Lr.* 3. 1. 10) [Mal.[2]].   *sorrow's* (Gildon[2]) Q 'sorrowes,'.

8. *platted* Q 'plattid', cf. l. 198 n.

14. *lattice* Q 'lettice', as in *All's* (F), 2. 3. 217 [Craig]. O.E.D. has several C 16–17 instances. For the image, cf. *Son.* 3. 11–12 [Mal.].

16. *conceited characters* 'emblematic devices' (Pool.).

18. *seasonéd...pelleted* Steev. notes as culinary, a pellet being a forcemeat ball. This is poss., but for 'the idea of salt tears acting as seasoning' and for the link with 'pelleted' in *Ant.* 3. 13. 165, see Muir, p. 159.

20. *shrieking* Q 'shriking'. Honigmann, pp. 88–9, discusses various occurrences of the word in *Troil.* (Q), describing it as 'a Sh. spelling not very common in 1609'. O.E.D. treats *shriek* and *shrike* as distinct words.

22. *her...ride* 'The allusion is to a piece of ordnance' (Mal.[1]); cf. ll. 281–2.

28. *commixt* Q 'commxit'.

29–35. *Her...negligence* S. Walker plausibly suggested indebtedness to Sidney's *Arcadia* (1590), III, 5

(=*Works*, ed. A. Feuillerat, 1, 376), 'In the dressing of her haire and apparell, she might see neither a careful arte, nor an arte of carelesnesse, but even left to a neglected chaunce', and *Arcadia* (1593) (=11, 168), 'she had cast on a long cloake...with a poore felt hat, which almost covered all her face, most part of her goodly heare...so lying upon her shoulders, as a man might well see, had no artificiall carelesnes'. Sh. prob. had an earlier part of the first passage in mind in *Lr.* 4. 3. 18–25 (see New Arden note).

30. *a...pride* I.e. a hand whose pride showed itself in carelessness: she thought she could get away with this negligence.

37. *beaded* (Gildon[1] 'beded') Q 'bedded', prob. just a variant spelling for the short vowel, see Kökeritz, pp. 201–2.

40. *Like...wet* A common conceit; cf. *A.Y.L.* 2. 1. 48–9 [Steev.].

41. *monarch's* (Gildon[2]). Capell MS.'s 'monarchs'' is also possible. *lets* Cf. *Ven.* 517 n.

42. *cries* See G.

43. *one* Cf. *Ven.* 293–4 n.

48. *feat and affectedly* Cf. Abbott, § 397, *J.C.* 2. 1. 224, 'fresh and merrily'.

51. *'gan* (Mal.[1]) Q 'gaue', which On. (<Knight) regards as poss., with 'give' intrans. = 'give oneself up to'. It is easier to suppose a misreading of 'gãne' with omitted macron. Cf. l. 118 n.

56. *Big* Perh. with a hint of the sense 'pregnant'.

60. *observéd...flew* Apparently indicates that he 'was also a philosopher of life' (Wyndham).

61. *fastly* Not very appropriate sense if it= 'hastily' (Schmidt); and 'near' [='fast (by)'] (Palgrave) is not closely parallel to any exx. in O.E.D. Possibly an error for 'softly' (spelt, as not uncommonly, 'saftly').

65. *comely distant* at a fitting distance. It is a matter of indifference whether or not we hyphenate, with Mal.¹.

78. *attended* Q 'atttended'.

79. *suit—...grace—* (Globe) Q 'suit...grace;'. Sewell first noted 'it...grace' as a separate phrase.

80. *O,* (Capell MS.) Q 'O' Gildon 'O!' Many have unnecessarily read 'Of' (Tyrwhitt).

81. *That...face* Cf. *Tim.* 4. 3. 262–4, 'the eyes and hearts of men...That numberless upon me stuck' [Pool.]; *Meas.* 4. 1. 59–60, 'millions of false eyes | Are stuck upon thee' [Jackson: see p. xxxvi].

86. *occasion* 'chance breath' (Craig).

91. *largeness* I.e. of imagination.   *sawn* Irregular, whether for 'seen' [Mal.¹] or 'sown' [Boswell]. The former seems more likely.

95. *seemed* Not a straightforward contrast of appearance and reality; presumably='was seen'.

96. *Yet...dear* Various puns have been seen in 'cost': on 'coat' (as in l. 236) [Wyndham], or on Fr. 'coste'='refuse silk' [Pool.]. But the meaning seems to be that his bare skin is more valuable by contrast with the 'phoenix down' on which some outlay ('cost') has been made.   *showed* Q 'shewed'; for nonsyllabic '-ed' after 'w', cf. *Ven.* 366 n.

100. *thereof* of his tongue.

104. *authorized* Sh. elsewhere (twice) so stresses, on the second syllable.

107–9. '*That...makes*' First marked as quotation by Mal.¹.

111. *became...deed* performed his feats becomingly.

112. *by th'* (Gildon) Q 'by'th', with which cf. *Oth.* (Q) 1. 3. 399, 'bit'h', 5. 2. 357, 'bi'th', *Ham.* (Q 2), 1. 5. 162, 'it'h' [Honigmann, p. 118, among spellings 'uncommon outside Sh.'].

115. *appertainings* Recorded only here and in *Troil.* 2. 3. 79 (Q; F 'appertainments'. A. Walker, note in this ed., regards 'appertainings' as 'possibly assimilated to the following "visiting"', but it may well be a Sh. substitution in transcribing; in general, see Honigmann, ch. 6).

118. *Came* (Sewell) Q 'Can'. Mal.[1] compared this same error in *Mac.* 1. 3. 98. If the MS. had 'cam', this would be an example of the 'absence of final e mute' for which see *MSH* 114.

119. *were* As if 'aids' and not 'trim' were the subject.

123-4. *sleep:* (Sewell)...*weep*, (Mal.; Sewell with no punct.) Q 'sleep,...weepe:'.

126. *will*, (Benson) Q 'will.'.

127. *general bosom* Cf. *Ham.* 2. 2. 566, 'general ear' [Steev.].

131. *Consents...desire*, (Mal.) Q 'Consent's... desire'.

132. *dialogued...say* I.e. have imagined his share in the dialogue.

139. *labouring* Wyndham conj. 'labour', which would certainly regularize the construction.

142. *mistress* Plural; cf. *Tp.* 1. 2. 173, 'Princesse' (where Rowe's 'princes' should be rejected), and Franz, §189a.

144. *in part* in shared ownership.

155. *precedent* So spelt in Q, not 'president', as usu. in Sh.

161. *wills* (J.C.M.) Q 'wits'. But the whole point is the arousing of *passions* in the attempt to blunt them by advice. The sp. 'wils' occurs twice in l. 133.

164. *forbod* Cf. *Lucr.* 1648 n.   *seems* Cf. *Ven.* 517 n.

169. *This man's untrue* Q 'This mans vntrue'. Edd. '"This man's untrue"'—surely sadly flat. Pool.

notes that Q is most naturally interpreted 'I could tell
more of his perfidy', but yields to Case's verdict that
this is 'fantastic'. Though 'say' = 'tell of' is not
precisely paralleled, it seems preferable to the usual
reading; that 'say' = 'assay' is also poss. In either case,
'could' = 'was able', not 'should be able'. For 'un-
true' = 'untruth', cf. *Son.* 113. 14 (if the Q text is
retained).

176. *city* A frequent metaphor for chastity; cf.
Lucr. 469 [Mal.²].

182. *woo* (Capell MS.) Q 'vovv'.

183. *offences* evidence of my wrongdoing.

192. *th'* Q 'th,'.

197. *here* (Benson) Q 'heare'.

198. *palèd* (Mal.²) Q 'palyd' Gildon 'pallid'.
Q.'s sp. is prob. just a variant of the '-id' ending found
in l. 8, though it could represent the pple of an un-
recorded vb. 'paly': Sarrazin, Supplement to Schmidt,
cites 'palied' from *I Return from Parnassus* (ed. J. B.
Leishman (1949), p. 87; Leishman accepts this as
simply = 'paled').   *red as blood* Proverbial (Tilley,
B 455).

204. *hair* (Benson) Q 'heir'.

207. *their...acceptance* I.e. my acceptance of
them.

208. *the* (Capell MS.) Q 'th'', against the metre.
This elision, as a graphic device, is not uncommon at
the time. Examples in Daniel's *Delia* (1592), where
the metre demands a syllable, are *Son.* 18. 4, 5, 'And to
th' Orient do thy Pearls remoue. | Yeelde thy hands
pride vnto th' yuory whight'; 27.12, 'Th' Ocean of my
teares must drowne me burning'; 40. 5, 'Th' Ocean
neuer did attende more duely'. Daniel is a poet in
whom genuine elision of 'th'' is very common. Of
these lines, only 27. 12 was later revised to remove the
anomaly.

212. *invised* Tentatively glossed by O.E.D. as
'unseen'. Given the odd vocabulary of the poem it is
prob. best to accept this, but the assumption of an easy
minim error would give an attested word, 'unused'=
'unusual'.

214. *Weak...amend* This property is described in
Pliny, *N.H.* xxxvii, 5 [Craig].   *radiance* App.
nonce-use for 'power of vision' (Mackail, p. 56).

215–16. *The...manifold* Edd. have made heavy
weather of this, but it seems fairly straightforward. All
the stones described symbolize qualities in the young
man, and the power of sapphire and opal to 'blend...
manifold' corresponds to his fickleness; 'blend' is pr.
indic.

224. *I* I.e. I being.

227. *similes* 'symbolical love-tokens' (Schmidt).

228. *Hallowéd* (Sewell) Q 'Hollowed'; cf.
Kökeritz, p. 225, *MSH*, p. 116.

229–30. *What...you* The drift is clear: the
servant of anyone's servant is indirectly the servant
of that person; 'for you' is obscure, since the similes
were not offered for her service, but Pool.'s gloss
'instead of you' seems unnecessary—the phrase simply
underlines that she is the real beneficiary. I follow
Q in having no internal punctuation in this line and
a half.

230. *comes* Cf. *Ven.* 517 n., 1128 n.

233. *Or* Mal.¹'s conj. 'A' is possible.

234. *her...suit* 'the solicitation of her noble
admirers' (Mal.¹).

235. *blossoms* 'Those who were full of youth and
rare promise' (Schmidt, comparing *R.II*, 5. 2. 46–7,
'Who are the violets now, | That strew the green lap
of the new come spring?').

236. *spirits* Cf. *Ven.* 882 n.

237. *kept...distance* remained coldly at a distance;

cf. the specific application to fencing in *Rom.* 2. 4. 21, and G. C. Moore Smith's note on 'keep a distance' in Bacon's *New Atlantis* (1900), Glossary.

238. *eternal love* love of what is eternal; for the relation of adj. to sb., cf. *Ham.* 1. 5. 21, 'this eternal blazon'.

241. *Playing* Pretty clearly corrupt. 'Playing' is prob. sound in l. 242, and caught up from it here. Mal.'s 'Paling' has met with some favour. He glosses, 'receiving within the pale of a cloister that heart which had never received the impression of love'; but the context calls for a metaphor parallel to 'mast'ring... strives', which would be a given by Capell MS. 'Planing'—'smoothing the place (in a pillow) which has not in fact had any impression made on it'. But the lost word need not have resembled 'Playing': other possibilities are Lettsom's 'Salving', or Sisson's 'Healing', with 'harm' (Lettsom) for 'form'.

242. *unconstrainèd* (Gildon²) Q 'vnconstraind'; 'which one is not obliged to wear' (Pool.).

251. *immured* (Gildon¹) Q 'enur'd', which some retain='hardened', 'habituated'. But the context demands the emendation; for the sp., cf. *L.L.L.* (Q), 3. 1. 123, 4. 3. 325.

252. *procured* (Benson) Q 'procure'. Edd., with commas after 'now' (Gildon¹) and 'all' (Mal.¹), explain 'she...now has procured her liberty to prove the whole experience of love'. It is not easy to understand 'has' from the context, and I should prefer to understand 'will be' out of 'would be', and to paraphrase, 'and now she wants to be induced to experience liberty in its fullest extent', i.e. she will meet any encouragement half-way.

260. *nun* (Capell MS.) Q 'Sunne'. The corruption is odd, but Q can scarcely be defended as='a very sun of sanctity' (Wyndham).

261. *ay* Q 'I': the normal sp.

262. *assail* assail her heart.

270. *kindred*, (Benson) Q 'kindred', perh. not entirely impossible in this poem, with 'kindred fame' = 'the reputation of one's family'.

271. *Love's...shame* Love's war against...shame is a peaceful one [Mal.¹, substantially].

272. *sweetens* As if 'Love', not 'arms', had been the subject.

273. *aloes* Italicized ('*Alloes*') in Q.

275. *bleeding* 'because every sigh was supposed to draw a drop of blood from the heart' (Pool.); cf. *M.N.D.* 3. 2. 97 n.

281–2. *dismount...levelled...sights* Metaphor from fire-arms (cf. l. 22) [Mal.]. There may be word-play on 'sight' = 'pupil of eye', which On. records as still current in Warwickshire. But more likely only (*a*) sight of a fire-arm, (*b*) power of sight (abstractly; for use in plur. see O.E.D.) are concerned.

284. *flowed* Q 'flowed'; cf. l. 96 and *Ven.* 366 n.

287. *encloses.* Q 'incloses,'.

290–1. *But...wear* Cf. *Ven.* 200 n.

293. *O* (Gildon¹) Q 'Or'.

298. *sober...civil* For the collocation, cf. *Rom.* 3. 2. 10–11, 'Come, civil Night, | Thou sober-suited matron all in black'.

299. *Appear* Cf. l. 4 n.

303. *Applied...cautels* 'applied, i.e. applicable, to his crafty designs' (Pool.).   *strange* Q 'straing'; cf. *Sir Thomas More*, 2. 4. 13, and *L.L.L.* 5. 2. 759 n.

305–8. *swooning...swoon* Q 'sounding...sound'; cf. *Lucr.* 1486 n. I normalise in accordance with the practice of this ed.: cf. *Troil.* 3. 2. 22 n.

312. *them* 'the *strange forms* of line 303' (Alden).

315. *preached pure maid* Cf. *A.Y.L.* 3. 2. 226, 'Speak sad brow and true maid' [Pool.].

319–20. *hovered*. (Gildon, with colon)...*lovered* (Gildon) Q 'houerd,...louerd.'.

323. *infected* See G.

324. *glowéd* (Collier¹) Q 'glowd', but 'bestowed' and 'owed' in ll. 326, 327 (and also, contrary to the rhyme, 'fore-betrayed' in l. 328, where Benson read 'fore-betrai'd').

GLOSSARY

Note. Where a pun or quibble is intended, the meanings are distinguished as (*a*) and (*b*). Notes such as 'here only' refer to what O.E.D. records.

ABIDE, submit to; Lucr. 486.

ABOMINATION, (i) abominableness; Lucr. 704; (ii) abominable act; Lucr. 921, 1832.

ABROAD, in the outside world; Comp. 137, 183.

ABUSE (sb.), (i) misuse; Ven. 166; (ii) corrupt practice; Ven. 792; (iii) offence; Lucr. 269, 1315.

ABUSE (vb.), misuse; Lucr. 864, 1529; (ii) maltreat; Lucr. 1267.

ABUSING, misuse; Lucr. 994.

ACCENT, (i) speech; Lucr. 566; (ii) modulation of voice; Lucr. 1719.

ACCOMPLISHED, perfect; Comp. 116.

ACCOMPLISHMENT, execution of a purpose; Lucr. 716.

ACCORD, agree; Comp. 3.

ACQUAINTANCE, body (here, pair) of friends (cf. *Oth.* 2. 1. 201); Lucr. 1595.

ACQUIT, atone for; Lucr. 1071.

ACTURE, action (here only); Comp. 185.

ACTION, (i) significant gesture; Lucr. 1403, 1433; (ii) (*a*) normal sense, (*b*) as (i); Lucr. 1323.

ADDICT, addicted; P.P. 20. 41.

ADDRESSED, prepared; Lucr. 1606.

ADJUNCT, annexed as a consequence; Lucr. 133.

ADON, Adonis (abbrev. form); Ven. 769, 1070; P.P. 6. 6; 9. 4.

ADVANCE, raise up; Lucr. 1705.

ADVANTAGE (sb.), (i) opportunity; Ven. 129; (ii) 'take advantage of (on)', make use of; Ven. Ded. 6–7; 405.

ADVANTAGE (vb.), benefit; Ven. 950.

ADVISED, (i) deliberate; Lucr. 1849; (ii) 'be advised', act only after consideration; Ven. 615.

ADVISEDLY, carefully, with deliberation or reflexion; Ven. 457; Lucr. 180, 1527, 1816.

AFFECTED (to), in love (with); Ven. 157.

AFFECTEDLY, lovingly; Comp. 48.

AFFECTION, love, desire; Ven. 387, 569, 650; Lucr. 271, 500, 1060; Comp. 146, 192.

AGENT, bodily organ; Ven. 400.

AIDANCE, aid; Ven. 330.

AIRY, insubstantial; Comp. 226.

ALARM, (i) sudden attack; Ven. 424; (ii) trumpet-call to arms, so, warning sound; Ven. 651; (iii) (*a*) (ii), (*b*) (i); Lucr. 473.

ALARUM, battle cry, call to arms (fig.); Ven. 700; Lucr. 433.

ALIGHT, alight from (here only trans.); Ven. 13.

ALLOW, approve; Lucr. 1845.

ALONG, at full length; Ven. 43.

AMAIN, at full speed; Ven. 5.

AMAZE, perplex; Ven. 684.

AMAZED, perplexed, bewildered; Ven. 469, 823, 925; Lucr. 446, 1356.

AMAZEDLY, perplexedly; Lucr. 1591.

AMPLIFY, make much of; Comp. 209.

ANATOMIZE, show minutely, in detail; Lucr. 1450.

ANNEXION, addition; Comp. 208.

ANNOY, auffering, grief; Ven. 497, 599; Lucr. 1109, 1370.

ANON, (i) again (answering 'sometime'); Ven. 279, 302; (ii) after a time; Ven. 700, 869; Lucr. 433.

ANSWER, (i) correspond to, come up to, satisfy; Ven. Ded. 13; (ii) repay, Lucr. 83.

ANTHEM, song of grief or mourning; Ven. 839; Phoen. 21.

ANTICS, grotesque figures; Lucr. 459.

ANTIQUITIES, ancient monuments; Lucr. 951.

APOLOGY, encomium; Lucr. 31.

APPAY, satisfy; Lucr. 914.

APPERTAINING, what belongs to a person; Comp. 115.

APT, readily; Ven. 354.

ARGUE, prove; Lucr. 65.

ARRIVE, tr., reach; Lucr. 781.

ART, artifice; Comp. 145, 174, 295.

As, (i) (i) as if; Ven. 323, 357; Phoen. 25 (or (ii)); (ii) (after 'so'), that; Lucr. 1372.

ASKANCE, turn aside (here only); Lucr. 637.

ASPIRE, (i) mount up; Ven. 150; (ii) mount up to; Lucr. 5.

ASPIRING, rising; Lucr. 548.

ASSAY (sb.), attempt; Lucr. 1720.

ASSAY (vb.), (i) attempt; Ven. 608; (ii) learn by experience; Comp. 156.

ASTONISHED, dismayed; Lucr. 1730.

ATTAINT (sb.), (i) infecting influence; Ven. 741; (ii) disgrace, stain; Lucr. 825, 1072.

ATTAINT (vb.), disgrace, dishonour; P.P. 18. 46.

ATTEND, tr., listen to; Lucr. 818, 1682.

ATTORNEY, advocate; Ven. 335.

AUTHOR, originator; Ven. 1006; Lucr. 523, 1244.

AUTHORIZED, sanctioned; Comp. 104.

AVAIL, be of use to; Lucr. 1273.

AVAUNT, be gone; Lucr. 274.

BACKED, ridden; Ven. 419.

BAIL, release by becoming bail for; Lucr. 1725.

BALK, let slip; Lucr. 696.

BAN, curse; Ven. 326; Lucr. 1460; P.P. 18. 32.

BANE, destruction; Ven. 372.

BAR (sb.), line (as impediment); Lucr. 327.

BAR (of), debar (from); Ven. 330 (without 'of'); 784; (with 'from') Lucr. 340.

BARE (sb.), naked surface; Comp. 95.

BARE (adj.), threadbare (fig.); Ven. 188.

BARN, enclose as in a barn; Lucr. 859.

BASE (sb.), 'bid a base'= challenge; Ven. 303 (as in game of 'prisoner's base', in which a player who leaves his 'base' is chased, and, if caught, made prisoner).

BASE (adj.), (i) menial; Ven. 395; Lucr. 1001; (ii) despicable; Lucr. 1000; (iii) (a) of mean rank, (b) mean, despicable; Lucr. 660; (iv) lowgrowing; Lucr. 664.

BAT, staff; Comp. 64.

BATE-BREEDING, causing strife; Ven. 655.

BATELESS, not to be blunted; Lucr. 9.

BATTLE, body of troops (fig.); Ven. 619.

BAY, position in which a hunted animal turns and faces the hounds; Ven. 877; P.P. 11. 13 (see note).

BEADED, made into beads; Comp. 37.

BEAR, (i) refl., behave; Lucr. 1096; (ii) sustain, keep going (a musical part); Lucr. 1132, 1135; (iii) 'bear back', move back; Lucr. 1417.

BEARING, deportment; Lucr. 1389.

BEGUILD, beguile; Lucr. 1544.

BEHOOF, advantage; Comp. 165.

BELDAM, old woman; Lucr. 953, 1458.

BELIED, filled with lies (cf. Cym. G. 'belie'); Lucr. 1533.

BEREAVE, take away; Ven. 439, 797; Lucr. 373, 835.

BETHINKING, action of thinking; Ven. 1024.

BETUMBLED, disordered (here only); Lucr. 1037.

BEWRAY, reveal (the identity of); Lucr. 1698; P.P. 18. 54.

BIDING, abode; Lucr. 550.

BLAME, sin; Lucr. 620.

BLAST, wither; Lucr. 49.

BLAZE FORTH, proclaim abroad; Ven. 219.

BLAZON, describe fitly; Comp. 217.

BLOT (sb.), (i) disfiguring mark; Lucr. 537; (ii) disgrace; Lucr. 1322.

BLOT (vb.), (i) obscure; Ven. 184; (ii) tarnish, sully; Ven. 796; Lucr. 1322, 1519.

BLUNT, rough, unfeeling, unpolished; Ven. 884; Lucr. 1300, 1398, 1504.

BOLLEN, swollen; Lucr. 1417.

BORROWED, counterfeit; Lucr. 1549.

BOW-BACK, arched back; Ven. 619.

BRAIDED, plaited; Ven. 271.

BRAKE, thicket; Ven. 237, 876, 913; P.P. 9. 10.

BRAVE (adj.), finely dressed; P.P. 12. 4.

BRAVE (vb.). challenge; Lucr. 40.

BREACH, place where something is broken; Ven. 1175.

BREAK, (a) break (lit. of the heart), (b) go bankrupt; Ven. 336.

BREATHING WHILE, time taken by a breath, very short period; Ven. 1142.

BREEDER, female; Ven. 282, 320.

BRINE, tears; Lucr. 796.

BRINISH, salt; Lucr. 1213.

BROKER, go-between; Comp. 173.

BRUISED, battered; Lucr. 110.

BULK, body; Lucr. 467.

BURDEN-WISE, as a burden or undersong; Lucr. 1133.

BUT, (i) only; Ven. 208, 347, 412, 414; (ii) except; Phoen. 32; (iii) that... not; P.P. 20. 40.

BY-PAST, bygone; Comp. 158.

CABIN, (i) cave; Ven. 637, 1038 (fig.); (ii) small room; P.P. 14. 3.

CABINET, dwelling; Ven. 854; Lucr. 442 (fig.).

CAGED, cage-like; Comp. 249.

CAITIFF, wretch; Ven. 914.

CALL, 'call all to naught' = abuse, decry vehemently; Ven. 993.

CAN, (i) may; Ven. 79; (ii) understand; Phoen. 14.

CANKER, worm; Ven. 656.

CANKERING, eating away; Ven. 767.

CAPITOL, temple on Capitoline hill; Lucr. 1835.

CARELESS, reckless; Ven. 556.

CARRIAGE, gun-carriage (fig.); Comp. 22.

CARRY-TALE, tale-bearer; Ven. 657.

CASE, clothes; Comp. 116.

CASTAWAY, ruined person; Lucr. 744.

CAUTEL, crafty device; Comp. 303.

CAVE-KEEPING, dwelling in caves; Lucr. 1250.

CEASELESS, unceasingly moving; Lucr. 967.

CHAFING, anger; Ven. 325.

CHALLENGE, lay claim to; Lucr. 58.

CHAMPAIGN, open and flat; Lucr. 1247.

CHANCE, (i) fortune; Lucr. 1596; (ii) happening; Lucr. 1706.

CHANNEL, gutter; Lucr. 1487.

CHAOS, (primeval) night; Ven. 1020; Lucr. 767.

CHAP, crack in the skin; Lucr. 1452.

CHARACTER, inscribe; Lucr. 807.

CHARM (sb.), spell; Lucr. 173.

CHARM (vb.), enthral; Lucr. 1404, 1681.

CHARMED, magically endowed; Comp. 146.

CHASE, hunted animal; Ven. 883.

CHECK, restrain; Lucr. 1490.

CHEER, (i) hospitable entertainment; Lucr. 89; (ii) look; Lucr. 264.

CHEER UP, encourage; Ven. 896; Lucr. 435.

CHERUBIN, cherub; Comp. 319.

CHEST, (a) breast, (b) box; Lucr. 761.

CHIVALRY, prowess in war; Lucr. 109.

CHURLISH, rough, violent; Ven. 616.

CIPHER, (i) show forth; Lucr. 207, 1396; (ii) decipher; Lucr. 811

CIRCLED, rounded; Lucr. 1229.

CIRCUMSTANCE, (i) circumstantial detail; Ven. 844; (ii) attendant fact; Lucr. 1262, 1703.

CITE UP, mention; Lucr. 524.

CLEANLY-COINED, cleverly invented; Lucr. 1073.

CLEAR, (i) bright; Ven. 860; (ii) innocent; Lucr. 382; (iii) translucent; Lucr. 1553.

CLEFT, twofold; Comp. 293.

CLEPE, name; Ven. 995.

CLIP, (i) embrace; Ven. 600; P.P. 11. 6.

CLOSE (adj.), closed; Lucr. 367.

CLOSE (vb.), enclose; Lucr. 761.

CLOSET, private room (fig.); Lucr. 1659.

CLOSE-TONGUED, uncommunicative; Lucr. 770.

CLOSURE, enclosure; Ven. 782.

CLOUD, become cloudy; Ven. 490.

CLOUDY, (i) (a) covered with clouds (Dian as moon), (b) gloomy, melancholy (Dian as goddess); Ven. 725; (ii) melancholy; Lucr. 1084.

COAST, approach; Ven. 870.

COAT, coat of arms; Lucr. 205.

COCKATRICE, fabulous reptile, able to kill by the breath or look; Lucr. 540.

COFFER UP, shut up in a coffer; Lucr. 855.

COLOUR (sb.), (i) pretext; Lucr. 267, 476; (ii) with quibble on military 'colour'; Lucr. 481.

COLOUR (vb.), disguise with specious appearance; Lucr. 92.

COMBUSTIOUS, combustible; Ven. 1162.

COMFORTABLE, cheerful; Lucr. 164.

COMMAND, authority; Lucr. 624.

COMMANDMENT, 'at commandment', at one's disposal; P.P. 20. 44.

COMMEND, entrust; Lucr. 436.

COMMISSION, due warrant; Ven. 568.

COMPACT (adj.), composed, (well) put together; Ven. 149; Lucr. 1423.

COMPACT (vb.), combine; Lucr. 530.

COMPARE, comparison; Ven. 8; Lucr. 40.

COMPASS, obtain possession of; Ven. 567; Lucr. 346.

COMPASSED, arched; Ven. 272.

COMPLAIN, (i) refl., bewail, utter complaints; Lucr. 598, 845; (ii) tr., complain of, bewail; Lucr. 1839.

COMPLEXION, appearance; Ven. 215.

CONCEIT, (i) power of comprehension, understanding, conception; Lucr. 701, 1298; P.P. 4. 9; 8. 8; (ii) fanciful design; Lucr. 1423.

CONCEITED, ingenious; Lucr. 1371.

CONCLUDE, decide; Lucr. 1850.

CONCLUSION, experiment; Lucr. 1160.

CONDUCT, guide; Lucr. 313.

CONDUIT, structure for distribution of water, made to spout from it, often in the shape of a human figure, allusively to persons weeping; Lucr. 1234.

CONFINE, limitation; Comp. 265.

CONFIRMED, fixed, unchangeable; Lucr. 1026, 1513.

CONFOUND, (i) throw into confusion; Ven. 827; Lucr. 290; Phoen. 41; (ii) ruin, destroy; Lucr. 160, 250, 1202, 1489.

CONFUSION, (i) agitation; Lucr. 445; (ii) destruction; Lucr. 1159.

CONGEST, gather together; Comp. 258.

CONJURE, adjure; Lucr. 568.

CONSORTED, associated; Lucr. 1609.

CONSTER, (mod. 'construe'), interpret; Lucr. 324; P.P. 14. 8.

CONSUME, evaporate; Lucr. 1042.

CONTENT, acquiesce; Ven. 61.

CONTRADICT, oppose; Lucr. 1631.

CONTROL, overpower; Lucr. 448, 678.

CONVERT, be changed; Lucr. 592, 691.

CONVERTITE, penitent; Lucr. 743.

CONY, rabbit; Ven. 687.

COPE, (i) tackle; Ven. 888; (ii) have to do (with); Lucr. 99.

COPESMATE, companion; Lucr. 925.

CO-SUPREME, joint ruler; Phoen. 51.

COUCH, cause to crouch; Lucr. 507.

COUNTERFEIT, likeness; Lucr. 1269.

COUNTERMAND, go counter to; Lucr. 276.

COUNTLESS, infinite; Ven. 84.

COUNTRY, belonging to one's country; Lucr. 1838.

COURAGE, sexual inclination; Ven. 276, ?294.

COURAGEOUSLY, lustfully; Ven. 30.

COURSE, (i) progress; Ven. 960; Lucr. 328, 500, 774; (ii) gallop; Comp. 109.

COURTESY, 'strain courtesy', stand on ceremony (here iron., hold back from attacking, out of fear); Ven. 888.

COY, gentle; Lucr. 669.

COZEN, defraud; Lucr. 387.

CRANK, zigzag; Ven. 682.

CREDENT, trustful; Comp. 279.

CREST (i) helmet; Ven. 104; (ii) ridge of the neck of a horse; Ven. 272, 297, 395.

CREST-WOUNDING, dishonouring the family crest (?with cuckoldry ref. [Prince]); Lucr. 828.

CREW, body of people (not derogatory); Lucr. 1731.

CRIMEFUL, criminal; Lucr. 970.

CROOKED, with bent back; Ven. 134.

CROP, gather, pluck; Ven. 946, 1175.

CROSS (sb.), hindrance; Lucr. 912.

CROSS (vb.), thwart; Ven. 734; Lucr. 286, 968.

CRY (sb.), bark of hounds in the chase; Ven. 693, 870, 885, 889.

CRY (vb.), beg for; Comp. 42.

CURELESS, incurable; Lucr. 772.

CURIOUS, (i) elaborate; Ven. 734; (ii) fastidious; Comp. 49.

CURIOUS-GOOD, elaborately skilful; Lucr. 1300.

CURST, fierce, savage; Ven. 887.

CURTAL, with docked tail; P.P. 17. 19.

CURTSY, bow; Lucr. 1338.

CYNTHIA, Diana (the moon); Ven. 728.

DAFF, (i) send away; P.P. 14. 3; (ii) take off; Comp. 297.

DAMASK, red; P.P. 7. 5.

DAME, mother; Lucr. 1477.

DANGER, power to harm; Ven. 639.

DARDAN, Dardania, the Troad, the peninsula on which Troy stood; Lucr. 1436.

DASH, stroke; Lucr. 206.

DATE, (i) duration; Lucr. 935, 1729; (ii) stipulated time (as on bond); Lucr. 26.

DAZZLE, become blurred; Ven. 1064.

DEAL, 'no deal', not at all; P.P. 17. 17.

DEATH, death's-head; Lucr. 1761.

DEATHSMAN, executioner; Lucr. 1001.

DEBATE, fight; Lucr. 1421.

DECAY, destruction, ruin; Lucr. 516, 808, 947; P.P. 14. 4.

DEFAME, infamy; Lucr. 768, 817, 1033.

DEFEATURE, disfigurement; Ven. 736.

DEFUNCTIVE, funeral; Phoen. 14.

DEFY, reject; P.P. 12. 11.

DELIVER, hand over; Lucr. 1333.

DEMURE, grave; Lucr. 1219.

DENIAL, refusal; Lucr. 242, 324.

DENY, refuse; Lucr. 513.

DEPENDING, impending; Lucr. 1615.

DEPRIVE, take away; Lucr. 1186, 1752.

DERIVE, take one's origin (from); Lucr. 1755.

DESCANT, (i) warble; Lucr. 1134; (ii) comment (at length); P.P. 14. 4.

DESCEND, come down from; Comp. 31.

DESPITE, (i) 'in despite', in disdain or defiance; Ven. 731; Lucr. 55; (ii) 'despite of', in defiance of; Ven. 751; Lucr. 732; (iii) 'my... despite', what has brought contempt on me; Lucr. 1026.

DESPITEFULLY, cruelly; Lucr. 670.

DESTINIES, the three Fates who determine the human lot; Ven. 733, 945.

DESTITUTE, forsaken; Lucr. 441.

DEVICE, (i) contrivance; Lucr. 535; (ii) manner of thinking; Ven. 789.

DIAL, clock; Lucr. 327.

DIALECT, manner of speech; Comp. 125.

DIALOGUE, express in dialogue form; Comp. 132.

DIAN, Diana, virgin goddess of the moon; Ven. 725.

DIAPASON, a bass in exact concord (i.e. in octaves) with the air; Lucr. 1132.

DIGNIFIED, raised to a position of dignity; Lucr. 660.

DIGRESSION, transgression; Lucr. 202.

DINT, impression, Ven. 354.

DIRECTLY, precisely; P.P. 2. 10.

DISCOVERY, (i) means of discovery; Ven. 828; (ii) disclosure; Lucr. 1314.

DISORDER, mental disturbance; Ven. 742.

DISPENSATION, 'make dispensation with'=set aside; Lucr. 248.

DISPENSE (with), pardon; Lucr. 1070, 1279, 1704.

DISPORT, pastime; Lucr.Arg. 18.

DISPOSING, management; Ven. 1040.

DISTAIN, sully; Lucr. 786.

DISTANCE, reserve; Comp. 151.

DISTEMPER, disturb; Ven. 653.

DISTRACT, divided; Comp. 231.

DIVE-DAPPER, dabchick; Ven. 86.

DIVORCE, that which causes separation; Ven. 932.

DONE, lost, destroyed; Ven. 197, 749; Lucr. 23.

DOOM, (i) Day of Judgement; Lucr. 924; (ii) judgement, sentence; Lucr. 1849.

DOTE, (i) be excessively in love; Ven. 837; Lucr. 207; (ii) act foolishly; Ven. 1059.

DOTING, foolishly fond, infatuated (in various emo-tional relationships); Lucr. 155, 1064, 1490.

DOUBT, fear; P.P. 14. 4.

DOWNWARD, turned downward; Ven. 1106.

DRAW, assemble; Lucr. 1368.

DRENCHED, immersed; Ven. 494.

DROUTH, thirst; Ven. 544.

DULL, (i) insensible; Ven. 340; (ii) inert; Lucr. 450.

DUMP, mournful melody; Lucr. 1127.

DUTY, (i) reverence, respect; Ven.Ded. 15; Lucr.Ded. 7, 11; 1352; (ii) action arising from this; Lucr. 14.

EAR, till, plough; Ven.Ded. 10.

EAT IN, corrode; Lucr. 755.

EBON, black like ebony; Ven. 948.

ECSTASY, frenzy; Ven. 895.

EFFECT, (i) manifestation of a being's nature; Ven. 605; Lucr. 251; (ii) resultant action; Lucr. 353.

ELEMENT, sky (fig.); Lucr. 1588.

ELYSIUM, abode of the blessed after death, hence, fig., perfect happiness, embodied in Adonis; Ven. 600.

EMPLEACHED, intertwined (first here); Comp. 205.

ENACT, decree; Lucr. 529.

ENCRIMSONED, red like crimson (first here); Comp. 201.

ENFORCE, obtain by force; Lucr. 181.

ENFORCED (i) forced (of lock); Lucr. 303; (ii) exercised with force; Lucr. 668.

ENFRANCHISE, set free; Ven. 396.

ENGINE, instrument; Ven. 367.

ENGIRT, encircle; Ven. 364; Lucr. 221, 1173.

ENPATRON, have under one's patronage; Comp. 224.

ENRAGED, inflamed with desire; Ven. 29.

ENSCONCE, hide; Lucr. 1515.

ENSUE, follow; Lucr. 502.

ENTERTAIN, (i) fill up; Lucr. 1361; (ii) maintain; Lucr. 1514; (iii) accept; Lucr. 1629.

ENTERTAINMENT, treatment; Ven. 1108.

ENTITULED (in), having a claim (to); Lucr. 57.

ENVIOUS, malignant; Ven. 705.

EQUAL, equally balanced; Lucr. 1791.

ESPOUSE, unite in marriage (fig.); Lucr. 20.

ESTATE, rank; Lucr. Arg. 25; 92.

ETHIOPE, negro; P.P. 16. 16.

EVER-DURING, everlasting; Lucr. 224.

EXCEED, (i) surpass; Ven. 292; (ii) be excessive; Lucr. 229.

EXCLAIM, (i) 'exclaim on', upbraid; Ven. 930; Lucr. 741; (ii) 'exclaim against', rail at; Lucr. 757.

EXCLAMATION, vociferous reproach; Lucr. 705.

EXTEMPORALLY, impromptu; Ven. 836.

EXTENUATE, make less; Ven. 1010.

EXTINCTURE, extinction (here only); Comp. 294.

EXTREMITY, utmost degree (here, of distress); Lucr. 969, 1337.

EYNE (old pl.), eyes; Ven. 633; Lucr. 643, 1229; Comp. 15.

FACE, surface; Lucr. 1744.

FACT, (evil) deed; Lucr. 239, 349.

FAINT, (i) weak-spirited; Ven. 401, 669; Lucr. 1209; (ii) (transf.) making feeble or faint; Ven. 739.

FAINTLY, like a coward; Lucr. 740.

FAIR (sb.), (i) beauty; Ven. 1083, 1086; (ii) beautiful person or thing; Lucr. 346, (the sun) 780.

FAIR (adj.) (i) courteous; Ven. 859; (ii) equitable; Lucr. 1692.

FALCHION, sword, more or less curved, with edge on the convex side; Lucr. 176, 509, 1046, 1626.

FALL, (i) befall; Ven. 472; (ii) let fall; Lucr. 1551.

FANCY, (i) love; Lucr. 200; P.P. 18. 4; (ii) person in love; Comp. 61, 197.

FANTASTIC, capricious; Ven. 850.

FANTASY, figment of the imagination; Ven. 897.

FASHION, appearance; Lucr. 1319.

FAULT, (i) 'cold fault', loss of scent; Ven. 694; (ii) sin, misdeed; Lucr. 238, 527, 629, 804.

FAULTFUL, sinful; Lucr. 715.

FAVOUR, appearance; Ven. 747.

FAWN, wag the tail with delight; Lucr. 421.

FEAR, (i) fear for; Ven. 642; (ii) frighten; Ven. 1094.

FEARFUL, timorous; Ven. 677.

FEAT, neatly; Comp. 48.

FEE, reward; Ven. 393, 609.

FEE-SIMPLE, estate belonging to owner and heirs for ever; Comp. 144.

FEELINGLY, with emotion; Lucr. 1112, 1492.

FEELING-PAINFUL, acutely painful; Lucr. 1679.

FENCE, defend; Lucr. 63.

FIELD, (i) field of battle; Ven. 108; (ii) battle; Ven. 894; (iii) (heraldry), surface of escutcheon, with quibble on (i); Lucr. 58.

FIGURE, represent symbolically; Comp. 199.

FIGURED, indicated by signs; P.P. 4. 10.

FILED, polished; P.P. 18. 8.

FILL, be satisfied; Ven. 548.

FINE, bring to an end; Lucr. 936.

FIT, be suitable; Ven. 327.

FLAP-MOUTHED, with broad hanging lips; Ven. 920.

FLATLY, prostrate; Ven. 463.

FLATTER, (i) please with suggestion (that); Ven. 978; (ii) encourage with pleasing, but false, hopes; Ven. 989; Lucr. 1061, 1559, 1560.

FLATTERING, (i) coaxing; Ven. 284; (ii) deceiving with false hopes; Lucr. 641.

FLATTERY, coaxing; Ven. 425.

FLAW, sudden burst of wind; Ven. 456.

FLEE, fly; Ven. 947.

FLOOD, (i) large body of water (river or sea); Ven. 824; (ii) river; Lucr. 266.

FLUXIVE, flowing (first here); Comp. 50.

FOIL (sb.), setting; Comp. 153.

FOIL (vb.), overcome; Ven. 114.

FOLD, conceal; Lucr. 1073.

FOLLY, wantonness, unchaste behaviour; Lucr. 556, 851.

FOND, foolish, infatuated; Ven. 1021; Lucr. 134, 216, 1094

FONDLING, foolish one; Ven. 229.

FONDLY, foolishly; Lucr. 207.

FOOL, wretch (term of pity); Ven. 578.

FOOTING, (i) footprint; Ven. 148; (ii) step; Ven. 722.

FOR, because; Lucr. 1142.

FOR WHY, because; Lucr. 1222; P.P. 10. 8, 10.

FORAGE, glut oneself; Ven. 554.

FORBEAR, leave alone; Ven. 526.

FORCE, (i) care for; Lucr. 1021; (ii) ravish; Lucr. 1657.

FORCED, committed under constraint; Lucr. 1071.

FORCELESS, frail; Ven. 152.

FORESTALL, anticipate; Lucr. 728.

FORGERY, deceit; P.P. 1. 4.

FORLORN, wretched; Ven. 251, 1026; Lucr. 1500.

FORTIFY, protect, Comp. 9.

FOUL, (i) ugly, unpleasant (with moral overtones); Ven. 133, 573, 773, 1105; (ii) dirty; Ven. 983; (iii) evil, vile; Lucr. 150, 173, 198, 199, 284, 346, 412, 546, 574, 612, 629, 700, 722, 886, 1208, 1623, 1704, 1824, 1852.

FRAUGHT, load; P.P. 17. 16.

FRENZY, distraction; Lucr.
1675.

FRESH, invigorating; Comp.
213.

FRET (sb.), ring of gut placed
on finger-board of stringed
instrument to regulate the
fingering; Lucr. 1140.

FRET (vb.), eat away; Ven.
767.

FROM, (i) different from, con-
trary to; Lucr. 113; (ii) at a
distance from; Lucr. 1144.

FROTHY, foaming; Ven. 901.

FROWARD, obstinate, perverse;
Ven. 570; P.P. 4. 14.

FRUIT, offspring; Lucr. 1064.

FULFIL, fill full; Lucr. 1258.

FUME, rage; Ven. 316.

GAGE (sb.), pledge, stake;
Lucr. 1351.

GAGE (vb.), pledge; Lucr. 144.

GALLED, fretted with salt
water; Lucr. 1440.

GAZE, 'stand at gaze', stare
(tech. of deer); Lucr. 1149.

GENDER, offspring; Phoen.
18.

GENERAL, (i) universal; Lucr.
924; (ii) 'in general', col-
lectively; Lucr. 1484.

GENTLE, well-born; Lucr. 851.

GENTRY, high rank by birth;
Lucr. 569.

GET, beget; Ven. 168.

GIDDY, revolving; Lucr. 952.

'GIN, begin (pa. ''gan'); Ven.
6, 46, 95; Lucr. 1228;
P.P. 13. 3; 16. 6.

GLASS, mirror; Ven. 1129;
(fig.) Lucr. 615, 619, 1526,
1758, 1763.

GO ABOUT, attempt; Ven. 319.

GOLDEN, precious; Lucr. 42.

GOOD-MORROW, good morning;
Ven. 859; Lucr. 1219.

GOVERN, control; Lucr. 602.

GOVERNESS, ruler; Lucr. 443.

GOVERNMENT, self-control;
Lucr. 1400.

GRACE (sb.), (i) divine favour;
Ven. 64; Lucr. 712; (ii)
charm, attractiveness;
Lucr. 1410; Comp. 285.

GRACE (vb.), put in a favour-
able light; Lucr. 1319.

GRAFF, grafted scion (fig.);
Lucr. 1062.

GRAINED, pronged; Comp. 64.

GRATE, rub against so as to
produce a harsh sound;
Lucr. 306.

GRAVE, (i) cut into; Ven. 376;
(ii) engrave (fig.); Lucr.
755.

GREEN, young and inexperi-
enced; Ven. 806.

GRIEVANCE, distress; Comp.
67.

GRIN, show the teeth; Ven.
459.

GRIPE (sb.), vulture; Lucr.
543.

GRIPE (vb.), grasp; Lucr. 1425.

GRISLY, grim; Lucr. 926.

GROOM, servant; Lucr. 671,
1013, 1334, 1345, 1632,
1645.

GROUND, main surface (of a
heraldic shield or a painting)
on which the device or pic-
ture is painted; Lucr. 1074.

GUARDS, caution; Comp. 298.

GUISE, habit; Ven. 1177.

GULF, voracious belly; Lucr.
557.

HABIT, clothing (fig.); Lucr.
1814.

HABITUDE, temperament; Comp. 114.

HAND, (i) 'in hand with', occupied with; Ven. 912; (ii) 'take in hand', be occupied with; Lucr. 1235.

HARBOUR, shelter; Lucr. 768.

HARD-BELIEVING, believing with difficulty; Ven. 985.

HARD-FAVOURED, of unpleasing face; Ven. 133, 931; Lucr. 1632.

HAUNT, habitually resort; Comp. 130.

HAVING, accomplishment; Comp. 235.

HEARSED, buried as in a coffin; Lucr. 657.

HEARTLESS, (i) cowardly; Lucr. 471, 1392; (ii) unsympathetic (if text sound); P.P. 17. 23.

HEAT, sexual desire; Ven. 311; Lucr. 48, 706.

HEAVE, lift, raise (without special implication of effort); Ven. 351.

HEAVED-UP, lifted up (cf. *heave*); Lucr. 111, 638.

HEAVINESS, sorrow, cause of sorrow; Lucr. 1283, 1602.

HEAVY, (i) (a) of great weight, (b) sleepy; Lucr. 1574; (ii) angry; Ven. 182; (iii) sorrowful; Ven. 839, 1125; Lucr. 743, 1326; (iv) (a) (iii), (b) deep, profound; Lucr. 1435; (v) sleepy, drowsy; Lucr. 121; (vi) (of sleep) deep, profound; Lucr. 163.

HECUBA, wife of Priam, king of Troy; Lucr. 1447, 1485.

HEIR, offspring, product; Ven. Ded. 8.

HELP, remedy; Ven. 93, 371; Lucr. 1056.

HELPLESS, unhelpful, unprofitable; Ven. 604; Lucr. 1027, 1056.

HIE, refl., hasten; Ven. 3, 323; P.P. 12.11.

HIGH-PITCHED, lofty; Lucr. 41.

HIS, its (usu. Sh. form; 'its' rare); Ven. 359, 756, 944, 1132; Lucr. 389, 532.

HIVE, headgear of plaited straw; Comp. 8.

HOLD-FAST, holding firmly; Lucr. 555.

HOLLA, stop!; Ven. 284.

HONEST, honourable; Lucr. 173.

HONESTY, chastity; Lucr. 885.

HONEY, sweet; Ven. 16, 452, 538.

HOPE, person who is the centre of one's hopes; Lucr. 1430.

HOT, sexually excited; Ven. 797; Lucr. 314.

HOTLY, (a) with burning heat, (b) with lascivious desire; Ven. 178.

HOVER, hesitate, waver; Lucr. 1297.

HUMOUR, (i) whim, caprice; Ven. 850; (ii) mental disposition; Lucr. 1825.

IDLE, useless, unprofitable; Ven. 770, 848; Lucr. 1016.

ILION, Troy; Lucr. 1370, 1524.

ILL, evil deed; Lucr. 304, 476.

ILL-ANNEXED, evilly added; Lucr. 874.

IMAGE, (i) representation (here, of person in a painting); Lucr. 1501, 1520, 1577; (ii) likeness; Lucr. 1753, 1762.

IMMODESTLY, because of un-chaste action; Lucr. 802.

IMPART, bestow; Lucr. 1039.

IMPOSITION, injunction; Lucr. 1697.

IMPOSTHUME, abscess; Ven. 743.

IMPRESSION, pressure; Ven. 566.

INCOME, advent; Lucr. 334.

INCREASE, (i) produce; Ven. 169; (ii) procreation; Ven. 791.

INCREASEFUL, productive; Lucr. 958.

INDENT, move in zigzags ('with the way'=along his way) (from separation of the two parts of a duplicate legal indenture, by indented per-foration); Ven. 704.

INFECTED, factitious; Comp. 323.

INFUSE, imbue; Ven. 928.

INSINUATE, ingratiate oneself (with); Ven. 1012.

INSTANCE, evidence, sign; Lucr. 1511.

INSULTER, triumphant person; Ven. 550.

INSULTING, triumphant; Lucr. 509.

INTEND, pretend; Lucr. 121.

INTENDMENT, what one in-tends, purpose, intent; Ven. 222.

INTEREST, right or title to possessions; Lucr. 1067, 1619 (or 'what one has a right in'), 1797.

INTRUDE, enter forcibly (trans.); Lucr. 848.

INVENTION, process of mental creation, creative power; Ven. Ded. 9.

INVISED, unseen(?); Comp. 212.

ISSUE, offspring; Ven. 1178; Lucr. 37, 522.

JADE, inferior horse; Ven. 391; Lucr. 707.

JAR, fight; Ven. 100.

JEALOUS, (i) apprehensive; Ven. 321; (ii) suspicious; Lucr. 800.

JEALOUSY, suspicion; Lucr. 1516 (elsewhere mod. sense).

JENNET, small Spanish horse; Ven. 260.

KEEP, dwell; Ven. 687.

KEN, sight; Lucr. 1114.

KEY-COLD, stone cold; Lucr. 1774.

KIND (sb.), (i) race; Ven. 1018; (ii) nature, disposi-tion; Lucr. 1147, 1242.

KIND (adj.), natural; Lucr. 1423.

LAGGING, tardy; Lucr. 1335.

LANGUISHMENT, mental dis-tress; Lucr. 1130, 1141.

LAUNDER, wet; Comp. 17.

LAP, wrap; P.P. 20. 24.

LATE, lately; Ven. 748, 1131.

LAWN, fine linen; Ven. 590; Lucr. 258, 259.

LAWND, glade; Ven. 813.

LEADEN, inert, spiritless; Ven. 34; Lucr. 124.

LEAGUE, (i) alliance; Lucr. 287, 383; (ii) union; Lucr. 689.

LEAVE, (i) abs., break off; Ven. 715; (ii) cease; Ven. 899; Lucr. 148.

LEISURE, leisure moment; Comp. 193.

LET (sb.), hindrance; Lucr. 330, 646.

LET (vb.), (i) cease; Lucr. 10; (ii) hinder; Lucr. 328.

LEVEL, range; Comp. 309.

LEVELLED, aimed; Comp. 22.

LEWD, bad, wicked; Lucr. 392, 971.

LIE, reside; Lucr. 834.

LIGHT (sb.), power of vision, sight; Ven. 1039; ?Lucr. 461.

LIGHT (adj.), cheerful; Lucr. 1434.

LIGHTLESS, (i) giving no light; Lucr. 4; (ii) dark; Lucr. 1555.

LIME, catch with birdlime; Lucr. 88.

LIMIT, region; Ven. 235.

LIMN (out), depict; Ven. 290.

LISTS, space enclosed by palisades, for tilting; hence, fig., place of encounter; Ven. 595.

LIVELIHOOD, animation; Ven. 26.

LIVELY (adj.), (i) intense; Ven. 498; (ii) living; Lucr. 1593.

LIVELY (adv.), in a lifelike way, to the life; P.P. 20. 17.

LIVERY (sb.), dress (fig.); Ven. 506, 1107; Comp. 195.

LIVERY (vb.), dress (fig.); Comp. 105.

LIVING, lifetime; Comp. 238.

LODE-STAR, guiding star; Lucr. 179.

LODGE, serve as a dwelling for; Lucr. 1530.

LOOK AS, just as; Lucr. 372, 694.

LOOK HOW, just as; Ven. 67, 815, 925.

LOOK WHAT, whatever; Ven. 299.

LORDING, lord; P.P. 15. 1.

LOSE, forget; Ven. 408.

LOVELY, amorous; P.P. 4. 3.

LOVER, provide with a lover (here first); Comp. 320.

LUST, (i) pleasure; Lucr. 1384; (ii) desire (not as strong as mod. 'lust'); Ven. 42.

LUST-BREATHED, inspired by desire; Lucr. 3.

LUXURY, lustfulness; Comp. 314.

MAIDEN, (i) befitting a maiden; Ven. 50; (ii) (fig.), of a fortress, etc., never conquered; Lucr. 408.

MAKE, (i) go; Ven. 5; (ii) commit; Lucr. 804.

MAKE AWAY, destroy; Ven. 763.

MANAGE (sb.), training of a horse; Comp. 112.

MANAGE (vb.), train a horse in its paces; here, of sexual intercourse; Ven. 598.

MAP, picture, image; Lucr. 402, 1712.

MARGENT, margin; Lucr. 102.

MARTYRED, disfigured; Lucr. 802.

MASTER, possess; Lucr. 863.

MATCH, agreement; Ven. 586.

MATE, check; Ven. 909.

MAUND, woven basket with handles; Comp. 36.

MAW, stomach; Ven. 602.

MEAN, means; Lucr. 1045.

MEASURE, dance; Ven. 1148.

MELTING, tearful; Lucr. 1227.

MICKLE, great; P.P. 15. 9.

MILCH, giving milk; Ven. 875.

MISS, fault; Ven. 53.

MISTRUST, suspect; Lucr. 1516.

MISTRUSTFUL, causing mistrust or suspicion; Ven. 826.

MOAN, lamentation; Lucr. 1108.

MODEST, chaste; Ven. 725.

MODESTLY, in accordance with chastity; Lucr. 1607.

MOE, more; Lucr. 1479, 1615.

MOIETY, small part; Lucr. Ded. 3.

MONUMENT, effigy; Lucr. 391.

MOOD, countenance expressive of disposition; Comp. 201.

MOODY, sullen; Lucr. 553, 1602.

MORALIZE (i) intr., interpret symbolically, by analogy; Ven. 712; (ii) interpret; Lucr. 104.

MORE, greater; Ven. 78; Lucr. 332.

MORROW, morning; Lucr. 1082, 1571.

MORTAL, (i) deadly, death-dealing; Ven. 618, 953; Lucr. 364, 724; (ii) of a human being, 'mortal stars'=eyes; Lucr. 13.

MORTALITY, mortal nature; Lucr. 403.

MOT, motto; Lucr. 830.

MOTE, speck of dust; Lucr. 1251.

MOTION, puppet-show; Lucr. 1326.

MOVE, anger; Ven. 623; Lucr.Arg. 42.

MOVER, living creature; Ven. 368.

MUSE, wonder; Ven. 866.

MUSIT, gap in fence; Ven. 683.

MUSTY, moist and fetid; Lucr. 782.

MUTINY, discord, strife; Ven. 651, 1049; Lucr. 426, 1153.

MUTUAL, common; Ven. 1018; Phoen. 24.

NAMELESS, having no legitimate name; Lucr. 522.

NAPKIN, handkerchief; Comp. 15.

NAY, denial (but text corrupt); P.P. 17. 8.

NEIGHBOUR, lie near; Ven. 259.

NEW, newly; Lucr. 1663.

NEWLY, anew; Lucr. 490.

NEXT, nearest; Ven. 1184.

NICE, exact, precise (in depiction or discrimination); Lucr. 1412; Comp. 97

NIGHTLY, used, manifested, at night; Lucr. 680, 1080.

NILL, will not; P.P. 14. 8.

NOTARY, recorder; Lucr. 765.

NOTE (i) stigma; Lucr. 208; (ii) distinction; Comp. 233.

NOUGHT, not at all; Ven. 631.

NUZZLE, push the nose; Ven. 1115.

OBJECT, (i) one that excites emotion (here, love); Ven. 255; (ii) spectacle; Lucr. 806, 1103.

OBSCURE, hidden; Ven. 237.

OBSCURELY, in hiding; Lucr. 1250.

OBSERVANCE, observant care; Lucr. 1385.

OCCASION, cause; Lucr. 1270.

O'ERSTRAWED, strewn over; Ven. 1143.

O'ERWHELM, overhang; Ven. 183.

O'ERWORN, (i) worn out by age; Ven. 135; (ii) spent; Ven. 866.

OF, by; Lucr. 22.

OFFICE, function; Ven. 1039.

ON, of; Ven. 160, 405, 544.

OR...OR, either...or; Lucr. 875, 1340.

ORATOR, spokesman; Lucr. 30.

ORB, globe; Comp. 289.

ORBED, spherical; Comp. 25.

ORIENT, bright; Ven. 981.

ORT, fragment (of food); Lucr. 985.

OTHER, others; Ven. 864.

OUT, away!; Lucr. 1016.

OUT OF, beyond; Ven. 567.

OUTBRAG, exceed in pride of beauty; Comp. 95.

OUTFACE, brazen out; P.P. 1. 8.

OUTWARD (pl.), external appearance; Comp. 80.

OUTWEAR, spend the whole of; Ven. 841.

OUTWORN, worn away; Lucr. 1761.

OVER-FLY, fly faster than; Ven. 324.

OVER-HANDLED, employed to excess; Ven. 770.

OVERLOOK, look down on; Ven. 178.

OVERRULE, hold sway over others; Ven. 109.

OVERSEE, see to; Lucr. 1205.

OVERSEEN, deceived; Lucr. 1206.

OVERSHOOT, pass or run beyond; Ven. 680

OVERSLIP, pass unnoticed by; Lucr. 1576.

OVERSWAY, prevail over by superior power; Ven. 109.

OWE, possess, own; Ven. 411, 523 ('owe me'=have for me); Lucr. 1803.

PACK, send away; P.P. 14. 21.

PACK, go away; P.P. 14. 29.

PAINTED CLOTH, wall-hanging painted or worked with figures and often mottoes or texts; Lucr. 245.

PALE (sb.¹), fence (here, fig., her arms); with quibble on sb.²; Ven. 230.

PALE (sb.²), pallor; Ven. 589.

PALE (adj.), causing paleness; Ven. 739.

PALMER, pilgrim; Lucr. 791.

PAMPHLET, small written composition; Lucr. Ded. 2.

PANDION, father of Philomela (see *Philomel*); P.P. 20. 23.

PARCEL, constituent part; Comp. 87, 231.

PARLING, speaking, parleying; Lucr. 100.

PART, (i) (theatr., here fig.), part one has to play; Lucr. 278; (ii) side; Lucr. 294.

PARTIALLY, in a biased manner; Lucr. 634.

PASSENGER, traveller on foot; Ven. 91.

PASSING, extremely; Ven. 297.

PASSION (sb.), lamentation; Ven. 832.

PASSION (vb.), grieve; Ven. 1059.

PATTERN (sb.), example framed from the model; Lucr. 1350.

PATTERN (vb.), provide with a precedent; Lucr. 629.

PAWN, stake; Lucr. 156, 1351.

PECULIAR, particular to, reserved for (one individual); Lucr. 14.

PEEP, appear; Lucr. 1251.

PEER, (i) show oneself; Ven. 86; (ii) make peep out; Lucr. 472.

PELF, treasure; P.P. 14. 12.

PELLET, form into small globules; Comp. 18.

PELT, throw out angry words; Lucr. 1418.

PENCILLED, painted; Lucr. 1497.

PENSIVED, sad (here only); Comp. 219.

PERFECT, thoroughly learnt; Ven. 408.

PERIOD, (i) end, conclusion; Lucr. 380; (ii) long pause, as at end of sentence; Lucr. 565.

PHILOMEL, nightingale; from Philomela, outraged by Tereus, her brother-in-law, who cut out her tongue to prevent her betraying him; she was changed into a nightingale; Lucr. 1079, 1128; P.P. 14. 17 (Philomela).

PHOENIX, incomparable; Comp. 93.

PHRASELESS, indescribable; Comp. 225.

PHYSIOGNOMY, art of judging character by the face; Lucr. 1395.

PIECE, increase; Comp. 119.

PILGRIMAGE, progress; Lucr. 960.

PILL, strip off; Lucr. 1167, 1169.

PINE, starve; Ven. 602 (trans.); Lucr. 905, 1115.

PIONEER, sapper; Lucr. 1380.

PITCHY, pitch dark; Ven. 821; Lucr. 550.

PITH, vigour; Ven. 26.

PLACE, residence; Comp. 82.

PLAIN, honest; Lucr. 1532.

PLAINING, lamentation; Lucr. 559.

PLAINT, lamentation; Lucr. 1364.

PLAINTFUL, mournful; Comp. 2.

PLANT, establish firmly; Ven. 557; Lucr. 887.

PLAT, braid of hair; Comp. 29.

PLAUSIBLY, with applause; Lucr. 1854.

PLEAT, fold (fig.); Lucr. 93.

PLUCK, pull (down); Ven. 30.

PLUTO, ruler-god of Hades; Lucr. 553.

POINT, appoint; Lucr. 879.

POOR, (i) petty ('poor abuses'), slight, insignificant; Lucr. 269; (ii) inadequate; Lucr. 323.

POSIED, bearing an inscription; Comp. 45.

POST (sb.), (i) 'in post', post-haste, at express speed; Lucr. 1; (ii) courier; Lucr. 926, 1333.

POST (vb.), (i) ride swiftly, post-haste; Lucr. Arg. 13; 220; (ii) hasten; P.P. 14. 21.

POWER, army; Lucr. 1368.

PRACTICE, deceit; P.P. 18. 9.

PRECEDENT, (i) sign, token; Ven. 26; (ii) example; Lucr. 1261.

PRECURRER, forerunner; Phoen. 6.

PREFER, present; Comp. 280.

PRESENT, immediate; Lucr. 551, 1263, 1307.

PRESENTED, offered; Ven. 405.

PRESENTLY, immediately; Lucr. 864, 1007; P.P. 13.4.

PRESS, crowd; Lucr. 1301, 1408.

PRESSED, weighed down; Ven. 430, 545.

PRETEND, propose; Lucr. 576.

PRETTY, considerable ('pretty while'); Lucr. 1233.

PREVENT, anticipate; Lucr. 966.

PREY, booty; Ven. 724.

PRICK, mark on a sun-dial; Lucr. 781.

PRIDE, (i) mettle (of a horse); Ven. 420; (ii) (height of) sexual desire; Lucr. 432, 438, 705; (iii) exalted position; Lucr. 662; (iv) love of display; Lucr. 864; (v) splendour; Lucr. 1809; Comp. 105.

PRIME, spring; Lucr. 332.

PRISON, imprison (fig.); Lucr. 642.

PRISONED, imprisoned; Ven. 362, 980.

PRIVILEGE, authorize; Lucr. 621.

PROCURE, cause; P.P. 17. 21.

PRODIGY, portent; Ven. 926.

PRONE, eager; Lucr. 684.

PROOF, experience; Comp. 153, 163.

PROPERTY, selfhood; Phoen. 37.

PROPORTIONED, regular; Lucr. 774.

PROTESTATION, solemn affirmation (of a resolution); Lucr. 1700, 1844.

PROUD, (i) spirited, high-mettled; Ven. 260, 884; (ii) sexually excited; Ven. 288; Lucr. 712; (iii) exalted; Lucr. 19.

PROVE, (i) try; Ven. 40; (with quibble on (ii)), 608; (ii) experience; Ven. 597.

PUBLISHER (OF), one who makes publicly known; Lucr. 33.

PURCHASE, win; Lucr. 963.

PURL, curl; Lucr. 1407.

PURPLE, blood-red; Ven. 1054, 1168; Lucr. 1734.

PUT BACK, repulse Lucr. 843; P.P. 18. 24.

QUALIFY, mitigate; Lucr. 424.

QUALITY, (i) nature; Lucr. 875, 1313, 1702; (ii) accomplishment; Comp. 99.

QUESTION, converse; Lucr. 122.

QUITTAL, requital; Lucr. 236.

QUOTE, observe; Lucr. 812.

RAGE (sb.), violence of passion; Lucr. 145, 424, 468, 909.

RAGE (vb.), be carried away by passion; Comp. 160.

RAGGED, (i) rough; Ven. 37; (ii) torn (fig.); Lucr. 892.

RANK, (i) full to overflowing; Ven. 71; (ii) licentious; Comp. 307.

RASCAL, of mean birth; Lucr. 671.

RATE, scold; Ven. 906; Lucr. 304.

RAVISH, spoil; Lucr. 778.

READ, 'read lectures'=teach lessons; Lucr. 618.

REASON, 'have reason', be right; Ven. 612.

REAVE, (i) deprive; Ven. 766; (ii) take away; Ven. 1174.

RECEIPT, what is received (here, food); Lucr. 703.

RECK, care for; Ven. 283.

RECREANT, cowardly; Lucr. 710.

RECURE, cure; Ven. 465.

REDRESS, mend; P.P. 13. 10.

REFLECT, shine; Lucr. 376.

REFUGE, excuse; Lucr. 1654.

REGARD, (i) thoughtful attention, deep reflexion; Lucr. 277, 1400; (ii) heed; Lucr. 305; (ii) view; Comp. 213.

REGISTER, one who keeps a record; Lucr. 765.

REIN, restrain; Lucr. 706.

RELENT, dissolve; Ven. 200.

RELENTING, softening (the heart); Lucr. 1829.

RELIEF, pasturage; Ven. 235.

RELISH, sing, warble; Lucr. 1126.

REMEMBER, 'be remembered', bear in mind; Lucr. 607.

REMISSION, pardon; Lucr. 714.

REMORSE, pity, compunction; Ven. 257; Lucr. 269.

REMORSELESS, pitiless; Lucr. 562.

REMOVE, depart; Ven. 81, 186.

REPEAL, recall from banishment; Lucr. 640.

REPETITION, mention, recital; Lucr. 1285.

REPINE, discontent; Ven. 490.

REPLICATION, reply; Comp. 122.

REPROBATE, depraved; Lucr. 300.

REPROVE, disprove; Ven. 787.

REQUIRE, request; Lucr.Arg. 4.

RESOLVE, dissolve; Comp. 296.

RESPECT (sb.), (i) reflexion; Ven. 911; Lucr. 275; (ii) heed, regard; Lucr. 201, 642, 1347.

RESPECT (vb.), (i) consider, take into account; Ven. 911; (ii) pay heed to; Lucr. 431.

RETIRE (sb.), retreat; Lucr. 174, 573.

RETIRE (vb.), (i) return; Ven. 906; (ii) draw back; Lucr. 303.

RETIRING, returning; Lucr. 962.

RETURN, turn again; Ven. 704.

REVEREND, respectful; Lucr. 90.

REVIVE, be rekindled; Ven. 338.

REWORD, re-echo; Comp. 1.

RIGHT (sb.), (i) claim; Ven. 759; (ii) 'do (one) right', do (one) justice; Lucr. 1027; (ii) what is due; Phoen. 16, 34.

RIGHT (vb.), do justice to; Ven. 220.

RIGHTFUL, just; Lucr. 1649.

RIGOL, ring, circle; Lucr. 1745.

RIGOUR, cruelty; Ven. 954.

RIOT, extravagance; Ven. 1147.

ROOT (sb.), stock; Lucr. 823.

ROOT (vb.), dig up with the snout; Ven. 636.

ROUND, circular movement; Comp. 109.

ROUSE, (i) drive from lair; Ven. 240; (ii) raise; Lucr. 541.

RUDE, rough; Lucr. 175.

RUDELY, roughly; Lucr. 170, 669.

RUDENESS, violence; Comp. 104.

RUFFLE, ostentatious display; Comp. 58.

RUIN, destruction, destructive effects; Lucr. 1451.

RUINATE, ruin; Lucr. 944.

RULE, 'be ruled by', follow advice of; Ven. 673.

SAD, serious, solemn; Lucr. 277, 556, 1081, 1386, 1610.

SADNESS, seriousness; Ven. 807.

SAINT, play the saint; P.P. 18. 44.

SAUCILY, rashly; Lucr. 1348.

SAVOUR, perfume; Ven. 747.

SAW, proverbial saying; Lucr. 244.

SCAPE, transgression (esp. sexual); Lucr. 747.

SCHEDULE, slip or scroll of paper with writing on it, here a letter; Lucr. 1312.

SCHOOL, 'set to school', teach; Lucr. 1820.

SCYTHE, mow down (fig.); Comp. 12.

SEAL MANUAL, seal affixed by one's own hand; Ven. 516.

SEARCH, probe (a wound) (fig.); Lucr. 1109.

SEARED, withered; Comp. 14.

SEASON (sb.), (favourable) time; Ven. 327; Lucr. 166, 879.

SEASON (vb.), add salt to; Lucr. 796.

SEATED, situated; Lucr. 1144.

SECURELY, without apprehension of evil; Lucr. 89.

SEED (pass.), run to seed, mature (here only, but cf.

ppl. adj. in *Troil*. 1. 3. 316 [Steev.]); Lucr. 603.

SEEK, have recourse (to); Lucr. 293.

SEEMING, apparently; Lucr. 1514.

SELD, seldom; P.P. 13. 7.

SENSELESS, (i) insensible; Ven. 211; Lucr. 1564; P.P. 20. 21; (ii) free from sensual sin; Lucr. 820.

SENSIBLE, (i) capable of feeling; Ven. 436; (ii) acutely felt; Lucr. 1678.

SENTENCE, maxim; Lucr. 244.

SENTINEL, guard; Lucr. 942.

SEPULCHRE, bury; Lucr. 805.

SERVE, (i) be opportune, favourable; Lucr. 166, 1019; (ii) gratify; Comp. 135.

SERVILELY, like a slave; Ven. 392.

SET, seated; Ven. 18; Comp. 39.

SET FORTH, praise; Lucr. 32.

SEVERAL, separate, distinct; Ven. 1067; Lucr. 1410.

SHADOW (sb.), (i) reflected image; Ven. 162, 1099; (ii) spirit, phantom; Ven. 1001; (iii) image of the imagination; Lucr. 460, 971; (iv) likeness; Lucr. 1457; (v) something unreal; Lucr. 270.

SHADOW (vb.), conceal; Lucr. 1416.

SHAG, shaggy; Ven. 295.

SHAME, be ashamed; Lucr. 1084, 1143.

SHAPE (sb.), outward appearance; Lucr. 597.

SHAPE (vb.), (i) transform by imagination; Lucr. 973; (ii) conform; Lucr. 1458.

SHARP, (i) hungry; Ven. 55; (ii) (of hunger) keen; Lucr. 422; (iii) cold, biting; Ven. 1085.

SHEAVED, made of straw; Comp. 31.

SHELF, sandbank; Lucr. 335.

SHIFT (sb.), expedient, trick; Ven. 690; Lucr. 920.

SHIFT (vb.), pass away; Lucr. 1104.

SHIFTING, (a) always moving, (b) deceitful; Lucr. 930.

SHINE, light; Ven. 488, 728.

SHOOT, act of shooting; Lucr. 579.

SHOW (sb.), (i) appearance; Lucr. 296, ?1507, 1514, 1580, 1810; Comp. 92; (ii) spectacle; Comp. 308.

SHOW (vb.), appear; Ven. 366; Lucr. 252.

SHREWD, malicious; Ven. 500.

SIGHT, (i) eyes; Ven. 183; Phoen. 35; (ii) gaze; Lucr. 104.

SIGHTLESS, impenetrable by vision; Lucr. 1013.

SILLY, (i) simple, unsophisticated; Ven. 467; Lucr. 1345; (ii) helpless, defenceless (conventional epith. of sheep); Ven. 1098; Lucr. 167.

SIMPLE (sb.), ingredient in a medicine; Lucr. 530.

SIMPLE (adj.), innocent, harmless; Ven. 795.

SINEW, nerve; Ven. 903.

SINGLE OUT, distinguish one scent (here the false scent) from another; Ven. 693.

SINGULAR, unique; Lucr. 32.

SISTERING, neighbouring; Comp. 2.

SITH, since; Ven. 762, 1163.

SLACK, diminish; Lucr. 425.

SLAKE, abate; Lucr. 1677.

SLANDER, disgrace; Ven. 1006; Lucr. 1054, 1207.

SLANDEROUS, bringing disgrace; Lucr. 1001.

SLEIDED, divided into filaments (see Per. G.); Comp. 48.

SLIP, error; Ven. 515.

SLUTTISH, dirty; Ven. 983.

SMELL, hound's 'scent'; Ven. 686.

SMOOTHING, flattering; Lucr. 892.

SNEAPED, pinched with cold; Lucr. 333.

So, provided that; Ven. 66, 180, 480, 514.

SOBER, dignified; Lucr. 1403; Comp. 298.

SOBER-SAD, solemnly dignified; Lucr. 1542.

SOD, boiled (fig.); Lucr. 1592.

SOFT, unmanly; Lucr. 200.

SOFTLY, quietly; Lucr. 176.

SOLEMN, awe-inspiring; Ven. 1057.

SOMETIME, (i) sometimes; Comp. 24; (ii) formerly, Comp. 58.

SOOTHING, flattering; P.P. 1. 11.

SORT, (i) consort (with); Ven. 689; (ii) choose (a suitable); Lucr. 899; (iii) adapt; Lucr. 1221.

SOUND (sb.), inlet of the sea; Lucr. 1329.

SOUND (vb.), (i) give a signal for; Lucr. 471; (ii) utter, proclaim; Lucr. 717.

SOUR (adj.), peevish; Ven. 449.

SOUR (vb.), cause to look sullen; Ven. 185.

SOUR-FACED, melancholy-looking; Lucr. 1334.

SOVEREIGN, supremely effective; Ven. 28, 916.

SOVEREIGNTY, supreme excellence; Lucr. 36.

SPEEDING, success (good or bad); P.P. 17. 16.

SPEND, (i) give vent to, 'spend ...mouths', bark loudly; Ven. 695; (ii) waste, consume; Lucr. 938, 1600; (iii) (a) expend, (b) utter, give vent to; Lucr. 1318; (iv) employ; Lucr. 1457; (v) 'spent', gone; Lucr. 1589.

SPILL, destroy; Lucr. 1801.

SPITE, vexation; Ven. 1133; Lucr. 1600.

SPLEEN, sudden impulse; Ven. 907; P.P. 6. 6.

SPORT (reflex. and abs.), amuse oneself; Ven. 154; Lucr. 907.

SPOT, disgrace; Lucr. 1053.

SPOTTED, polluted; Lucr. 721, 1172.

SPRING, (i) young shoot (of a plant); Ven. 127, (fig. for 'down'), 656; Lucr. 869, ?950; (ii) as the season of flowers, fig. for early life (not easy to distinguish from (i)); Lucr. 49, 604; (iii) fig., source; Lucr. 1455.

SPRITE (i) mood; Ven. 181; Lucr. 121; (ii) phantom; Lucr. 451; (iii) disembodied spirit as opposed to the body; Lucr. 1728.

SPURN AT, fig., disdain, scorn; Ven. 311; Lucr. 880, 1026.

STAIN (to) (sb.), one who eclipses; Ven. 9.

STAIN (vb.), (i) tinge; Lucr. 56; (ii) disgrace, defile, dishonour; Lucr. 168, 1655, 1743, 1836; (iii) make dim; Lucr. 1435.

STAINED (i) full of disgrace; Lucr. 1059, 1316; (ii) defiled; Lucr. 1181.

STALK, move cautiously like a fowler; Lucr. 365.

STALL, tie as in a stall; Ven. 39.

STARING, truculent; Ven. 1149.

STATE, (i) exalted position; Lucr. 666, 1006; (ii) condition; Lucr. 1066; (iii) dignity; Lucr. 1809.

STAY (sb.), delay; Lucr. 328.

STAY (vb.), (i) 'stay the field', continue the fight; Ven. 894; (ii) stop; (intrans.) Lucr. 311, 423, 1275; (trans.) Lucr. 323, 917, 1364.

STELL, ?fix, ?portray; Lucr. 1444.

STICK, hesitate; P.P. 18. 51.

STILL (adj.), (i) quiet, silent, Lucr. 167; (ii) constant; continual; Lucr. 702, 803.

STILL (adv.), always, continually (passim).

STILL (vb.), quiet; Lucr. 813.

STILL-PINING, always hungry; Lucr. 858.

STILLITORY, still; Ven. 443.

STIR, (i) disturbance (here, war); Lucr. 1471; (ii) mental agitation; Ven. 283.

STOLE, robe; Comp. 297.

'STONISH, bewilder; Ven. 825.

STOOP, (i) bend; Ven. 1028; (ii) submit, yield; Lucr. 574.

STOP (sb.), sudden check (in horse's 'career'); Comp. 109.

STOP (vb.), (i) close, shut up; Ven. 46, 331; (ii) mark as with 'stops' on a printed page, punctuate; Lucr. 327.

STORE, abundance; Lucr. 97.

STORM, make a storm in; Comp. 7.

STORY, tell the story of; Ven. 1013.

STRAIGHT, immediately; Ven. 1091; Lucr. 217, 1634.

STRANGENESS, aloofness; Ven. 310, 524.

STRANGER, belonging to those not familiarly known; Lucr. 99.

STRICT, tight; Ven. 874.

STUFF UP, fill out; Lucr. 297.

SUBTLE, (i) moving imperceptibly; Lucr. 926; (ii) deceitful, crafty; Lucr. 957, 1541.

SUBTLETY, craft; Ven. 675.

SUDDENLY, immediately; Lucr. 1683.

SUFFER, permit, allow full scope to; Ven. 388; Lucr. 1832.

SUFFICE, satisfy; Lucr. 1112.

SUGGEST, tempt, prompt; Ven. 651; Lucr. 37; P.P. 2. 2.

SUPPOSE, picture to oneself, imagine; Lucr. 133, 377.

SUPPOSED, imaginary; Lucr. 455.

SUPREME, ruler; Ven. 996.

SURCEASE, cease; Lucr. 1766.

SURMISE, thought, contemplation; Lucr. 83, 1579.

SURVEY, inspection; Ven. Ded. 12.

SUSPECT, suspicion; Ven. 1010.

SWAIN, peasant; Lucr. 1504.

SWEET, sweet thing; Lucr. 867.

SWOLLEN, bursting (with anger); Ven. 325.

SYMPATHIZED, (of feelings) matched, answered by; Lucr. 1113.

SYMPATHY, agreement, conformity; Ven. 1057; Lucr. 1229.

TAINT, (i) corrupt, deprave; Lucr. 38; (ii) sully, dishonour; Lucr. 1182.

TAINTED, corrupted; Lucr. 1746.

TAKING, state of alarm; Lucr. 453.

TALENT, treasure (pl.); Comp. 204.

TANTALUS, in Greek myth., punished in Hades for his sin (variously defined in different accounts) by having his thirst and hunger tormented by water receding when he is about to drink and fruit always just eluding his grasp when about to be plucked, hence 'tantalize'; Ven. 599; Lucr. 858.

TARRIANCE, waiting; P.P. 6. 4.

TEDIOUS, (i) long and tiresome; Ven. 841; Lucr. 1379; (ii) (a) long (if narrated), (b) painful; Lucr. 1309.

TEEN, distress; Ven. 808.

TELL, count; Ven. 277, 520.

TEMPERING, (of wax) softening; Ven. 565.

TENDER (sb.), offering; Comp. 219.

TENDER (adj.), (i) youthful; Ven. 32, 127, 1091; (ii) finely sensitive in perception; Lucr. 695.

TENDER (vb.), regard favourably; Lucr. 534.

TENOR, purport; Lucr. 1310.

TEREU, vocative of 'Tereus' (see *Philomel*), imagined to be what the nightingale says; P.P. 20. 14.

TERMLESS, indescribable; Comp. 94.

THAT, so that; Ven. 242; P.P. 16. 7, 20. 15.

THICK, fast; Lucr. 1784.

THICK-SIGHTED, not seeing clearly; Ven. 136.

THINK, (i) bear in mind; Lucr. 493; (ii) 'think long', grow weary with waiting; Lucr. 1359.

THIS (adj.), 'by this', by this time; Ven. 175, 697, 877, 973, 1165; Lucr. 1079, 1268, 1772.

THOROUGH, through; Lucr. 1851.

THRALL, enslaved; Ven. 837.

THREADEN, made of thread; Comp. 33.

THREAT, threaten; Ven. 620; Lucr. 331, 508, 547.

THRENE, lament; Phoen. 49.

THRONG, press upon; Lucr. 1417.

TICKLING, pleasurably touching; Lucr. 1090.

TIDE, flow (of tears); Ven. 957, 979.

TIMELESS, unseasonable; Lucr. 44.

TIMELY, early; P.P. 10. 3.

TIRE, feed ravenously; Ven. 56.

TITAN, god of the sun; Ven. 177.

TO, in addition to; Lucr. 1589.

TOKEN, mark (of disease); Lucr. 1748.

TOWARD, compliant; Ven. 1157; P.P. 4. 13.

TOWER, soar aloft in circles before swooping; Lucr. 506.

TOY (sb.), trifle, trifling ornament; Lucr. 214.

TOY (vb.), dally amorously; Ven. 34, 106.

TRANCE, stupor, daze; Lucr. 974, 1595.

TRAVAIL, wearisome journeying; Lucr. 1543.

TREATISE, talk, tale; Ven. 774.

TRENCH, cut like a trench; Ven. 1052.

TRIM (sb.), array; Comp. 118.

TRIM (adj.), fine; Ven. 1079.

TROPHY, emblem or memorial placed over a tomb; Ven. 1013.

TROTH, (i) faithfulness; Lucr. 571, 885; (ii) plighted troth; Lucr. 1059.

TRUCE, 'take truce', make peace; Ven. 82.

TRUE, honest; Ven. 724; Lucr. 748.

TRUMPET, trumpeter; Phoen. 3.

TRUSTLESS, treacherous; Lucr. 2.

TRY, prove; Ven. 280; Lucr. 353.

TUNE, utter, sing; Ven. 74; Lucr. 1107, 1465.

TUSH, tusk; Ven. 617, 624.

'TWEEN, between; Ven. 269; Lucr. 247.

TYPE, distinguishing mark; Lucr. 1050.

TYRANNY, cruelty, pitiless violence; Ven. 737; Lucr.Arg. 41.

TYRANT (sb.), cruel, pitiless person; Ven. 797, 931.

TYRANT (adj.), cruel, pitiless; Lucr. 851; Phoen. 10.

UNADVISED, unintentional; Lucr. 1488.

UNAPPROVED, unconfirmed; Comp. 53.

UNAPT, (i) disinclined; Ven. 34; (ii) unfit; Lucr. 695.

UNBACKED, not taught to bear a rider; Ven. 320.

UNCONTROLLED, (i) never yielding; Ven. 104; (ii) uncontrollable; Lucr. 645.

UNCOUPLE, set one's hounds loose; Ven. 674.

UNCOUTH, strange; Lucr. 1598.

UNDERTAKE, be surety for; Comp. 280.

UNDISTINGUISHED, confused; Comp. 20.

UNDONE, ruined; Ven. 783.

UNEXPERIENT, inexperienced (first here); Comp. 318.

UNFOLD, disclose, make known; Lucr. 754, 1146.

UNHALLOWED, unholy, wicked; Lucr. 192, 392, 552.

UNHAPPY, bringing misfortune; Lucr. 1565.

UNLIVE, deprive of life; Lucr. 1754.

UNNOTED, unnoticed; Lucr. 1014.

UNRECALLING, not to be recalled (here only); Lucr. 993.

UNRESISTED, irresistible; Lucr. 282.

UNRIPE, immature; Ven. 128, 524; P.P. 4. 9.

UNSAVOURY, distasteful; Ven. 1138.

UNSEASONABLE, not in season for being hunted; Lucr. 581.

UNSHEATHE, dislodge; Lucr. 1724.

UNSOUNDED, unfathomed; Lucr. 1819.

UNTREAD, retrace; Ven. 908.

UNTUNED, having lost its melodiousness; Lucr. 1214.

UNTUTORED, not improved by instruction; Lucr.Ded. 4.

UPHEAVE, lift (cf. *heave*); Ven. 482.

UP-TILL, up against; P.P. 20. 10.

URCHIN-SNOUTED, having a snout like a hedgehog's; Ven. 1105.

USE, interest; Ven. 768.

VADE, fade; P.P. 10. 1, 2; 13. 2, 6, 8 (ppl. adj.).

VAIL, lower; Ven. 314, 956.

VANITY, vain, worthless pursuit; Lucr. 894.

VANTAGE, (i) opportunity, 'at vantage', in a position favourable to oneself; Ven. 635; (ii) 'urging for vantage', putting in the most favourable light; Lucr. 249.

VASSAL (sb.), (i) (*a*) servant, (*b*) base, abject person; Lucr. 429; (ii) servant; Lucr. 666, 1360.

VASSAL (adj.), base, subordinate; Lucr. 608.

VASTLY, in a waste or desolate manner; Lucr. 1740.

VAULTY, cavernous; Lucr. 119.

VENGE, avenge; Lucr. 1691.

VENOMED, poisoned; Ven. 916.

VENT, (i) utterance; Ven. 334; (ii) aperture, outlet; Lucr. 310, 1040.

VERDURE, smell, fragrance; Ven. 507.

VERY, mere; Ven. 441.

VESTAL, priestess of Vesta in Rome, vowed, to chastity, whose duty it was always to keep a sacred flame alight in Ven.'s temple; Ven. 752; hence, maiden vowed to chastity; Lucr. 883.

VILLAIN, servant; Lucr. 1338.

WAIL, (i) weep (of eyes); Lucr. 1508; (ii) bewail; Lucr. 1799.

WAIT, 'wait on', accompany; Ven. 1137; Lucr. 275, 869, 910, 1006.

WANT, be in want; Lucr. 97, 557.

WANTON (sb.), (a) frolicsome person, (b) lascivious, unchaste person; Lucr. 401.

WANTON (adj.), (i) sportive, frolicsome; Ven. 777; P.P. 16. 4; (ii) unchaste, immodest; Ven. 809; Lucr. 104, 320; (iii) (a) (i), (b) (ii); Lucr. 401.

WASTE, (i) spend (neutral sense); Ven. 24, 583; (passing into unfavourable sense) Ven. 130; (ii) destroy; Ven. 749; (iii) wear away; Lucr. 959.

WAT, name for a hare; Ven. 697.

WATCH, stay awake; Ven. 584; Lucr. 1575.

WATER-GALL, secondary rainbow; Lucr. 1588.

WEAR, wear out; Ven. 506.

WEED, garment; Lucr. 196.

WELKIN, sky; Ven. 921; (fig. for 'face') Lucr. 116.

WELL-BREATHED, sound in wind; Ven. 678.

WHEN AS, when; Ven. 999.

WHERE, whereas; Lucr. 792.

WHE'ER, whether; Ven. 304.

WHETHER, which of the two; Ven. 304; P.P. 7. 17, 14. 8.

WHILES, while; Lucr. 1135.

WHO, WHOM, which; Ven. 306, 630, 956; Lucr. 1119, 1805.

WILFUL, (i) willing; Ven. 365; (ii) eager; Lucr. 417.

WILL (sb.), (i) desire, esp. carnal desire; Lucr. 128, 129, 243, 247, 302, 352, 417, 486, 495, 614, 625, 700, 728, 1299, 1633; (ii) 'by (one's) will', voluntarily; Ven. 479, ('good will') 639.

WILL (vb.), be resolved, determined, to; Ven. 769.

WINDOW, shutter; Ven. 482.

WINK, (i) close the eyes; Ven. 90, 121, 122; Lucr. 458, 553; (ii) close (intrans.); Lucr. 375, 1139.

WIPE, brand; Lucr. 537.

WISTLY, intently; Ven. 343; Lucr. 1355; P.P. 6. 12.

WIT, (i) intelligence; Ven. 472, 690, 1008; Lucr. 153, 964, 1809, 1816 (plur.), 1820; (ii) person of a turn of mind (defined by qualifying adj.); Ven. 850.

WITHAL, (i) with; Ven. 847;
(ii) therewith; Lucr. 467.

WITHHOLD, detain by holding
fast; Ven. 612.

WITHOUT, outside; Lucr. 393.

WITTILY, cleverly; Ven. 471.

WONDER, wonder at; Lucr.
1596.

WOOD, mad; Ven. 740.

WOODMAN, hunter; Lucr.
580.

WORN-OUT, past, departed;
Lucr. 1350.

WOT, knows; P.P. 17. 6.

WRACK, (i) shipwreck; Ven.
454; (fig.) Lucr. 966; (ii)

destruction, ruin; Ven. 558;
Lucr. 841, 1451.

WRACK-THREATENING, threat-
ening ruin; Lucr. 590.

WREAKED, avenged; Ven.
1004.

WRETCH, term of pity; Ven.
680, 703; Lucr. 269.

WRETCHED, (i) contemptible;
Lucr. 999; (ii) very un-
happy; Lucr. 161, 1136,
1501, 1665, 1826.

WRINKLE, frown; Lucr. 562.

YOKING, acting like a yoke;
Ven. 592.